The Making
of an Abolitionist

The Making of an Abolitionist

William Lloyd Garrison's Path to Publishing
The Liberator

DENIS BRENNAN

McFarland & Company, Inc., Publishers
Jefferson, North Carolina

LIBRARY OF CONGRESS CATALOGUING-IN-PUBLICATION DATA

Brennan, Denis, 1945–
 The making of an abolitionist : William Lloyd Garrison's path to publishing The Liberator / Denis Brennan.
   p. cm.
 Includes bibliographical references and index.

 ISBN 978-0-7864-7425-7 (softcover : acid free paper)
 ISBN 978-1-4766-1535-6 (ebook)

 1. Garrison, William Lloyd, 1805–1879. 2. Abolitionists—United States—Biography. 3. Liberator (Boston, Mass. : 1831) 4. Printers—United States—Biography. 5. Journalists—United States—Biography. 6. Antislavery movements—United States—History—19th century. I. Title.
 E449.G25B74 2014
 326'.8092—dc23
 [B]   2014013249

BRITISH LIBRARY CATALOGUING DATA ARE AVAILABLE

© 2014 Denis Brennan. All rights reserved

No part of this book may be reproduced or transmitted in any form or by any means, electronic or mechanical, including photocopying or recording, or by any information storage and retrieval system, without permission in writing from the publisher.

On the cover: *The Liberator* masthead, 1850, designed by Hammatt Billings; William Lloyd Garrison portrait (Library of Congress); slaves on Smith's Plantation, Beaufort, South Carolina, 1862, photographer Timothy H. O'Sullivan (Library of Congress)

Printed in the United States of America

McFarland & Company, Inc., Publishers
 Box 611, Jefferson, North Carolina 28640
   www.mcfarlandpub.com

For Margaret ... who never stopped believing

Acknowledgments

As with all human endeavors, this book is not the product of one person's efforts, so it is incumbent upon me to recognize those who have contributed to its completion and publication. My sincere appreciation goes to all those who have willingly and freely given of their time, talent, and effort on my behalf. There have been so many who have assisted me in a variety of ways that any effort to name them all would be futile and undoubtedly incomplete. I apologize to all for this omission but without exaggeration it is surely true that most of the value found in this book resulted from their generosity. Whatever faults, flaws, omissions or errors remain are certainly mine alone.

The librarians and archivists at many institutions have graciously, and often patiently, answered a stream of inquiries. The Newburyport Town Library, the American Antiquarian Society, the Boston Public Library, the Massachusetts Historical Society, the New York State Library, the State University of New York at Albany Library, and the Schaffer Library at Union College in Schenectady were consistently helpful as well as quick to offer suggestions to improve my research practices and to enhance my research results.

The scholarly inspiration of several mentors at the University at Albany deserves specific recognition and my earnest gratitude. Graham J. Barker-Benfield has been a constant source of inspiration and gentle persuasion since I first met him in an undergraduate course more years ago than I wish to admit, Richard Hamm was always available to discuss, advise, and challenge me to dig just a little deeper, and Ron Bosco provided a balance and perspective that tempered my historical mind with a sense of the literate. My gratitude to these three cannot be fully expressed and I am proud to consider them not only colleagues but friends. Additionally, at Union College, my fellow faculty members have listened, advised, and cheerfully encouraged my work, while the college has provided me the opportunity to practice my craft in the classroom.

In addition, inspiration and encouragement has always come from my four children, Timothy, Norah, Ian, and Daniel. They have supported Dad's academic career with humor and patience while they also motivated me forward. I am humbled by their care, understanding, and encouragement. In particular, Daniel merits individual and distinct commendation for serving as my personal editor. He read, commented, and suggested revisions to several drafts with patience, intelligence, and aplomb. The final version was markedly improved through his efforts.

Finally, there is one person to whose faith, caring, patience, understanding, and love I can singularly ascribe credit for completing this book. Thank you, Margaret — this is as much your accomplishment as mine.

Contents

Acknowledgments vii
Preface 1

ONE: The Printer's Stand 7
TWO: The "mere boy" 28
THREE: Political Machinations 53
FOUR: Religious Apathy 83
FIVE: A Change of Heart 104
SIX: On Trial in Baltimore 129
SEVEN: **"And I will be heard"** 153
EIGHT: "The press is able to cope" 174

Chapter Notes 181
Bibliography 199
Index 207

In a small chamber, friendless and unseen,
Toiled o'er his types one poor, unlearned young man;
The place was dark, unfurnitured, and mean;
Yet there the freedom of a race began.
Help came but slowly; surely no man yet
Put lever to the heavy world with less:
What need of help? He knew how types were set,
He had a dauntless spirit, and a press.
  — from "To W.L. Garrison" by James Russell Lowell

Preface

On December 29, 1865, after thirty-five years of weekly publication, the final issue of *The Liberator* came off the press. Only a few days earlier, the Thirteenth Amendment had been declared ratified by three-fourths of the states and was officially verified by Secretary of State William Seward as a part of the United States Constitution. In 1831, in the paper's inaugural editorial, William Lloyd Garrison had promised, with strident and uncompromising words, that *The Liberator* and its editor would not be silenced until "every chain be broken, every bondman set free." His promise was now fulfilled. In 1865, the language in his "VALEDICTORY" avoided the fiery rhetoric of his youth, perhaps evoked a sense of fatigue, and suggested the heavy physical toll taken by the long years of struggle. Nevertheless, in its own way, it was no less uncompromising. He recognized those who argued that the victory was only partial, that his retirement was a mistake, and that political and social equality for the freedmen remained to be vindicated. While acknowledging that reality and promising not to abandon the cause, he insisted that *The Liberator* had accomplished its objective and asked that he "be permitted to take a little repose in my advanced years."

Garrison's decision to end publication of *The Liberator* reflected, as its establishment had also demonstrated, the independent character of its editor and publisher. Throughout its existence, Garrison had been determined to remain unbound by outside influences — the final decision about what to publish and what language was appropriate was the editor's alone. Any person's decision to fully embrace the cause of abolition, as he had done, required, he believed, a commitment that could not be mitigated or moderated by concessions with other philosophies or institutions. On December 15, 1837, he wrote in *The Liberator* that anyone who embraced the cause of abolition "loving his creed, or sect, or party, or any worldly interest ... more than the cause of bleeding humanity ... will prove himself unworthy of his abolition profession."

Such an uncompromising stance did not win friends, and likely contributed to the splintering of the abolitionist movement around 1840, but it reflected Garrison's experience in the years between his printing apprenticeship in Newburyport and his momentous decision to begun publication of *The Liberator* in Boston in 1831. His training at the printer's stand in Ephraim Allen's office had convinced him of the power of the press to educate citizens and permit them to participate fully in American society and politics. Indeed, this was more than simply a "power" but a responsibility and duty of the editor. Later, his experience as an editor and a co-editor of several newspapers convinced him that, with regard to the issue of slavery, compromise with church or political leaders meant negotiating the "cause of bleeding humanity," compromising his own voice and the voice of freedom, and bargaining with principle. *The Liberator* and its editor could not be bound by any organization or institution.

While Garrison's strident and singular message about the evils of slavery is undeniably clear from the day *The Liberator* first appeared, the single consistent message that he delivered in his previous printing experiences, from the last years of his apprenticeship until January 1831, was not abolition. His most consistent message was about the power of the press: the importance of newspapers in American social and political life, the moral obligations of the editor to provide the information the American citizen needed, the duty of citizens to enter the marketplace of ideas, and the role of the newspaper (and its editor) to provide the means for the political and religious institutions to reach the public and, to paraphrase Thomas Jefferson, help them to keep their opinions right.

The decision to publish in Boston only materialized in the last months before *The Liberator*'s first issue appeared, but in retrospect once his chosen career in the printing profession began, the path to January 1, 1831, can be clearly traced. Abandoned by his father as a very young child, Garrison experienced a peripatetic decade traveling around New England with family. He had little opportunity for formal education before eventually returning, without family, to his hometown, Newburyport. After other failed attempts to find a trade, he was indentured to Ephraim Allen as a printer's apprentice. For the next seven years, he worked in the dank, malodorous, and physically demanding atmosphere that was the printer's trade; however, that atmosphere was also filled with opportunity, which Garrison engaged with vigor. The printer's office became his college and provided the education he had been denied. He read and wrote, never abandoning the hard work and manual labor associated with the arts and mysteries of his chosen trade. In time, he became a writer, editor, and trusted manager in Allen's office. He observed and commented in the paper on local, national, and international social and political issues with energy that belied his youth, albeit a youth whose life had become defined, structured, and steadied by his trade. His passion for democratic politics and the faith his mother instilled in him, along with the press, were the foundations of his life.

Garrison's faith in the nation's political institutions, however, was quickly tested after he completed his indenture. With Allen's financial assistance, Garrison edited his own newspaper in Newburyport, *The Free Press*. Demonstrating his burgeoning independent spirit he challenged, perhaps foolishly, the political establishment in the town, which he believed had abandoned pure Federalist political ideology. He even managed to irritate his former master and current benefactor. Furthermore, local political leaders did not appreciate his independent and clarion voice. After six months, he was forced to relinquish his paper but not without defiantly declaring that no amount of coercion would undermine his principled search for truth. In this first editorial effort, he learned that political independence had a price.

He left his hometown for Boston and the company of other aspiring printers and editors. Once settled, he was quick to enter Bostonian political debates. After several months of temporary journeyman efforts, he found a second editorial position. As editor of the *National Philanthropist*, Garrison, for the first time in any substantive way, was introduced to the world of antebellum reform. *The Philanthropist* was the first newspaper devoted solely to temperance reform and the new editor embraced it wholeheartedly. Although his commitment to temperance was certainly robust, advocacy of social reform could not fully silence his appetite for discussion of political issues, which many *Philanthropist* readers, and the paper's publishers, eventually found tiresome and distracting. Soon another editorship was completed, but not, of course, without a Garrisonian flourish. His final editorial comment expressed contempt for anyone who could not appreciate the rationality of his editorial topics and opinions.

While political commentary undoubtedly contributed to Garrison's demise as editor of *The Philanthropist*, it was certainly not the only reason. It was also strongly influenced when he met Benjamin Lundy in Boston in March 1828. The famous Quaker abolitionist and self-trained publisher was touring New England to rally support for his anti-slavery newspaper in Baltimore and the cause of anti-slavery in general. The tour accomplished little except to light a fire in Garrison's heart. From that meeting forward, the battle to end slavery became the principal issue in his life; however, any possibility of collaboration with Lundy was put on hold. Meanwhile, Garrison was recruited to publish a newspaper in Bennington, Vermont. The *Journal of the Times* was a pro–John Adams election publication which Garrison accepted less on account of his support for Adams than the promise of complete editorial freedom. With Adams' victory in Vermont almost certain, the editor had leave to fill the paper with articles about a variety of reform ideas, including, temperance, peace, morality, education, Indian rights, and anti-slavery. Adams did indeed win Vermont but lost the presidency to Andrew Jackson, whom Garrison considered completely unfit for the office. Jackson's victory was an affront to American democratic ideals and Garrison wrote about the impending danger his election meant for the nation.

He was unabashed in his disgust with Andrew Jackson and dismayed by the acquiescence of the nation's voters, who were so easily manipulated into electing a person so clearly incompetent. Meanwhile, another experience further tested Garrison's faith in the American political system. In Bennington, he had organized one of the largest anti-slavery petitions ever submitted to the U.S. Congress. It was dismissed out of hand. Congressional rejection of the rather benign anti-slavery petition, which requested little more than a plan to end the slave trade in the nation's capital, was surely additional evidence of the want of political morality. While certainly discouraged, these setbacks were not yet signs of irredeemable political depravity. Garrison was not prepared to despair of the power of the power of the press to help restore political righteousness in the nation's leaders.

As his patience with political leadership was tested, he also reflected on similar failures on the part of American ministers and churches. Benjamin Lundy returned to New England in early 1829 and once again his pleas for the enslaved millions were greeted with indifference not only by the political establishment but by nearly every minister in the region, including in Boston. The ministers invited to meet with Lundy counseled moderation, told him that anti-slavery activity on their part was meddling in affairs that were not their concern, and expressed fear that those efforts would give offence that could forestall a solution. When Garrison was invited to deliver an Independence Day speech at the Park Street Church, his growing concerns about political corruption and ministerial apathy became the twin subjects of his address, "Dangers of the Nation." Specifically, he proclaimed that "our politics are rotten to the core," and that "infidelity in our land" was a reality. Garrison warned that the continued failure of the political and religious institutions to battle the scourge of slavery would make the free-states of the North subservient to slave-power apologists and complicit in sinful and evil practices.

Nevertheless, he had not lost hope that both institutions would recognize their obligations and professed his desire to be their coadjutor in bringing an end to the scourge of slavery.

Soon after the speech, Lundy's call to Baltimore was received and Garrison's co-editorship of the *Genius of Universal Emancipation* began. Here he hoped to be heard by political and religious leaders and provide assistance as they came together to lead the struggle to end slavery. It was not meant to be, not the least on account of Garrison's own changing perspectives. A combination of personal reflection and interaction with black communities in Boston had driven Garrison beyond mere anti-slavery to the realization that the only legitimate anti-slavery position was to call for *immediate* emancipation — the sinner does not stop sinning gradually. Furthermore, his contact with black leaders and the black community in Baltimore led him to question the wisdom of colonization and argue more forcefully for full civil and political rights for free (and freed) blacks. These new perspectives, in combination with his aggressive language, enraged Southern slaveholders and their supporters, and did not always sit well with the gentle Quaker, Benjamin Lundy. Ironically, however, it was a libel case instigated by Francis Todd, a shipowner from Garrison's hometown, Newburyport, that ended his editorship in Baltimore after six months. Todd resented Garrison's accusations about the transportation of slaves on one of his ships and sued for libel. Trial in a slave state and the inevitable guilty verdict forced Garrison into a Baltimore jail for nine weeks. Garrison embraced prison as a badge of honor and, while jailed, considered his options to continue his campaign.

After his release, Garrison's plans were in flux but his goal, destroying slavery, was fixed. He considered the possibility of reviving his relationship with Lundy or the possibility of establishing his own abolitionist paper in Washington, D.C. What better place to challenge the monster of slavery than in its home territory. He toured from Baltimore to New England seeking support, but with very limited success. However, what he did find, widespread throughout the supposedly "free" New England states, was apathy and indifference toward the enslaved — most disturbingly for Garrison, in his hometown of Newburyport.

During the final few months of 1830, as he struggled to decide how he would proceed, Garrison came to two realizations. First, he and his press must do more than provide support in the battle, but must lead; the political and religious establishments were morally bankrupt. After years urging political and religious action, it was clear that neither institution intended to lead the fight to end slavery; rotten politics and infidelity were not prepared to yield or repair the error of their ways. The "Dangers of the Nation" were stolid and impassive. Second, while slavery in the southern states was intransigent and unyielding, indifference toward slavery in the northern states was equally so. Thus, Boston, Massachusetts, was as culpable as Washington, D.C., or Richmond, Virginia. *The Liberator*, as he wrote in his first issue, would therefore raise "the standard of emancipation ... within sight of Bunker Hill, and in the birthplace of Liberty." Emancipation had to be won in the North before the South could succumb. Furthermore, the printer's stand, where Garrison composed and set his type as an apprentice, as a journeyman printer, as a young editor, and as a publisher, was the sole remaining bulwark of liberty. It was there that Garrison would take his own stand, beholden to no other party or creed, and wage battle with slavery and its apologists for the next thirty-five years. Success was hardly assured, but his voice would be heard.

ONE

The Printer's Stand

ON DECEMBER 29, 1865, in his valedictory editorial for *The Liberator*, William Lloyd Garrison called his paper the "original 'disturber of the peace'" and expressed pride in the challenges it had faced since before the day it first appeared.

The Liberator had been repudiated, he wrote, "by Southern slaveholding villainy on the one hand, and Northern pro-slavery malice on the other" and was rejected by anyone "claiming to be Christian or patriotic." With great pride he relished the confrontation created by the paper's publication and the defiance it offered to the political and religious institutions of 1831. No small measure of Garrison's pride was in consequence of the fact that *The Liberator* had accomplished its thirty-five-year-old goal: "the extermination of chattel slavery." But, in addition, *The Liberator* represented a journalistic endeavor unlike any other. It was a journal, he wrote, that had "vindicated primitive Christianity, in its spirit and purpose" and "the Declaration of Independence, with its self-evident truths." Garrison conceded that there was much work which remained to be done in order to secure the rights of the freedmen but, for now, it was especially appropriate, he argued, "to let its existence cover the historic period of the great struggle." *The Liberator* had not only defined the battle for emancipation, and vindicated the rights of the oppressed, but its existence, Garrison believed, was an example of the power of the press to disturb the peace of the complacent and to be "a terror to evil doers."[1]

Garrison's life as an abolitionist, reformer, non-resister, supporter of women's rights, and persistent advocate for social change was fundamentally driven by and dependent on his career as a journalist. He did not take up the journalist's profession in order to pursue the issues he advocated; he was first a printer, later a writer, and finally a journalist. As Garrison himself explained, in a letter written only a few months before his death to fellow printer and reformer George W. Stacy,

> My connection with the printer's craft, is to me a source of unspeakable pride and delight, and it had everything to do with shaping my career and literally putting into my hands the great instrumentalities for the final overthrow of the slave system. Had I not been a practical printer — an expert compositor and able to work at the press — there had been no Liberator.[2]

For Garrison, the printer's trade and the practice of journalism became the means to achieve abolition. When the nation's political and religious leaders abandoned their duty to fight for the enslaved — for those who were being denied political liberty and Christian compassion — Garrison turned to the printing press and the principles of free speech to lead the battle.

It is perhaps little wonder that Garrison sought to have his voice heard in society. He was the third of four children, abandoned by an alcoholic father when he was only three years old, separated from his beloved mother Frances (more commonly called Fanny) from age twelve until her death seven years later, and eventually an apprentice while virtually an orphan in his hometown of Newburyport, where he received little formal education, save the school of the printing office. Throughout his life Garrison was unwilling to compromise in his expression of what he believed were fundamentally important goals or ideals. After removal to Baltimore with his mother, brother and sister when he was only twelve, he refused to stay and returned alone to Newburyport to plan his life. As a young apprentice, he was committed to finding some means of educating himself and preparing himself for a useful career. Then, as a young master printer, in his first editorial effort at *The Free Press*, he took on the politicians of Newburyport and the local Federalist Party organization for perceived slights to orthodox Federalist political beliefs. He insisted on remaining faithful to what he believed were the fundamental tenets of Federalism, while others were prepared to forego them, he asserted, in the interest of political expedience. In his second editorship, at the *National Philanthropist*, he embraced the cause of temperance and other reform issues which emphasized universal values and morals, and which sought to return American society to a balance that it seemed to have lost. Later still, in Bennington at the *Journal of the Times* and in Baltimore at the *Genius of Universal Emancipation*, the issue of slavery took center stage in his life.

Slavery was, he believed, at odds with both the teachings and ideals of

Christianity as well as with the ideological political principles upon which the United States was founded. When both failed to challenge slavery's continued existence, he answered the call as his experience and training had taught him. The Church and political parties, which had sustained and encouraged him as he grew, seemed to have succumbed to what, in later years, he called a "compromise with the devil" in which essential truths were willingly and capriciously forsaken. Once the battle was joined, Garrison could compromise no longer, not until victory was in sight. His chief tool in the battle was his printing press—a weapon (although he may have eschewed that particular term) that he believed had the power to influence and change the world. He could not compromise the conduct or independence of his press without diluting the cause and his goal.

Those who have examined Garrison's life and contributions have tended to consider his career at the press as an auxiliary to his career in abolition. Certainly this is a justifiable perspective in examining the years following *The Liberator's* first appearance. Over the years, writers have reflected on Garrison's prophetic presence as the moral center to a revitalized anti-slavery movement; on the central role he played in achieving emancipation, or conversely for some, his marginal role; on the new philosophical dimensions he contributed to abolition; and on the psychological dynamics within his life that generated his interest in reform and fueled his passionate, aggressive style. For Garrison, however, printing was the crucial component in his unyielding effort to reform American society. By the time he began publishing *The Liberator* in 1831, printing and publishing remained the only well from which he could draw the resources necessary to fight for the abolition of slavery. Only infrequently has this fact been the subject of historical inquiry into Garrison's life. Yet the press was undeniably a fundamental element of his life. From 1818 until 1865, Garrison's cosmos revolved around the physical realities of weekly newspaper publication. In a like fashion, after emancipation and after *The Liberator* was discontinued, numerous letters and articles written by Garrison appeared in a variety of newspapers. Addressing the public in print continued to be the principal means for him to express his concerns about the persistent problems in American society. Between 1866 and 1878, Garrison wrote over one hundred articles for *The Independent*, which was edited by his friend Theodore Tilton, on a variety of subjects, but he wrote especially about Reconstruction, President Andrew Johnson's impeachment, and the failure of the nation to support the civil rights of the freedmen in the South. An advertisement in that paper on November 21, 1878, identified Garrison as one of its "distinguished writers and contributors."

The earliest commentators about Garrison's life and influence came from those who knew him while he was still alive. All acknowledged his role as editor of *The Liberator,* but none chose to focus on Garrison's commitment to the press as a basic instrument of reform. Two of these commentators were close friends and fellow abolitionists, Samuel J. May and Oliver Johnson. Neither May's *Some Recollections of Our Antislavery Conflict* nor Johnson's *William Lloyd Garrison and His Times* purport to be biographies of Garrison, but both treat him with great reverence and as central to the antebellum abolitionist movement. For May, Garrison "by moral and religious means" directed the completion of the "great work which the American revolutionists commenced," and furthermore argued that the nation had, at the time of the book's publication, only just begun to recognize the extent of his contributions.[3]

Johnson was even more effusive in his praise for Garrison's foresight, steadfastness, and guidance. Throughout his book, Johnson repeatedly returned to his major theme: Garrison was the moral center of the abolitionists' struggle, and if the center were abandoned, the battle may have been lost. "It is not too much to say," Johnson argued, "if the moral agitation had ceased, and Garrison and his friends retired from their work ... the Slave Power would have held the country more firmly than ever in its grasp."[4] While Johnson gave some credit to the political abolitionists for their part in the struggle, he clearly believed that Garrison's ceaseless campaign provided the impetus for the kind of political action which Garrison himself shunned. Eight years after his book was published, Johnson wrote that after Garrison's death he took it as his duty to write "in defense of him and of the movement he founded and led," especially in light of recent commentary which claimed that Garrisonians had "accomplished little or ... had indeed done nothing but mischief." He dedicated his book not just to Garrison but to "all the heroes of the [abolition] struggle" while staunchly maintaining that triumph in the struggle was dependent on the moral agitation begun and sustained by Garrison.[5]

Another contemporary, Henry Wilson, was more qualified in his praise for Garrison than either May or Johnson. Wilson rose through the Massachusetts' political system to become a United States senator in 1855, and served as chairman of the Senate Committee on Military Affairs during the Civil War. In that capacity, John Meyer argues that Wilson "ranks with Lincoln and Stanton as the three most responsible on the civilian side for winning the Civil War."[6] In 1872, he was elected vice president for Ulysses Grant's second term, and in that year he published the first volume of a four-volume work, *The History of the Rise and Fall of the Slave Power in America.* With regard to Garrison, Wilson wrote that he "evinced singular personal independence, rare moral courage, and an uncompromising fidelity to his convictions and to the claims of humanity,"[7] but also voiced reservations about the originality and uniqueness of Garrison's contributions. Garrison did not, Wilson argued, discover any new truths about slavery, was not the first to espouse immediate emancipation, and his use of severe language and his refusal to cooperate with either political or church associations limited his influence, especially after 1840. In summary, Wilson described Garrison as unoriginal, lacking any significant leadership abilities, clearly mistaken in eschewing political abolition, and ultimately un-deserving of credit for slavery's eventual demise.

Both before and after Wilson's book was published, Garrison expressed his own frustration with the author's analysis. Before publication, Wilson had sent parts of his manuscript for Garrison's appraisal. Garrison wrote a long letter to Wilson in which he questioned Wilson's treatment of the "Garrisonian abolitionists, so called." Garrison called his corrections "few & trifling," but they were in fact rather substantial. Garrison asserted that the political and religious anti-slavery activism of the 1840s and 1850s was only made possible by the moral agitation that preceded them. Furthermore, Garrison took exception to Wilson's allegation that Garrisonian abolitionism grew ineffective after 1840 and argued that Lincoln's election was, in fact, made possible by the moral regeneration they inspired.[8] After the book's publication, Garrison reiterated his criticism of Wilson in a letter to the historian Henry Adams. Adams had written to Garrison to request his response to Wilson's book, which Garrison declined for "private reasons." While he did tell Adams that Wilson's history was "meritorious," he nevertheless complained that it "disproportionately magnifies the political" efforts to abolish slavery. In Garrison's estimation, Wilson gave his readers the impression that the contribution of Garrisonian activists was "a very subordinate instead of a most potential one to the end of the struggle."[9] Wilson would not be the last of Garrison's post-emancipation critics, only the last that Garrison would be able to address personally.

Without doubt Garrison certainly had significant positive influence on the four-volume biography of his life published by two of his sons five years after his death. Wendell Phillips Garrison and Francis Jackson Garrison's work, *William Lloyd Garrison, 1805–1879: The Story of His Life Told by His Children*, fully appreciated the radical nature of their father's moral agitation, and lovingly presented their father as the principal guiding force in the anti-slavery struggle. While certainly the objectivity of the authors can be considered suspect, it remains to this day the single best source for anyone initiating an investigation into Garrison's life. His sons completed a project that many had beseeched their father to undertake after *The Liberator* ended publication: writing the story of his own life. In March 1873, a group of prominent citizens, led by Edmund Quincy, Samuel E. Sewell, John Greenleaf Whittier, Maria Weston Chapman, and many others, wrote Garrison and requested that he prepare his autobiography.[10] He reminded his friends that in 1866, he had agreed to write a history of the anti-slavery struggle and as of yet "the first sentence remains to be recorded." From issues relating to his health, to concerns about the size and complexity of the work, Garrison laid out enough roadblocks to support doubt that he ever seriously considered undertaking the task.[11] Although he never said so directly, the paralysis which incapacitated his wife Helen in 1863, and about which he expressed some culpability for the time spent agitating for abolition and for his failure to provide sufficient economic support, may have also been a factor.[12] In a letter to his son, Wendell, about the request, Garrison expressed his reluctance to write his autobiography, saying, "I doubt if I shall at any time be able to do more than leave some reminiscences and sketches for you and my other children to dispose of as you ... think best."[13] In their biography, Garrison's sons explained that his disinclination to write his autobiography was because "he preferred discussing the topics of the day to recording his life-experiences for posterity."[14] One can only speculate whether their analysis and perspective represented a polite rationalization or more truly represented their father's ongoing journalistic inclinations.

The first single-volume biography of Garrison, *William Lloyd Garrison: The Abolitionist* by Archibald Grimké, was published at the beginning of the last decade of the nineteenth century. Grimké was born into slavery in South Carolina, was nephew to famous abolitionists Angelina and Sarah Grimké, eventually graduated from Harvard Law School, became a leader in the civil rights struggle at the turn of the century and an associate of W.E.B. DuBois, and participated in the formation of the National Association for the Advancement of Colored People (NAACP) in 1909. In light of Grimke's life and experience, it is not surprising then that he presented Garrison as an American hero and an example for current and future generations. He relied heavily on the Garrison sons' four volumes and his most important accomplishment may have been in condensing those volumes to a more readable scale. Substantively, however, he offered little or no new information or perspectives on Garrison's life.[15]

Neither do the two other late nineteenth-century works in which Garrison received significant historical notice: James Schouler's *History of the United States of America Under the Constitution*, published in 1892, and James Ford Rhodes' *History of the United States from the Compromise of 1850*, published in 1893. But if no new information emerged, the two did present widely divergent perspectives on Garrison's contribution to abolition. For Schouler, Garrison was a dangerous radical who, far from eschewing violence, "tended to anarchy" and "sent not peace, but a sword." Garrison and his associates, he charged, willfully encouraged the slaves to insurrection and precipitated a division within the nation that only widened the division between North and South. Somewhat grudgingly, Schouler granted that Garrison was right to regard slavery as morally reprehensible. Still he argued that emancipation was eventually achieved by "enlightened statesmen," and not by Garrison's "appeal to terrorism."[16] Rhodes' perspective was much more in line with the appraisals of Johnson and May. He presented Garrison as the moral conscience of northern commercial, political, and religious authorities who had become abettors to slavery. Furthermore, Rhodes supported Garrison's own claim that his policies and actions were responsible for the existence of the Republican Party and for the election of Abraham Lincoln in 1860.[17] If no new information or analysis is offered in the two works, they do at least articulate the broad scope of divergent, but generally dichotomous perspectives about Garrison that are often reflected in later studies and scholarly analysis.

The first twentieth-century study of Garrison was a spirited and enthusiastic biography of Garrison published in 1921 by John Jay Chapman, *William Lloyd Garrison*. For Chapman, Garrison had become the forgotten man of an anti-slavery movement that was increasingly dismissed as insignificant in popular contemporary society. Early in the century, historians of southern history, such as U.B. Phillips, avowed justification for American slavery and dismissed the benefits of emancipation. Phillips described southern plantations as schools "constantly training and controlling pupils who were in a backward state of civilization." Those "pupils" were, of course, Africans who, in Phillips' determination, were experiencing "an essentially slow process of transition from barbarism to civilization."[18] Abolition, abolitionists, and emancipation interfered with this process. Rather, Chapman believed Garrison was "the central figure in American life" in the thirty years before the Civil War began, and argued that he "changed this nation as much as one man ever did ... or any nation in the history of the world."[19] While Chapman offered an eloquent defense of Garrison and the abolitionist struggle, his biography bordered on the hagiographic and, despite his effort, failed to restore Garrison to a place of historical prominence.

In fact, a dozen years later, Gilbert Barnes' reappraisal of the abolitionist movement, *The Antislavery Impulse, 1830–1844*, displayed a diametrically opposite perspective and denigrated Garrison. Barnes argued that Garrison's role in the abolitionist movement was at best marginal and, at worst, a serious hindrance to the movement's success. The abolitionist movement, in Barnes' re-interpretation, emerged from the religious revivalism of Charles Finney, and the driving force was not Garrison in New England, but Theodore Weld and the rebels from Lane Seminary in Cincinnati. Garrison was "simply a notorious name, a term of opprobrium, a grotesque of abolition fanaticism." Moreover, the only contribution made by the Garrisonian abolitionists in New England was in creating and sustaining the legend that Garrison had inspired the anti-slavery impulse and was its leading voice, when, it truth, he was "dead weight."[20]

While not fully embracing Barnes' depiction of Garrison as marginal to antebellum abolition, several scholars reinforced James Schouler's judgment which had pictured Garrison as a dangerous extremist. In *The Coming of the Civil War* by Avery Craven, and in *On Freedom's Altar: The Martyr Complex in the Abolition Movement* by Hazel Catherine Wolf, Garrisonian abolitionism was harshly criticized. For both authors, the extremism of the message and the actions of Garrison and his followers unduly alarmed the southern planters to the point of helping to precipitate a war, which may not have been necessary if cooler, more responsible leaders had prevailed. In addition, Wolf pictured Garrison as a professional agitator who "stumbled upon antislavery" and embraced it as his life's work because it fit his ambition for attention and recognition. He welcomed the kind of martyrdom which, she argued, was viewed as an American tradition from early colonial times through the Revolution, and he employed that martyr complex to vindicate his righteous anger against slavery, as well as to advance his own reputation.[21] A few years later, Stanley Elkins' *Slavery: A Problem in American Institutional and Intellectual Life* argued, in line with Barnes' analysis, that Garrison's individualist approach to abolition was successful only in generating a "personal legend" for his own benefit and aggrandizement. As a result, "Garrisonism" ultimately drove the abolition movement "from organization to fragmentation, from consolidated effort to effort dispersed, diffuse, and pervasive." Whatever opportunity abolitionism had to create a cohesive institution to challenge the power of institutionalized and institutionally supported slavery was thus lost on account of Garrison's ego and fanaticism.[22]

In the 1950s there were two other significant works on Garrison, Ralph Korngold's *Two Friends of Mankind: The Story of William Lloyd Garrison and Wendell Phillips and Their Relationship with Abraham Lincoln*, and Russell Nye's *William Lloyd Garrison and the Humanitarian Reformers*. Both treated Garrison much more sympathetically than Barnes, Craven, Wolf, or Elkins. Korngold's rather brief biography relied heavily on secondary sources but strove to present Garrison in a more positive light, and to demonstrate that he was a significant abolitionist leader who directly influenced events in the United States from the 1830s through the Civil War. While not completely convincing, Korngold at least offered a substantive challenge to the attempts by Barnes and others to entirely marginalize Garrison's career. Nye's analysis falls somewhere between Barnes and Korngold. Like Barnes, Nye is inclined to minimize Garrison's direct influence on emancipation but, like Korngold, he argued that Garrison was "a person of real historical importance." Garrison became a "symbol to his generation" of the discord created by his moral agitation against slavery. While Southerners concentrated their anger and fear against his rhetorical vitriol, Northern consciences were besieged by his persistent call for an immediate end to slavery, the immorality of which few denied but the existence of which most considered inconsequential to their lives and societies — and a political decision beyond their right to influence, much less decide.[23]

Along with the observance of the centennial commemoration of the Civil War and contemporary attention to civil rights issues, two informative biographies of Garrison were published in 1963. The first, Walter Merrill's *Against Wind and Tide: A Biography of William Lloyd Garrison*, owes a great debt to the access (provided for Merrill by the Garrison family) to previously unpublished documents and letters. Later, these became part of a six-volume collection of Garrison's letters published by Merrill and his co-editor, Louis Ruchames, between 1971 and 1981. In his biography, Merrill treated Garrison's life in full and not solely as the abolitionist agitator and moral iconoclast who had dominated previous works on Garrison. He offered a picture of Garrison's relationship with his family, friends, and fellow abolitionists, and showed him as a reformer who fought against more than slavery, but also against war, prejudice, passivity, and a variety of other moral sins. Furthermore, Merrill disputed Barnes' thesis, which gave Theodore Weld principal credit for leading the anti-slavery crusade, and argued that Garrison deserved "primary credit for bringing the problem of slavery to the attention of the nation."[24] The second biography published in 1963, *The Liberator, William Lloyd Garrison: A Biography*, by John L. Thomas, also offered a broad examination of Garrison's life. Thomas acknowledged Garrison's courage and his importance to the moral agitation that led to the end of slavery. He also presented solid evidence of Garrison's influence on Weld and other reformers in the west, which further undermined Barnes' contention that a western anti-slavery movement emerged independent of Garrison. But ultimately, for Thomas, Garrison was a kind of tragic hero. Garrison's perfectionist philosophy and moral authoritarianism on slavery ignited the abolitionist movement, but his inability to provide effective leadership and his refusal to compromise doomed the movement from achieving one of its fundamental goals: full civil rights and racial equality.[25]

Four years later, Aileen Kraditor's *Means and Ends in American Abolitionism: Garrison and His Critics on Strategy and Tactics, 1834–1850* challenged Elkins' and Thomas' appraisal of Garrison's individualism as divisive and ultimately destructive of the anti-slavery movement. Kraditor claimed that she did not intend to rehabilitate Garrison's image, but she certainly did nonetheless.[26] The schism that occurred in the anti-slavery movement in 1840 was not, according to Kraditor, the result of personal pique, but the consequence of fundamental ideological differences. Garrison was certainly at the center of the controversy, but debate in 1840 over the "woman question" and abolitionist connections with political organizations were representative of more essential differences within the movement. Garrison and his followers wanted fundamentally radical change unlike other, more reform-minded abolitionists. For Garrisonians, the social, religious, and political institutions were fundamentally flawed and required much more than minor revisions or simple reform. In addition, both factions diverged on the proper tactics for developing support for abolition. The Garrisonians, in Kraditor's analysis, were not fanatical individualists. They encouraged an inclusive abolitionist movement that did not impose specific socio-religious beliefs on its members. Rather it was the anti–Garrisonians who wanted an exclusive abolitionist movement and who forced the schism. For Kraditor, Garrison was more consistent in his abolitionist and social reform agitation than either the moderate or political abolitionists, and she implied in her conclusion that adherence to his ideals may have prevented secession and the Civil War.[27]

Several books in the 1970s addressed the history of antebellum anti-slavery directly and, as part of that subject, an evaluation of Garrison's contribution could not be ignored. In *The Abolitionists: The Growth of a Dissenting Minority* by Merton Dillon, the author argued that while abolitionists were never more than a minority in America, a portion of their agenda was adopted by the majority of American society. Regardless of this achievement, however, abolition was a failure because it intended, in the fullest understanding of the term, not only to end slavery, but also to create a society that accepted racial equality. At the heart of this failure was the schism in the movement in 1840 and, while Dillon does not single out Garrison as the sole culprit and exclusively responsible, he does argue that Garrison's role was especially divisive.[28] The two anti-slavery societies that emerged from the schism were both essentially powerless. The movement became dominated by political abolitionists who accomplished emancipation, but were nevertheless incapable of creating a racially egalitarian society. For Ronald Walters in *The Antislavery Appeal: American Abolitionism After 1830*, published in 1976, the importance of the 1840 schism has been overstated. He examines Garrison's role in the affair and concludes that the similarities between the two sides far exceeded the differences. In fact, the "appeal" of anti-slavery was that it was not a fanatical or extreme sentiment in antebellum society. In Walters' analysis, anti-slavery was one of several efforts, including the system of slavery itself, to impose some order on a rapidly changing society. Distinctively, for Garrison, slavery was beyond the moral foundation on which this new order could be built. This moral foundation was expected by many abolitionists to be enough to convert the nation and bring an end to slavery, according to James Stewart Brewer in *Holy Warriors: The Abolitionists and American Slavery*. Garrison was one of those warriors whose anti-slavery agitation in the 1830s did not produce conversion, but rather a harsh backlash of violence, mob action and suppression of civil liberties. In turn, this backlash fed the fear of a "slave power" conspiracy that eventually resulted in the Civil War. Stewart gives greater sway, however, to pre–Garrisonian influences, such as the Enlightenment and the Great Awakening, in the development of anti-slavery sentiment in the United States. Furthermore, in the final analysis, according to Stewart, neither Garrison nor any other abolitionists can take credit for ending slavery. "It was," he wrote, "the Union armies and generals who led them, together with African American activists in the North and South, who turned emancipation from a hope into an imperative."[29]

Lawrence Friedman's *Gregarious Saints: Self and Community in American Abolitionism, 1830–1870* continued the focus of abolitionist studies, like Stewart's, which emphasized actions and behavior among the abolitionists themselves. They were, for Friedman, neither failed radicals nor successful agitators, but "evangelical missionaries who contributed quite inadvertently and secondarily to sectional tensions and the Civil War."[30] Friedman presented a sophisticated analysis of three different abolitionist communities, in Boston, New York City, and upstate New York. These communities shared both a common origin in nineteenth-century American evangelization movements and a common inclination to draw together for support, as was a common characteristic of many antebellum reform movements. The differences that separated these various abolitionist communities and which defined their individual focuses were, for Friedman, established early in the 1830s and not by the schism at the end of the decade. Garrison was the center of the family-like community Friedman called the "Boston Clique." Within this clique Garrison worked hard to maintain his fatherly image, to treat other members with care and respect, both to limit discord, and to maximize unity within the group. This was no easy challenge in light of friction within the members of the "Boston Clique," the dissent between Boston and the other abolitionist communities, and, for all three communities, changing attitudes about women, race, politics, and the use of force. The image of Garrison that emerged from Friedman's book is more thoughtful and nuanced than any previous depiction and suggested that the depth of his character had, as of 1982, yet to be fully measured.

The most recent complete biography of Garrison is a masterful effort to provide a fully developed interpretation of his life, while also restoring his reputation as the most important force behind antebellum abolition. Henry Mayer's *All on Fire: William Lloyd Garrison and the Abolition of Slavery* dismissed the harsh, impatient, and impractical agitator of some earlier biographies, and pictured Garrison as a much more engaging, practical, interesting, and even humorous individual. Furthermore, Mayer believed that Garrison has been denied the recognition that his foresight and courage earned him in the struggle for emancipation. Garrison deserved, Mayer argued, "a place as central in the history of the nineteenth century as that of Dr. Martin Luther King, Jr. in the history of the twentieth."[31]

Mayer's may yet be a minority view, but his analysis suggests that Garrison's reputation has come full circle, from the adulation of May, Johnson, and his children, through the reassessments and marginalization of the early to mid-twentieth century, to a current revitalization and renewal. Certainly, neither Mayer nor any of Garrison's other biographers ignored his career in printing and neither do they dismiss *The Liberator* as insignificant or unimportant for the abolitionist cause. Like them, Mayer told the story of Garrison's apprenticeship, his early experiences as an editor, his struggle to publish *The Liberator* and keep the paper afloat, and his agonizing decision to cease publication after emancipation was secured. For all, however, the centrality of newspaper publishing to abolitionism, Garrison's contributions to American journalism or effective manipulation of 19th century journalism are either overlooked or downplayed. One reason for the lack of emphasis on his printing career is that Garrison's journalistic practices did not conform to the common trends investigated by historians of journalism. General studies of American journalism have been inclined to focus on two journalistic trends in the first half of the nineteenth century — newspaper and editorial involvement in the political process and the emergence of the "penny press."[32]

The second of these early nineteenth-century trends in journalism, the "penny press," was born nearly three years after the first issue of *The Liberator*, but clearly reflected a trend in American newspaper publishing which Garrison found offensive, even repulsive. It was initiated when the first edition of Benjamin Day's *New York Sun* hit the streets of the city in September 1833. The "penny press" era had begun. By emphasizing local news and sensational occurrences, and marketing the paper directly to the consumer for one-sixth the price of a conventional newspaper, one penny paid by individual issue rather than three dollars (or more) for an annual subscription, the *Sun* became the first successful newspaper for the masses. Within a few months it had the largest circulation of any newspaper in the nation and within a decade the "newspaper revolution" it began made the "penny press" available to nearly every citizen in the country.[33] By the time the Civil War began, these new newspapers produced many changes in journalism, from altered layouts and appearance, to a focus on topics that were of interest to ordinary citizens rather than society's elite, and to a lessening of the influence of partisan politics in newspapers' business affairs.[34]

With this transformation, the newspaper industry increasingly became more accustomed to dealing with newspaper readers as consumers rather than as voters. This was a change too far for Garrison. Although by the Civil War he had completely rejected politics and politicians as useless in the anti-slavery struggle, newspapers and newspaper editors' responsibility for promoting social and moral change remained paramount and, for Garrison, unchanged. The sensationalism of the "penny press" and its appeal to citizens' baser instincts diminished the editor of such a newspaper who flagrantly dismissed his obligation to inform and direct moral and ethical behavior. Nevertheless, by the end of the century, the change instigated by Day and the *New York Sun* contributed to an increasingly commercialized press that treated news primarily in terms of marketability and profit. This transformation, according to Gerald Baldasty, resulted from the combined effect of publishers' decreasing dependence on political parties for monetary support and increasing dependence on advertising and publicity.[35]

The first of these early 19th century trends, newspaper editorial contributions to and influence of the political process, was strongly evident in Garrison's training and experience during his apprenticeship at the *Newburyport Herald*, which will be detailed in the next chapter. The American newspaper press that Garrison learned to manipulate so successfully in the 19th century had come of age in the 18th century, principally during the period of resistance that preceded the American Revolution and Independence. Prior to the imposition of the Stamp Act in 1765, colonial newspapers were little more than advertising bulletin boards run by printers who rarely risked their livelihood by delving too deeply into partisan politics.[36] During revolutionary turmoil, however, political neutrality was unacceptable as Sons of Liberty, Committees of Safety, and Committees of Correspondence in local towns and villages enforced unequivocal commitment to the patriot agenda. Consequently, partisan journalism emerged — perhaps less committed to "freedom of the press" than to economic viability, or, as Arthur Schlesinger wrote, "liberty of speech [belonged] solely to those who spoke the speech of liberty."[37] For instance, John Mein and Thomas Fleeming, publishers of *The Boston Chronicle*, made what they believed was an honest effort to present both Patriot and Tory viewpoints. However, Samuel Adams and the Boston Committee of Safety found neutrality, or what we might today call objectivity, unacceptable; Mein was assaulted, hung in effigy and eventually sought protection from the British military.[38]

Moreover, cooperation among pre-revolutionary colonial printers had been unwittingly encouraged earlier by revisions in British colonial affairs which had permitted Benjamin Franklin to restructure the colonies' postal system a decade before the Stamp Act Crisis of 1765. One of the most important changes Franklin instituted was to permit printers to exchange newspapers without cost via the postal system. Afterward, news traveled more routinely between the colonies and a sense of intercolonial accord (not yet unity) began to develop. As a result, in the wake of changes in post–1763 British policies, an awareness of common issues and problems relating to these policies grew. When resistance was galvanized, "of the many ways of [influencing] men's minds none ... equaled the newspaper."[39] These printers did not lead revolutionary conflict but provided support for the movement; by 1775, there were forty-two newspapers—not a remarkable number, but double the number just ten years earlier, and all except a few were committed as "engines of opinion" in support of the rebel cause.[40] Reflecting on this period later in his life, John Adams wrote:

> The Revolution was in the Minds of the People ... before a drop of blood was drawn at Lexington. The Records of the thirteen Legislatures, the Pamphlets, Newspapers in all the Colonies ought to be consulted ... to ascertain the Steps by which the public Opinion was enlightened and informed.[41]

For Adams, the great engine to build support for revolution was the newspaper press and the information it disseminated from 1763 to 1774.

In the years following the Revolution, the press initially returned to some semblance of their non-partisan perspectives of the pre-revolutionary days, although they were now expected to be auxiliaries for the new American government and to represent "the legitimating force behind the new government."[42] For Thomas Jefferson, the nation's citizens were "the only censors of their governors" and required "full information of [government] affairs through the channel of the public papers ... [since] ... the basis of our government [is] the opinion of the people, the first object should be to keep that right."[43] In light of this expectation, the new government supported the press in a variety of ways. National and State guarantees of press freedom (at least until the Sedition Act of 1798) stifled attempts to control publications; there were no taxes on printing; publishing government documents provided regular income to many printers; and the continuation of the postal exchange combined with low postage on newspapers promoted circulation. In the early 1790s, newspapers "accounted for 70 percent of the mail by weight, but for only 3 percent of the postage." In addition, ironically, newspaper expansion was assisted by the lack of technology which inhibited the emergence of a single "national" newspaper, and encouraged the growth of decentralized "newspaper networks."[44]

Meanwhile, the political environment matured in the face of conflict, especially between Thomas Jefferson and Alexander Hamilton, over interpretation and meaning of the United States Constitution. This occurred first in the debate over the creation of the National Bank but later focused more sharply over an understanding of the limits to the national government's powers. The political conflict and the tensions the conflict exposed escalated through most of the decade and significantly contributed to the passage of the Sedition Act of 1798: a national government attempt to suppress an oppositional press and prosecute one political party, Jefferson's Republican Party. This, in turn, presaged the tumultuous presidential election of 1800. One consequence of these events was the creation of our political party system, something unanticipated, unexpected, and unwanted by the founding generation.

This political system, composed of the Federalist and the Republican parties, formed around Hamilton and Jefferson. Not least because both leaders eschewed political parties (or factions), the leadership of these early American political organizations devolved to newspaper editors, who often held strong political convictions and stood firmly on one (or the other) side of the partisan divide. Additionally, in return for financial support, they willingly published explicitly fractious essays and arguments. The influence of the newspaper editor initially had waned in the post-revolutionary years; he was still a "meer mechanic" whose craft denied him access to the title of "gentleman."[45] The title would remain elusive, but the creation of these partisan political newspapers enhanced the editor's influence. According to Jeffery Pasley, the emergence of these papers established the direction of American politics, and "from the 1790s on, no politician dreamed of mounting a campaign, launching a new movement, or winning over a new geographic area without a newspaper." For the next fifty years and as a permanent political party system emerged, the creation of a newspaper was "the first concrete act of party building."[46]

In what may be viewed as the apex of this political war, the presidential election of 1800 pitted Federalist John Adams against Republican Thomas Jefferson in the first openly partisan political party confrontation in U.S. history. It was a brutal and vicious battle waged largely by decentralized newspaper political networks. The majority of newspapers were controlled by Federalists, but Republican advocates and editors learned quickly to use them more effectively. Regardless, the arguments for newspapers on both sides often "pandered to hatred, disgust ... [and] ... relied on invective, falsehood and distortion."[47] Considering the outcome of the election, Jefferson's victory in 1800 demonstrated that his press was undoubtedly more successful; consequently, much of the credit for his election belongs not with the elite gentlemen and "natural aristocrats" who supported him, but with the artisans and "meer mechanics" of a burgeoning newspaper industry.[48]

Jefferson won, but the implications of the Republican victory in 1800 were not lost on Alexander Hamilton and other Federalist leaders. Many of them had denigrated the influence of uneducated printers and newspaper editors, who were supposed to be followers rather than leaders of public opinion. Federalist Party leaders reversed their position and created new newspapers or modified existing papers to reflect a new reality about newspapers and political dependence on the printer's craft.[49] Hamilton, for example, provided the funds for the New York *Evening Post* which first appeared in November 1801, and a few months later he proposed a plan for a nationwide Federalist organization. Hamilton's plan was founded on his belief that "men are rather reasoning than reasonable animals ... for the most part governed by the impulse of passion," and his speculation that the Jeffersonian-Republicans had been particularly effective in courting this "human passion." He called for a national organization to challenge the Republican Party's success. It was an organization which sounds very much like the internal structure of a modern political party. Called the "Christian Constitutional Society," its objectives were to support Christianity and the United States Constitution; the society's organization would include a national central council, statewide sub-councils, and local sub-councils within each state. The means to accomplish its objectives were, in Hamilton's words, "the diffusion of information" by newspapers and pamphlets. "Wherever," he wrote, "there is a press, clubs should be formed, to meet once a week, read the newspapers, and prepare essays." Under Hamilton's direction, the Federalists would use the growing partisan newspaper phenomenon to combat the Republicans, or as he preferred to label them, "the Jacobins."[50]

Isaiah Thomas, the first historian of American newspapers, published his *History of Printing in America* in 1810. His work recorded the consequence of the political newspaper expansion, and included a list of all newspapers published at that time, with their political party affiliation. Of the 366 newspapers, only 13 percent were neutral while the remaining 87 percent were evenly divided as committed to either Federalist or Republican political ideology.[51] More recently, Jeffery Pasley estimated the number of newspapers in 1810 at closer to 400 and calculated the rate of growth by decade from 1790 to 1820 at 148 percent, 52 percent, and 48 percent, respectively.[52] No doubt these statistics are hardly as impressive as the rate of growth in the political blogosphere of the last few decades, but considering the physical challenges associated with printing and newspaper publication at that time, it represents remarkable growth and an important accomplishment.

In the wake of Jefferson's victory in 1800, the Republican Party became dominant. Despite Hamilton's proposal and perhaps as another consequence of his death in 1804 after his duel with Aaron Burr, for a brief period the new political party system faded, and with it the usefulness of party newspapers. But in the second decade of the century, as the Jeffersonian party itself began to splinter (especially in the aftermath of the disastrous Embargo of 1807 and the War of 1812) and as the process of democratization expanded, new political conflicts emerged. In the resurgent political party system, organization and voter participation were critical and, as Gerald Baldasty noted, "central to the process of party organization [at that time] was the partisan editor and the partisan newspaper." Editors served on the central organizing committees of the party and, the newspaper was the principal method of communicating with party members and the electorate — especially considering postal regulations and the "exchange."[53] Furthermore, a subscription to a newspaper indicated membership in a political party and the newspaper editors held the party together between elections.[54] Political parties depended on *partisan* newspapers to disseminate information to the electorate and believed they were the most effective means of convincing them what was right and how they should use their vote. "News" for these papers was not factual or objective (as we might understand those terms today) and consequently, nothing was more disliked than "neutrality" in an editor. A paper which claimed neutrality simply was not worth reading.

By the election of Andrew Jackson in 1828, these newspapers and their editors had re-defined the meaning of democracy, broadened its application, extended democracy to more United States citizens, and contributed significantly to the creation of the United States' modern political party system. The term "democracy" begs for some clarification. Perhaps it can best be understood as a process that moves toward inclusion, based on the historical and social conditions within any particular society or culture at a given moment. The historian Sean Wilentz, who has written extensively about early national race and class in the Unites States, provides a good working definition; he describes democracy as "a historical fact, rooted in a vast array of events and experiences, that comes into being out of changing human relations between governors and the governed."[55] The notion of "changing human relations" explain why we can consider our nation in 1790 a democracy while its social structure (with 20 percent of the population in slavery) and restricted suffrage (with property limitations for men and the exclusion of women) would certainly be un-democratic in the present-day United States. The newspapers and editors of the late 18th and early 19th centuries made significant contributions toward changing the relations between the governors and the governed in the nation's early history. Printers refashioned their role in American society; they increasingly saw themselves and their newspapers as more than auxiliaries to the political leadership of a "natural aristocracy" and promoted a kind of leveling of American democracy which was not the expectation of, nor desired by, the founding generation.

The partisan political newspaper "was part of an exceptionally dynamic political era, and political activists believed in the efficacy of newspaper propaganda."[56] With the resurgence of parochial political organizations and the supposed democratization of the common man in the Jacksonian era, "the partisan editor and the partisan newspaper" became a critically important element in electioneering. Editors were party organizers, if not party leaders, and the newspaper was an invaluable tool for communicating with the party faithful.[57] By mid-century, Michael Schudson has argued, the "world of journalism was not well differentiated from politics" as journalists and editors used their profession as a path into the political world. This pattern held sway even after the Civil War and was perhaps most especially exemplified by the 1872 presidential candidacy of Horace Greeley, founder and longtime editor of the *New York Tribune*.[58]

Garrison fully engaged in the first of these trends, newspapers' political involvement, both in his apprenticeship and in his early editorial experiences, but essentially ignored the "penny press," although his journalistic inclinations were decidedly as democratic. Newspapers, for Garrison, were meant to be a vehicle for transmitting information to the public, for engaging in discussion and debate, and for creating an educated citizenship who could discern the truth from competing interests and perspectives—that is, to influence the relationship between the governors and the governed. For him, therefore, *The Liberator* could never treat its readers as consumers for profit and, despite his own eventual rejection of the political process as corrupt, *The Liberator* was intended to influence and persuade the America body politic. As a journalist, Garrison was part of a less well-examined trend in American journalism which Hazel Dicken-Garcia called the "information or news role." In this role, newspaper editors moved away from political and mercantile interests and stressed the editors' responsibility to provide to the individual citizen information which was "useful in life's conduct, decision making, and participation in the political system."[59] Dicken-Garcia acknowledged Garrison's participation in this kind of journalism, and, in a similar vein, Michael Schudson noted that *The Liberator* engaged in the "associational model" of journalism in which readers joined in community and communicated with one another.[60] Garrison, however, did more than simply participate in this trend in journalism. He was one of its first proponents and practitioners, not only in *The Liberator*, but in his very first editorial endeavor, *The Free Press* in Newburyport.

Notwithstanding this fact, biographical and historical appraisals of Garrison have primarily dedicated their attention to an analysis of his contribution to abolitionism with a limited focus on the role of printing in his life; a role which Garrison himself described as essential to his reform activity. His children and his contemporaries set the tone, and through the vicissitudes of historical interpretation, Garrison's reputation has fallen and risen based primarily on a perspective of his importance, or lack thereof, to abolition in the antebellum era. One exception to this focus on Garrison's abolitionism was an article titled "'The Organ of An Individual': William Lloyd Garrison and *The Liberator*" by Robert A. Fanuzi. Garrison, according to Fanuzi, jealously guarded his editorial control and independence at *The Liberator*, but while doing so, his egotism constrained him from publishing a newspaper that fully served the interests of a rational and informed citizenry.[61] While Fanuzi, unlike other commentators, directly addressed Garrison's printing career, he viewed it as a means by which Garrison aggrandized his own importance; Fanuzi does not adequately address how Garrison used the press as an effective instrument to provide information, to promote education, to contribute to an increasingly democratic United States, and to advocate reform.

Another exception offers a much different perspective on Garrison's publishing career. In an article titled "Tocqueville, Garrison and the Perfection of Journalism," David Paul Nord acknowledged that Garrison protected his editorial control of *The Liberator*, but also argued that few historians have recognized that "journalism was central to Garrison's understanding of emancipation and of the nature of a good society."[62] In the 1830s, America's most famous European visitor, Alexis de Tocqueville, recognized the important role that newspapers exerted in American society. He suggested that newspapers were necessary to create associations, to voluntarily unite individual efforts, and to encourage cooperation among a nation's citizens. "So," he wrote, "the more equal men become and more individualism becomes a menace, the more necessary are newspapers. We should underrate their importance if we thought they just guaranteed liberty; they maintain civilization."[63] Like Tocqueville, in Nord's analysis, Garrison believed that newspapers served democracy by bringing like-minded individuals together in a forum that encouraged debate over public policy decisions. Furthermore, Nord asserted that Garrison resisted efforts to make *The Liberator* the official voice of any organization not only because of his own personality and self-centered pride, but in order to retain the paper's status as a place for open discussion. Slavery, he believed, could not stand in the light of open and free discussion which would eventually expose the truth. Garrison believed, Nord contended, that dynamic reform required two elements, agitation and discussion. Both were critical elements of both Garrison's overall reform efforts and his plans for *The Liberator*.

Garrison's apprenticeship and his formative training as a newspaper editor developed and matured during the era of Tocqueville's commentary and, as part of that training, he fully ingested the conception of the newspaper's obligation to sustain national strength and vitality. His passionate commitment to be part of what he, in his own words while in Bennington, Vermont, called a "new race of editors" reflected his expectation of editorial integrity on the part of all newspaper publishers.[64] His disappointment in the behavior of many in the printer's fraternity was no small part in his decision to publish *The Liberator* and insist on rigid personal editorial control.

The Liberator also shared something in common with the American Tract Society's efforts to reach people in the United States with an old message in a new form. As described by Nord, in an article without reference to Garrison, Tract Societies intended to use modern techniques to provide readers with traditional religious teachings and literature.[65] The tract message distributed by the colporteurs who worked for these societies was not simply that reading mattered, nor simply that reading had the potential to evangelize and change people's lives, but rather that reading must also be focused on the proper message in order to achieve the proper result. Popular literature, especially novels, and increasingly the sensationalist press, offered too many opportunities for sin and licentiousness to take hold of individual lives. Tract publications were intended to use the appeal of the current style of literature in combination with modern mass media technology to deliver "a timeless message" of salvation.[66] In *The Liberator*, Garrison's message also reached back to a morality about slavery that he believed had been abandoned by the two institutions that were supposed to instruct and direct the republic, politics and church. As a result of their withdrawal from the most critical moral matter of the era, Garrison applied the power of the press, the only institution remaining within his power to influence, to lead the struggle for reform and emancipation.

The principal focus of this book then is to assert the process by which printing, the press, and newspaper publishing became central to Garrison's life and emerged as his primary tool in the abolition struggle. Emancipation would not become a reality until the end of the Civil War, but for Garrison the die was cast on January 1, 1831, with the publication of the first issue of *The Lib-*

erator. After uninterrupted weekly publication for thirty-five years and less than a year before his death, a group of Boston printers, members of the Franklin Typographical Club, and invited guests gathered at Young's Hotel in Boston on October 14, 1878, to celebrate the sixtieth anniversary of Garrison's first day as an apprentice in Newburyport, Massachusetts. Two days earlier, Garrison had visited Newburyport, where his apprenticeship in the printing trade had begun on October 13, 1818, and where he once more took a composing stick in hand. "Standing at case," ready to select and set type as he had learned to do as an apprentice so many years ago, he set three of his own sonnets which were published in the next day's *Herald*.[67] Speaking to the assembled guests at the celebration, Garrison recalled his most recent venture "at case" with relish and delighted in telling them that his old hands still worked quickly and that his finished work contained no errors. Furthermore, it was fitting, Garrison explained, that they came together to celebrate his apprenticeship because he had "always engaged in setting up types" and it was this engagement that formed both his career in printing and his career in reform. Some of his fellow printers, Garrison acknowledged, may not have fully endorsed his anti-slavery labors, but all of them endorsed the printing press as an instrument of change in the world. "I need not say, Mr. President," Garrison declared,

> how mighty an instrumentality the press is in regard to the progress of mankind. Ours is "the art preservative of all arts," and it stands at the head of all. Every craft is honorable, it is useful, but the printing craft is that which takes hold of the mind and intellect and soul. It is the power to move the world, and it is moving it. Some one has wittily said that the greatest stand in the behalf of civilization is the ink-stand, but I would add that it is the printer's stand, with a well-assorted case, and a compositor at that case with active brains and active hands putting "thoughts that breathe and words that burn" into type to help the age onward and upward.[68]

In his life, the "printer's stand" for Garrison was at first the physical instrumentality of newspaper publishing, but later became his personal commitment to emancipation for the nation's four million slaves. He deftly employed it to replace the preacher's pulpit and the politician's platform, especially after he determined that church and politics had abandoned the cause of abolition. Garrison did not choose this path lightly, nor without some reluctance, but, once chosen, he would not relinquish his stand until emancipation became a reality.

Two

The "mere boy"

AT WILLIAM LLOYD GARRISON'S funeral on May 28, 1879, Wendell Phillips eulogized his longtime friend and fellow abolitionist. He recalled Garrison as a young man who was passionately committed to ending slavery in the United States and marveled at the "mere boy ... with neither training or experience ... [who confronted] ... church, commerce, and college." Phillips wondered:

> What created such life under these ribs of death? Whence came that instinctive knowledge? Where did he get that sound common sense? Whence did he summon that almost unerring sagacity which, starting agitation on an untried field, never committed an error, provoking year by year additional enthusiasm; gathering, as he advanced, helper after helper to his side! I marvel at the miraculous boy. He had no means. Where he got, whence he summoned, how he created, the elements which changed 1830 into 1835 — 1830 apathy, indifference, ignorance, icebergs, into 1835, every man intelligently hating him, and mobs assaulting him in every city — is a marvel which none but older men than I can adequately analyze and explain.... Well, that dungeon of 1830, that universal apathy, that deadness of soul, that contempt of what called itself intellect, in ten years he changed into the whole country aflame. He made every single home, press, pulpit, and senate chamber a debating society, with *his* right and wrong for the subject.[1]

Phillips can be forgiven some hyperbole in a funeral eulogy, but he raised a question for which no completely adequate answer has been offered.

There is no denying the style of Garrison's rhetoric as an adult and as a newspaper editor. He chose not to equivocate and the uncompromising tenor of his language was calculated to evoke an emotional response — to influence, but not necessarily to win friends. "On [slavery], I do not wish to think, or to speak, or write with moderation," Garrison editorialized in the inaugural issue of *The Liberator*. "Tell a man whose home is on fire to give a moderate alarm ... I will not retreat a single inch —**and I will be heard**."[2] He was heard, yet Phillips' comments at Garrison's funeral in 1879 raise a reasonable question: what was it in Garrison's youth that prepared this "boy" to challenge "church, commerce, and college" in so dramatic a fashion to achieve first the enmity of a nation, and later, its honor?

There is little in Garrison's upbringing to suggest that a prominent career awaited him. If anything, his early years suggested little promise for the future. His father, Abijah Garrison, was born in Nova Scotia on June 18, 1773, went to sea as a youth and eventually became a sea captain — seemingly a successful workingman. His mother, Frances Maria Lloyd (Fanny), was born in 1776 in New Brunswick, was described as a "strikingly beautiful woman," who was also strong willed and independent. When she informed her Episcopal parents that she was determined to be baptized and become a Baptist, they forced her to leave their house. When Abijah met Fanny he was immediately smitten and pursued her until she agreed to marry him. They married in December 1799 and settled in St. John, New Brunswick, where two children were born, James Holley in 1801 and Caroline Eliza in 1803. Commercial decline in New Brunswick encouraged Abijah to move his young family to Newburyport, Massachusetts, in the spring of 1805; William Lloyd was born there on December 10.

Less than three years later, in July 1808, Abijah abandoned his family, returned to New Brunswick and was never seen again. There is certainly no justification for parental abandonment, but several events that took place in 1808 were likely contributing factors in Abijah's decision to leave his family. The commercial prosperity of seafaring Newburyport had disintegrated since the imposition of Jefferson's Embargo, which had effectively shut down all international commerce and devastated the New England shipping industry. In addition, the death of his daughter, Caroline, from eating poisonous flowers, and the birth of a new daughter, Maria Elizabeth, represented additional burdens which he interpreted as justification to seek solace in the bottle. Fanny loathed his appetite for drink and had been struggling for several years to break Abijah's penchant for alcohol.[3] With his father's abandonment of the family, young William, who was not yet three years old, was one of three children of a single mother abandoned by her parents and her husband, living in a foreign country at the beginning of long period of economic depression for seafaring New England.[4] Clearly, this situation did not represent an auspicious beginning.

Fanny supported her three young children by working as a practical nurse, but over the next ten years she moved frequently and the fatherless family was often separated. These travels and the family's poor financial condition severely limited William's exposure to formal education. From 1812 through 1815, during the second war with England, Fanny took his older brother, James, to live and work in Lynn, Massachusetts, while seven-year-old Lloyd (the name by which his mother generally chose to address him) remained in Newburyport with Deacon Ezekiel Bartlett. His four-year-old sister, Elizabeth, also remained in Newburyport but stayed with a different family. Prior to this family breakup, Lloyd had attended the primary school in Newburyport on School Street, but while staying at the Bartlett's home he moved to a grammar school nearer their home. Deacon Bartlett was affiliated with a struggling Baptist church and earned a meager living for his family as a woodcutter. He treated Lloyd kindly but because of the Bartlett's financial condition, Lloyd had to quit school after three months to earn money toward his board. In addition, "he [had] not shown himself an apt scholar," according to his first biographers, "being slow in mastering the alphabet, and surpassed even by his little sister Elizabeth."[5]

In 1815, Lloyd and his family were reunited in Lynn, Massachusetts, where his mother secured an apprenticeship for him with a Quaker shoemaker named Gamaliel Oliver. Before the end of the year, however, Fanny decided to move the family to Baltimore where she was promised work for both herself and her boys at a new shoe factory planned by a friend who was another Lynn manufacturer. Unfortunately, soon after they arrived in Baltimore, the factory failed and the family again separated. Older brother James, who had already caused Fanny much concern because of his rowdy acquaintances and love of alcohol, followed in his father's footsteps and ran away to sea. He was not heard from for twenty-five years. With great reluctance, Fanny allowed Lloyd to return to Newburyport and the care of Deacon Bartlett. Lloyd, she wrote to her friend Frances Farnham, was "discontented" in Baltimore and eager to return to his friends and to school in Newburyport.[6] Fanny and Elizabeth Garrison remained in Baltimore. Although Lloyd corresponded with his mother during their separation, they would not meet again until June of 1823, shortly before Fanny's death.

Back in Newburyport in 1816, Lloyd was allowed to return, for at least part of the year, to the "Grammar School on the Mall" and received one final dose of formal education.[7] Seven years later, in a letter to his mother Garrison made a rare comment about the deficiency of his education. "I do not understand one single rule of grammar," he wrote, "having a very inferior education."[8] In 1817, with his formal education ended, Lloyd was apprenticed to a cabinet maker in Haverhill, Massachusetts. His mother and Deacon Bartlett believed that the young man's future success depended on learning a trade, and although Lloyd knew that they were right, he hated the work they had chosen for him. After six weeks, the twelve-year-old ran away, but he was quickly found and returned to his master, who, having no interest in training a reluctant learner, released Lloyd from his apprenticeship indenture. Garrison returned to Deacon Bartlett's home and several abortive efforts were made to find a situation for the fourteen-year-old. Finally, on October 18, 1818, Lloyd was apprenticed to Ephraim Allen, publisher and editor of the *Newburyport Herald,* for a seven-year term.[9]

Allen had received his training as a printer in Boston from Isaiah Thomas and began working at the *Newburyport Herald* as a journeyman printer in 1801. He soon purchased the *Herald* and for most of the next three decades, until 1834, was editor and publisher. He was later remembered for his energy and strong work ethic: he "so conducted the press under his control, as to secure the approbation and support of the community with which he was identified."[10] His newspaper became locally popular and survived challenges from many other newspaper enterprises in Newburyport, including Garrison's short-lived *Free Press* in 1826. He was respected for conducting the *Herald* in the best interests of the whole community and after his death in 1846 his obituary acknowledged that it was difficult to separate the history of Newburyport with the life of the town's most esteemed editor.[11]

It was in Allen's printing office where the young Garrison's informal education began. He embraced the "arts and mysteries" of the printing trade, which had changed little from the technology Gutenberg employed in the middle of the fifteenth century. The fundamentals of the process still required four actions: inking, positioning the paper, application of pressure, removal and drying of the finished product.[12] Presses had evolved and were improved, but the fundamental processes had not substantively changed. At the beginning of the nineteenth century, a printer, like Allen, working with a standard wooden press could produce about 200 sheets per hour. Beginning in the late 1820s, with the development of the "bed and platen press" and the addition of steam power, production reached 1000 sheets per hour.[13] Greater printing production capabilities in the 1830s helped to make the "penny press" possible. However, these changes did not begin, at least in the United States, until 1819 — and even then only on an experimental basis and certainly did not soon reach Newburyport. Innovation and change certainly altered the traditional printing press, but if Gutenberg entered a typical early nineteenth century printer's office, he would have little trouble identifying and learning to operate the latest version of his press.[14] Learning the trade's "arts and mysteries" were the first step of Garrison's instruction and education; during his seven years and two months of apprenticeship, the talent and temperament of one of the reform era's most controversial and influential journalists were formed.

Unfortunately, evidence of the form and structure of this "informal" element of Garrison's education has not been easy to uncover. Garrison kept no diary or journal during his youth, but we can be fairly certain that he shared similar experiences with other craft apprentices of the early nineteenth century. The system of apprenticeship was in decline as a method of developing new trade craftsmen by then and by the time of the Civil War, apprenticeship was almost fully replaced with a more flexible, less complex, but also less craft-based system, which more adequately reflected the needs of modern industrial growth. For a lucky few, this change meant more education and success, but for most it meant low wage factory labor. In the printing trade however, the decline in apprenticeships was delayed; consequently, those lucky enough to work in the system, like the young Garrison, found a new focus on educational opportunities beyond the new and limited practices of eighteenth-century apprenticeship.[15]

Traditionally, the system of apprenticeship had served a number of important purposes, including the transmission of craft skills and job training from one generation to the next, the teaching of impressionable youth the value of work, the inculcation of proper moral development, and, not the least benefit, it was a form of social control for potentially troublesome young men. Apprenticeship in the nineteenth-century United States was primarily a male institution and the relatively rare instances of female apprenticeships "provided only legal guardianship and training in female work rather than the learning of a craft."[16] Garrison joined the ranks of the apprentice at a time of significant change. The American Revolution had created disruption in the system as many apprentices ran away to become soldiers and fight in the war. In addition, the democratization of American society stressed the importance of the individual, and Republican ideology conflicted with the absolute power normally granted to the master. After the war and into the nineteenth-century, the master's authority, and with it apprenticeship itself, was further challenged by the publication of books which explained the previously "secret" elements of various crafts, by evangelical religion which emphasized individual responsibility, and by market forces including the development of factories and the cash wage system. All these combined to make many masters and artisans reluctant to commit themselves to a long term agreement which included the health and well-being of a potentially disruptive young man. Conversely, young men became reluctant to commit themselves to a long-term contract to learn a trade that did not promise long-term financial success.[17] The Embargo of 1808 and the financial disaster known as the Panic of 1819 further exacerbated the decline in apprenticeships, but for Garrison and others in the printing trade, the decline was less severe until the emergence of the steam-powered presses of the late 1820s and 1830s.[18]

While the apprenticeship system itself was in decline, at another level, many young apprentices nevertheless benefited from institutions created by early nineteenth-century reformers seeking to aid individual self-improvement. Despite a call for improving educational opportunities during the eighteenth century, the primary purpose of education in the early nineteenth century was the pursuit of knowledge by the elite — the gentlemen who were presumed to be the natural leaders of society. However, the ideals of self-improvement, the growth of popular involvement in public life, and the democratization of the post–War of 1812 era led Garrison and others like him to pursue knowledge as well. Robert Gross examined this phenomenon as it was experienced in Concord, Massachusetts, after the Revolution. "A new social landscape took shape," he argued, as the eighteenth century ended, in which various voluntary associations were formed to pursue community improvement. For Concord, this included a Library Society intended "to spread knowledge and virtue — without which, it was believed, the republic could not survive."[19] Similarly, Alan Taylor, in his study of social growth and change in post–Revolutionary frontier New York State, described the importance that Judge William Cooper placed on establishing social associations, such as lodges, academies, libraries, and a local newspaper, as an integral part of creating a prosperous and successful village like Cooperstown in the final decade of the nineteenth century.[20] In addition, although not usually considered among antebellum reforms, Joseph Kett argues that "the popular pursuit of knowledge possessed close ties to temperance and school reform and it acquired some of the features of a reform movement."[21] Ronald Walters defined antebellum reform as "one of several means by which antebellum men and women attempted to impose moral direction on social, cultural, and economic turmoil."[22] In this light, including the pursuit of knowledge with other antebellum reforms is apt. The diffusion of knowledge was part of the republican ideology of liberty and democracy on which many antebellum reforms were built. Consequently, "apprentices were invited to Lyceums, public lecture series," and other educational activities, especially in times of economic depression.[23]

This pursuit of knowledge and the promotion of change in educational self-improvement often benefited from local movements, such as library associations, educational societies, improvement movements, and in a few places, formal educational academies. For instance, the Panic of 1819 led Boston merchant William Wood to create a library with donated books, exclusively for apprentices. He was concerned that the lack of work brought on by the economic decline left too many apprentices idle—a dangerous situation which potentially could lead to anti-social behavior.[24] Generally, the books included in the library were tightly controlled and excluded novels or adventure stories, which were considered unsuitable for the mechanic class. Even as late as 1833, the Philadelphia apprentice library still maintained a policy of banning novels which were deemed to be "not suited for the laboring class" because the sensationalism of a novel could destroy the apprentice's masculine character.[25] Wood's idea was a success and he traveled around the country to explain his concept and to advocate his program. Apprentice libraries were organized in many cities around the nation, including Providence, New York, Philadelphia, Baltimore, and Charleston. In addition, with libraries founded in places close to Garrison's home, such as Salem, Massachusetts, and Portland, Maine, word of such an important development very likely made its way to Newburyport, especially to the printing office. As it did, Garrison quickly prepared himself to engage these opportunities.

In addition to the potential benefit of these social and cultural changes, life inside a printing office, despite the physical demands, tedious and repetitive work in a dank and foul-smelling work area, also promised opportunities for self-improvement and served as "a more or less effective shirt-sleeved substitute for the university."[26] Among the first jobs an apprentice printer like Garrison learned was to set type. Standing in front of a set of cases with compartments for single-letter type (upper-case letters were above compartments for lower-case letters), the apprentice composed lines of text on a "composing stick" which was later transferred to the galley tray for printing.[27] Obviously, this required him to read the text he set. These texts varied widely: simple advertisements, poetry, news reports of local, national, or international interest gleaned from the numerous newspapers the printer received in exchange with other newspaper editors, editorial comments on politics or social happenings, letters to the editor, as well as excerpts from novels.

Especially in a political hotbed like Newburyport, where a dying Federalist Party struggled to remain alive and relevant, conversation in the cramped confines of the small office probably encouraged thoughtful as well as animated conversations which an intelligent young apprentice could hardly ignore. A younger generation of Federalists had tried after President Jefferson's inauguration in 1801 to re-organize and re-energize the party but, in the wake of the Hartford Convention and the Treaty of Ghent, ultimately failed. By 1815, Federalist "was an epithet, a smear word."[28] Garrison's later writings demonstrate that he engaged with a wide range of subjects and issues, but in their biography, Garrison's children said he took a particular "interest in politics, and ... studied the writings of Fisher Ames, and was a fervent admirer of Timothy Pickering and Harrison Gray Otis."[29] All three men were influential New England Federalists who as scholars, authors, or politicians helped to form the young Garrison's political ideology. Pickering and Otis were still actively involved in Massachusetts politics and that involvement would certainly have been actively discussed in a printing office like Allen's and as well become a source of political education for a young apprentice. Perhaps the demoralized and widely ridiculed Federalism that Garrison embraced in the Newburyport printing office as a youth helped to prepare him to face the hatred and vitriol that he earned when he embraced the appellation of "abolitionist."

One of the most influential newspaper editors of the nineteenth century, Horace Greeley, began his printing apprenticeship a few months after Garrison's ended in 1825. He later reflected on the opportunity for reading and education that an apprenticeship in a printing office provided, and suggested that it was a better means of acquiring knowledge "than by spending four years in college."[30] In a similar vein, author and literary critic William Dean Howells recalled the activity inside his father's country printing office, which, although a few decades after Garrison's apprenticeship, likely compared favorably with Ephraim Allen's office. "There was always a good deal of talk going on," he remembered, "when it was not mere banter it was mostly literary; we disputed about authors among ourselves, and with the village wits who dropped in."[31] Howells' father, like Allen, combined in his printing office the jobs of journalist, printer, and editor. Garrison, as Howells himself asserted, could fairly claim: "journalism became my university, the printing-office was mainly my school."[32]

While we are only able to speculate about the intellectual influences of social organizations and the printing office, one of the realities of Garrison's life as an apprentice about which we can be certain are the relationships he developed with his fellow apprentices and other young men in the Newburyport community. Tobias H. Miller and Thomas Bennett worked in the *Herald* office in the early years of Garrison's apprenticeship. Miller worked as a journeyman at the *Herald* in order to earn the tuition to enter the Andover Seminary, and Garrison fondly remembered the "Reverend" Miller in a speech given in Boston in 1878. Miller had "by his beautiful spirit and fine example," Garrison said, "a great influence upon my mind."[33] Bennett was an "adventurer and amateur classicist" who was working on a translation of Cicero's orations.[34] While Garrison was searching for work in Boston in 1827, Bennett provided him with food and lodging.[35] Garrison's closest friends, William Goss Crocker and Isaac Knapp, were nearer his age and circumstances. Both were apprentices at the printing office and bookstore of W & J Gilman on State Street, just a few doors away from Allen's shop. Like Garrison, Crocker was a communicant at the Newburyport Baptist Church. They maintained correspondence after both left Newburyport and until Crocker's death in Liberia in 1844 while serving there as a missionary.[36] Isaac Knapp, in a fashion not dissimilar to Garrison's early years as a journeyman printer, drifted in and out of various newspaper positions until he joined with Garrison as his partner in the publication of *The Liberator*.

Garrison, Crocker, and Knapp spent many evenings in a room over the printing office of W & J Gilman "engaged in reading, study and literary composition."[37] While there is no record of the particular books they read and studied, there were at least two sources from which they could have chosen. Just like many other New England towns, Newburyport had its own library called the Newburyport Athenaeum, which had been incorporated in 1810 "for the purpose of promoting learning" and reportedly contained between ten and twelve thousand volumes.[38] In addition, the W & J Gilman Bookstore ran the "Merrimack Circulation Library"—a ready source of material for the young apprentices. Its catalogue from 1821 lists nearly 1,500 books, including political treatises, histories, novels, poetry, and an extensive collection of the works of William Shakespeare.[39] In a newspaper advertisement, the circulating library claimed "about 2,000 volumes, including all the celebrated 'Waverly Novels' ... [and] ... are continually making additions."[40] Walter Scott's Waverly Novels were a particular favorite of the young Garrison, according to his children's biography.[41] The annual subscription fee to the Merrimack Library was $5, but by meeting where Crocker and Knapp worked, at the location of the subscription library itself, the boys relieved themselves of the financial obligations of membership and had easy access to a significant number of books for their own use and education.

In addition to his apprentice acquaintances, Garrison also attracted the attention of at least one man of great influence in Newburyport, Caleb Cushing. Cushing was destined to have a long career in public service, including four terms in the United States House of Representatives, commissioner to China, Mayor of Newburyport, associate justice of the Massachusetts Supreme Court, President of the National Democratic Convention in 1860 (which nominated John C. Breckinridge for President of the United States), and he was nominated by President Grant to serve as chief justice of the United States Supreme Court. His nomination was rejected by the Senate and he was instead appointed minister to Spain.[42]

After graduating from Harvard and being admitted to the bar in 1821, Cushing returned to his home in Newburyport. He opened a law office "in the chamber under the Herald Printing Office" and began the practice of law.[43] In 1822, Cushing undertook the duties of editor and publisher of the *Newburyport Herald* while Ephraim Allen was out of town for a number of months. By this time, Garrison had completed more than four years of his apprenticeship and was a well-trained and trusted journeyman printer who supervised all the printing aspects of the paper's publication; therefore, he worked closely with the new editor.[44] Several years earlier, in October 1820, Cushing had published a twenty-two-page article in Edward Everett's *North American Review* in which he denounced slavery, defended the fundamental humanity of blacks, and argued that they were capable of "elevation, order, and improvement."[45] While serving as editor, Cushing published a series of opinion pieces in the *Herald* on the issue of slavery including one on July 12, 1822, about the Denmark Vesey insurrection which had occurred in South Carolina two months earlier. His article expressed a rather pessimistic appraisal about the future of slavery and its long-term impact on the nation. Without unequivocally condemning it, Cushing certainly registered disapproval and suggested that because of the particular conditions of American slavery, it was doubtful to end without violent and severe repercussions. Unlike slavery in Rome, for instance, race and skin color was determinate of the condition. Furthermore, men in the southern states were naturally reluctant to willingly forego the economic benefits of the system. Consequently, neither emancipation nor colonization were realistic options. In light of these factors, Cushing predicted a day in the future when slaves will take up arms "to vindicate their freedom" and that "we see nothing to prevent a repetition of the horrors of Saint-Domingo."[46] He may have been the first to introduce Garrison to anti-slavery sentiments and the potential dangers which slavery posed to the United States.

For the duration of his editorship, Cushing "commended the young writer, encouraged him to persevere, and lent him books from his own library."[47] Garrison acknowledged Cushing's encouragement in a letter to Fanny Garrison in May 1823.[48] Cushing had commended to the *Herald*'s readers a new series of articles written by Garrison (under a pseudonym) and identified him as "a correspondent who ... has favored us with a number of esteemed and valuable communications."[49] A few months before his death, in a letter to one of his children, Garrison wrote that after Cushing discovered that he was responsible for several anonymous letters published in the *Herald*, he "took a special interest in me, giving me compliments and words of encouragement."[50] In the final years of his apprenticeship, Cushing was a link for Garrison between the life of a lowly apprentice and the more refined and intellectual life of Newburyport's elite.

Another outlet for the diffusion of knowledge, in addition to the printing office and libraries, was the local debating club. Across the country, hundreds of these organizations emerged alongside the public orations that had become a national pastime and an American public ritual.[51] Alexis de Tocqueville took note of this particularly American phenomenon when he wrote about his experiences with ordinary Americans: "an American does not know how to converse, but he argues; he does not talk, but he expiates. He always speaks to you as if addressing a meeting."[52] When a debating society was organized in Boston in 1821, the *Herald* reported its establishment but also noted that a similar organization had existed in Newburyport "some time since."[53] According to Caleb Cushing, who was one of the Newburyport club's founders as well as an active participant, the club first met on January 5, 1821, and thereafter continued to meet regularly for several years. For Cushing, debating societies were of particular value in light of the "popular character of our government," which made oratorical skills valuable. "A well regulated debating society," he argued, "is an excellent school of instruction and experience in this important qualification."[54] Garrison and other apprentices were certainly not members of the Newburyport Debating Society, but Cushing and other influential citizens of the town were.

In addition to its educational role, the Newburyport Debating Society also became an important component of the town's social life. For many years the society organized the annual celebration of Independence Day and provided an orator for the occasion. Furthermore, the society had a published constitution which outlined the procedures for meetings, a "Committee on Questions" to organize the discussion, and rules for membership which required new members to receive approval of two-thirds of the membership.[55] On August 31, 1824, when the Marquis de Lafayette, the French hero of the American Revolution, visited Newburyport, thousands of citizens, including Garrison, lined the streets to welcome him, despite persistent inclement weather. One third of the official select committee chosen to greet him and accompany him through the town were members of the debating society.[56]

Garrison was certainly well aware of the Newburyport Debating Society because the *Herald* regularly published the dates of the society's meetings and the subjects for discussion and debate. The first meeting mentioned in the *Herald* was scheduled for Wednesday, March 28, 1821, and the question for debate was "Has the fanaticisms of the dark ages been productive of more evil than good to man kind?"[57] Perhaps Garrison attended some of the meetings as Cushing's guest, but considering his age, social status in town and the rules of the society, which allowed members to bring only visitors "who may be strangers in town," it is certainly doubtful that, even if he attended, he was allowed to participate in the debate.[58] According to Cushing's history, the Newburyport Debating Society was re-organized in 1823 and "consisted not merely of persons desirous to engage in its regular exercises, but of a large number of others, who joined as auditors only." We cannot know for certain, but perhaps Garrison was one of those "auditors."[59]

Sometime around the end of 1824, the Newburyport Debating Society disbanded. An announcement in the *Herald* requested all members to pay their one dollar per year dues immediately so "the accounts of the society may be speedily closed."[60] Four weeks later, a notice appeared acknowledging receipt by the Newburyport Female Asylum of $56.01 from the "late Newburyport Debating Society."[61] According to Cushing, the Society ended "in consequence of the dispersion of some of the active members of the Society," and he referred to a new society that was organized to take its place.[62] Two new organizations later appeared in the columns of the *Herald*. The first sporadic notices of meetings for the "Forensic Association" were published between January 18 and April 15, 1825. Then, beginning on June 28 and continuing regularly for the rest of the year, which was also the last year of Garrison's apprenticeship, notices for meetings of the "Franklin Debating Society" were commonly seen. The second of these groups was founded by Garrison and counted among its members his friends, Knapp and Crocker.[63]

The Franklin Debating Society may have been the successor to the Newburyport Debating Society which Cushing had referenced, and it may be that it became more prominent after the latter dissolved. In discussing the Franklin Debating Society's role in the July 4 celebrations for 1826, Currier's *History of Newburyport* explained that it was "practically the Newburyport Debating society re-organized," but makes no mention of Garrison's involvement with either the organization or the festivities.[64] Nevertheless, there is no question that Garrison's club was certainly in existence before the Newburyport Debating Society disappeared and at least a year prior to the club's first notice in the *Herald*. In July 1824, Garrison delivered what may have been his first public address, before the members of the Franklin Debating Club on the occasion of the Independence Day celebrations.[65] By this time, Garrison had published more than a dozen pieces in the *Herald* and had begun to develop his distinctive aggressive style. Apparently, this address, which may have been Garrison's inaugural public address, was very important to him. A friend reported that he could be found practicing his speech in the "groves and green fields on the outskirts" of Newburyport.[66]

The address began with a paean to the glory of Independence Day itself—a day which "ushered into existence the freest, and which is destined to eventually be the mightiest Republic on earth!" He praised the triumph of freedom over despotism and acclaimed the goodness and selflessness of George Washington, who helped colonial patriots to "trample under feet with indignation the chains which he severed, when he found [them] enslaved." The revolution which Washington led was the "pole-star of attraction" for all other nations to imitate in order to understand how to seek and win their freedom. He expressed regret that the example of the United States was not being followed around the world quickly enough, yet predicted a future in which the unassailable truths of the Declaration of Independence "will be sufficient to raise a torrent, that will overwhelm tyranny in one mass of undistinguished ruin."[67] The bright, shining light of America had become, in the eyes of a young and enthusiastic journeyman printer, the new "city on a hill" for the rest of the world to admire. The address was full of passion and praise for the political ideology and even the military power of the United States, ran to nearly 5,000 words, and was anonymously published at the *Herald* office "By A Member." Willfully or not, Garrison was clearly preparing to be heard.

The debate subjects for the Franklin Debating Society that appeared in the *Herald* in the last six months of 1825 indicate a wide range of topics. Some of the subjects for debate might be considered inconsequential, such as "Was the assassination of Julius Caesar justifiable?" or fanciful, such as "Are theatrical exhibitions beneficial to the public?"[68] Nevertheless, the club also debated more substantive questions, such as "Are capital punishments justifiable?" or "Will the Union of the States be permanent?" or "Was it justifiable in our forefathers to dispossess the natives of their territories?"[69] Without doubt though, the image of Garrison, who was only two weeks past his twentieth birthday when his apprenticeship ended in December 1825, and his friends Knapp and Crocker sitting together and passionately arguing these topics, evokes some sense of youthful angst. Still, this was one source of Garrison's effort, according to Phillips' eulogy, to make "every single home, press, pulpit and senate chamber a debating society."[70]

The *Boston Statesman* praised the formation of debating societies for "the great good [they] have effected in our several communities" and reminded readers that "in such a *school* did the great Franklin lay the foundation for his useful life; & through the incitement of such societies we believe that many future Franklins will rise to adorn and benefit our country."[71] While we cannot be certain how grand Garrison's visions of his future success were at this time, we cannot doubt the connection he probably felt with America's most famous printer's apprentice, Benjamin Franklin. Among the books listed in the *Catalogue of the Merrimack Circulating Library* was *The Life of Franklin, Written By Himself*, there is good reason to believe that Garrison had read it and was familiar with another printer apprentice's life story. Naming his debating club in honor of Franklin may not have been very original on Garrison's part, but it does reflect a man who believed that his ambitions were not beyond his grasp and whose schools, like Franklin's, were the printing office and his own "Junto."[72] It was the lessons learned in this "university" that helped create a man prepared to use the printing press to reform the nation and emancipate its slaves.

The structure of Garrison's education, that is, the printing office, the libraries, the acquaintances, and the private groups in which he participated, helps to give some insight into the broad outlines of his development. In addition, Garrison's own writings during his years of apprenticeship provide another, more direct and more concrete, source. Including his 1824 Independence Day speech, a total of twenty-eight published letters and newspaper articles have been located. One poem, "To a Young Lady," which appeared in the *Herald* on April 29, 1825, may also be attributed to Garrison since it was signed by "A.O.B." ("An Old Bachelor," one of his pseudonyms). During his career, Garrison published hundreds of his own poems and this one seems to fit his style. Most of these letters were written for publication in either the *Newburyport Herald* or *The Salem Gazette*, which was published by Ferdinand Andrews, a cousin of Caleb Cushing.[73] Unfortunately, only three of the extant letters were personal in nature and these three reveal little about Garrison's personality or educational pursuits.

Garrison was sixteen years old when, in Franklinesque fashion, he submitted an anonymous letter to the editor of the *Herald* under the pseudonym "An Old Bachelor." According to the story his children record, the letter arrived in the printing office while Garrison was setting type and he watched anxiously as Ephraim Allen opened and read it. Allen was so delighted with the letter that he read it aloud to all present and then handed it to Garrison to set for publication.[74] We may reasonably wonder if this story became embellished over time, but the publication of the letter is certainly not in doubt.[75] A second letter was sent and published, and Allen let it be known that he welcomed more correspondence from "A.O.B."[76] Both letters were purportedly written by an elderly unmarried man, angry about a "Breach of Marriage" lawsuit judgment.[77] The *Herald* had recently reprinted an article about a man who was ordered to pay $750 for "keeping company two years with a lady, and not offering to marry her during that period."[78] The sixteen-year-old Garrison, who only later became a staunch supporter of both women's rights as well as women's participation in public affairs, wrote at the time that "women in this country are too much idolized and flattered ... and inflated with pride and self-conceit." In an accompanying editorial note, Allen bade his readers to "not take offence at the querulous reflections of our correspondent the 'Old Bachelor'" but it is interesting to note that the well-recognized Garrisonian style of challenging and confrontational rhetoric was already present in his first published article. Garrison took Allen's request for more correspondence to heart and continued to submit letters. In the next year, another eleven of his letters were published in the *Herald*. Sometime during that year, Caleb Cushing, then filling in as editor for Allen, discovered the identity of "An Old Bachelor." He kept Garrison's secret while he encouraged the young apprentice to read, study, and write more.[79]

In his published collection of Garrison's letters, editor Walter Merrill includes ten of the twenty-eight extant apprenticeship documents. His analysis of these letters helps to identify some of the literature which Garrison had read or with which he was at least familiar.[80] Only one of this group of ten letters was written after August 1824, when Garrison was eighteen years old. Garrison referred to four of Shakespeare's plays, *All's Well That Ends Well*, *Hamlet*, *Macbeth,* and *Othello*. Other references included Alexander Pope, Cicero, scriptural passages from the Bible, and political references to *The Letters of Junius*. The author of the *Junius* letters is unknown, but sixty-nine letters under that name and which were critical of the policies of King George III were published in the London *Public Advertiser* between 1769 and 1772. The letters espoused a "Radical Whig" ideology that appealed to many colonists in British North America in the decade of resistance that preceded revolution. They were a part of the "flood of newspapers, pamphlets, and letters ... from opposition sources in England" that recorded evidence to demonstrate that the "true Whig" principles of the Glorious Revolution had been abandoned and that the resulting corruption threatened to destroy the rights of all Englishmen.[81] In his career as an abolitionist editor, Garrison clearly embraced a similar perception about abandonment of American Revolutionary ideology.

The use of literary, scriptural, and political references in his letters continued for the rest of Garrison's life as he turned to the very serious business of abolition and radical reform. This practice may have reflected a conspicuous display of erudition by a person who felt deprived of education in his youth; an affectation assumed by a person seeking to belong to a higher social circle; simply the habit of a person who learned to love poetry and literature; or some combination of all three. What is apparent was that Garrison made considerable efforts to fill in the gaps in his formal education, had a persistent thirst for knowledge, and enjoyed displaying that knowledge.

Most of the works that the young Garrison authored were published in local newspapers in several series of short essays. They exhibit his interest in a variety of subjects, but most frequently the focus was on politics, government, or patriotism. A marked exception to this pattern appeared in the *Herald* of May 31, 1822, under the title "THE SHIPWRECK." Supposedly the story of an incident experienced by "An Old Bachelor" in his youth, Garrison attempted this one time only, to tell a fictional adventure story. Much as he may have admired Walter Scott, Garrison must have realized that narrative fiction was not his forte; he abandoned the genre. More typical was a series of three essays about current affairs in "South America" that appeared in July 1822. Presumably Garrison was addressing the Latin American countries, especially perhaps Mexico, which had recently liberated itself from Spain, and he commended the citizens of those countries for overthrowing tyranny. He cautioned against allowing their freedom to be usurped by military despots, with an especially severe warning to these newly freed nations if they continued to seize, threaten, or rob American citizens. He acknowledged that his language might be "deemed too harsh by many" but he made no apologies — something he continued to do throughout his career. Uncharacteristic of the later Garrison, however, he avowed a willingness to use force to resolve disputes. He threatened that if the rights of American citizens were not respected, then we "will finish with cannon what cannot be done in conciliatory and equitable manner." In conclusion, he offered the United States as an example of how freedom can be justly distributed to all, as well as beneficial for all, and suggested that if they learned well from our experience, someday "the nations of North and South America may cordially unite" if the patriots of "South America" finally secured their own liberty.[82]

One final letter for 1822 appeared in August and used the threatened conflict between Russia and Turkey as a pretext to comment on the actions of "public journalists." This may represent Garrison's earliest effort to publicly address the special duties and responsibilities associated with newspaper publishing. The obligation of newspaper editors to provide honest, non-partisan, and accurate information for the public was often the focus of Garrison's editorial commentary in the future and became a foundational justification for *The Liberator*. In this letter, he decried the number of conflicting rumors that appeared in various newspapers speculating about the possibility of extended conflict between Russia and Turkey. Garrison assumed that the conflict was about to end. This prediction became only one of many examples of Garrison's failure in forecasting future events; the war continued until 1829.[83] More significantly, his article targeted the practices of "the public newspapers" which employed "idle rumors" to promote interest in national and international events. Such rumors not only damaged the public interest, "A.O.B." argued, but also often caused significant injury to the commercial trader who relied on newspaper reports to make business decisions.[84] This letter clearly demonstrated that the printer's apprentice understood the power of newspapers to influence public opinion, provoke public reaction, and achieve social or political change. If at the present moment Garrison viewed this journalistic power as dangerous when built on a foundation of "idle rumors," it was a power which became for him an essential tool and one he learned to wield effectively, when built on the foundation of truth and justice, as was the case in his campaign to eradicate slavery.

As discussed earlier, during the winter of 1822-23, Caleb Cushing took over editorial duties at the *Herald*. With his encouragement, Garrison's next two series of articles appeared in the spring of 1823. For the first series, Garrison assumed a new pseudonym, "One of the People," and offered three essays on "Our Next Governor."[85] The majority of the citizens in Newburyport remained supporters of the Federalist Party, even as the party disintegrated both in New England and nationally. The party's initial decline in national politics came with the election of Jefferson in 1800 and only accelerated in the aftermath of the Hartford Convention in 1814 where New England Federalists had met from December 15, 1814, to January 5, 1815, to discuss possible revisions to the United States Constitution. The delegates resented the economic hardships imposed by the Embargo Act and the War of 1812, both of which they believed were especially harsh on the people of New England. Outside of the northeastern region, many believed that the real purpose of the convention was to plan New England's secession from the Union. This belief contributed to accusations of disloyalty and treason which only seemed to be confirmed when the convention's demands reached Washington as news of the Treaty of Ghent ending the war and Andrew Jackson's extraordinary victory in New Orleans were received as well. The convention was a leading cause in the final dissolution of the Federalist Party; they appeared to have committed "political suicide" by opposing a war "that most Americans believed had ended in a glorious victory."[86]

Stanley Elkins and Eric McKitrick concede that Federalism "persist[ed] in regional pockets" for some time and one of the most persistent pockets was the Newburyport of Garrison's youth and the county of Essex in Massachusetts.[87] Garrison was not an exception and he emphatically voiced support for Harrison Gray Otis, the Federalist candidate for governor in 1823. Otis was a wealthy Boston lawyer who had served in various local, state, and federal political offices; he was also an organizer, leader, and staunch defender of the disastrous Hartford Convention, which in addition to discrediting the Federalist Party, effectively crippled Otis' national political career.[88] Garrison compared Otis' principles to the "pure principles of the immaculate Washington," and described the election as a choice between the principles of the

Federalists and the lies of the Democrats. Despite Garrison's declarations that there did not remain "a shadow of doubt of [Otis] being called to the gubernatorial chair by an overwhelming majority," Otis received only about 46 percent of the votes to 53 percent for the Republican candidate, William Eustis.[89] Although a Federalist had been elected governor of Massachusetts in each of the previous three elections, by 1823 the power of the Federalist Party was now clearly on the wane, even in one of its traditional strongholds.

Within weeks, Garrison returned as "An Old Bachelor" with a three part series titled "A Glance at Europe."[90] France, backed by the Holy Alliance, which was a loose confederation of European powers intent on stifling liberal politics on the continent, was attempting, he asserted, to restore Ferdinand of Spain to its throne. The two greatest evils to befall Spain, according to Garrison, were the Inquisition and, perhaps as a punishment from God, the imposition of arbitrary power, but, he asserted, the citizens of Spain had learned from the American Revolution and had released themselves "from the chains of oppression." This success was now threatened, "A.O.B." contended, and other rumors suggested that attempts might be made to restore Spain's authority over her lost colonies in Latin America. Garrison viewed the Holy Alliance as an instrument of repression which intended to "extirpate the rights and privileges of nations and to dig up and destroy the seeds which Liberty has planted." He did not foresee any current threat to the United States, but clearly Garrison was beginning to understand that when liberty was threatened for some, it was threatened for all—an idea that would be reflected in the motto which appeared on the masthead of the first issue of *The Liberator*: "Our Country Is the World—Our Countrymen Are Mankind" although he was far from fully embracing that philosophy just yet.[91] As far as the current situation in Europe was concerned, it seemed to Garrison to be a stalemate between the continents' great powers. However, from his vantage point and with his limited understanding of international politics, he could not have predicted that the threat of renewed European influence in North America would result in the December 1823 proclamation of what later became known as the Monroe Doctrine.

For the next thirteen months, Garrison did not write any articles that were published or are extant. One cause for this withdrawal from print may have been connected to his mother. In June 1823, Allen finally allowed Garrison enough time off to travel to Baltimore to visit his mother, who was very sick. He had written a long letter to Fanny Garrison in May which provided details about the many roadblocks Ephraim Allen imposed before allowing him time to leave to visit her. Allen originally agreed to let him travel in the fall of 1822, but business circumstances forced him to renege; he then promised to allow Garrison to go the following spring, but that was cancelled as well. Allen was hardly supportive of a son's wish to visit a sick mother and only finally agreed to let Garrison go if he would "*hire a journeyman*" to replace him. In the letter, he also explained how he had used his leisure time "usefully and wisely ... [to expand] ... the intellectual powers and faculties of my mind," and had authored several articles which were published in the *Herald*.[92] She responded to her son's letter with a plea for him to come visit, but also warned him against spending too much time "writing political pieces" and not enough time seeking truth in the Bible and praying to understand God's will in his life.[93] Garrison finally made the journey to Baltimore and spent a few weeks with his mother; he returned to Newburyport in August 1823 to complete the final years of his apprenticeship. Within a month, on September 3, 1823, Fanny Garrison died. Her death, as well as her advice, may have been influential in his year's absence from print.

Garrison's absence was not long-lived and his return to print in 1824 also brought a new name, "Aristides," and a new venue for publication, *The Salem Gazette*. In the first of two letters to the editor, Garrison inserted himself into a book war being waged between Timothy Pickering and John Adams during his son's first presidential election campaign.[94] In what was supposed to be confidential correspondence between John Adams and William Cunningham dating from 1809, Adams had harshly attacked both Alexander Hamilton and Timothy Pickering, whom Adams accused of acting as Hamilton's agent while Pickering had served as Adams' secretary of state, in order to maintain influence over his cabinet. The letters were published by Cunningham's son in 1823 in an effort to discredit John Quincy Adams' campaign efforts by destroying the reputation of the candidate's father. In 1824, Pickering published his own book in response.[95]

Garrison's assumption of the new pseudonym "Aristides" recalled its use by Noah Webster in a letter to Alexander Hamilton in 1800. Webster had chastised Hamilton for his actions in opposing John Adams' presidential aspirations; those actions, Webster argued, divided the Federalist Party and threatened to help Jefferson win the election.[96] In 1824, Garrison saw a similar problem as partisans for Pickering and Adams published books about letters written by John Adams in an effort to influence John Quincy Adams' chances in the 1824 presidential race. Nearly three-quarters of the first letter pilloried the "partisans of John Q. Adams for the Presidency" who attacked Pickering. Garrison specifically singled out Robert Walsh, editor of the *National Gazette*, as one of many "wiseacres ... fearful that the *spotless* character of their idol may be tarnished by the fingers of *truth*." Garrison adamantly supported the staunch Federalist, Pickering, and confidently predicted, "The name of PICKERING will live when that of Adams will be lost in oblivion."[97]

The second letter of this pair is almost totally devoted to criticism of Walsh, the *Gazette* editor, for an unwarranted "mass of scurrility and falsehood" against Pickering. Garrison argued that any critic, such as Walsh, needs "four requisite qualifications — *candor, modesty, good sense,* and *impartiality*" all of which to some degree Walsh lacked.[98] While these two letters clearly defended the reputation and Federalist ideology of Pickering, they also demonstrated Garrison's growing awareness of the power exerted by an influential editor such as Philadelphia's Robert Walsh, about whom Garrison remarked, "Were it not that his *name* might carry some influence with it, his violent invectives might pass unnoticed." Despite his impassioned outpouring of support, Garrison paradoxically argued that Pickering did not need Garrison's words to protect him from the animosity of his enemies but, with reason and truth as his guard, his enemies' "poisoned arrows will fall harmless at his feet." These letters reveal fundamental characteristics of the mature Garrison, the editor who would be heard, who believed passionately in clear ethical editorial responsibilities for newspapers publishers, and who became an advocate for open discussion and reasoned debate as the path to the discovery of truth.

Remaining focused on the upcoming presidential campaign, "Aristides" appeared again in next month's *Salem Gazette* with an open letter to another of the candidates, Andrew Jackson. Assuming a respectful but matter-of-fact tone, and calling himself "a plain, unlettered man," Garrison attempted to explain to the General why "the cool, the discerning, and the dispassionate body of your fellow countrymen, perceive your unfitness for the office to which you ... are aspiring." The most important reasons for Jackson's "unfitness" were his opposition to the Hartford Convention of 1814 and his published comments which called for the leaders of the convention to be punished. Garrison accused General Jackson of having the same kind of blind ambition that was the downfall of Caesar and Napoleon, argued that his chance for election was "lost irretrievably," and called on Jackson's patriotism to convince him to abandon the effort.[99] Perhaps Garrison wrote this letter in the guise of a different Aristides — the Athenian who was believed to have been a general in the battle of Marathon — and maybe thought that from one general to another Jackson would take his advice. If that were the case, Garrison clearly did not understand Andrew Jackson very well.

The 1824 campaign for president was again the theme for Garrison's most ambitious collection of essays, a six-part series titled "The Crisis."[100] It seems likely that by using this title Garrison meant to recall Thomas Paine's series by the same name published during the American Revolution. Published in sixteen installments between 1776 and 1783, *The Crisis* pamphlets began with the famous line "These are the times that try men's souls" and were written in plain language that significantly bolstered the morale of Washington's troops during the Revolutionary War.[101] As a Federalist, Garrison was not a fan of the Thomas Paine who had supported the French Revolution, but in his youthful exuberance it is reasonable to assume that he saw the 1824 election in the same light as the struggle of 1776. The particular "crisis" which Garrison envisioned in 1824 was the presidential election results in the state of Massachusetts. The national election was a four-way race between Andrew Jackson, Henry Clay, John Quincy Adams, and William Crawford; however, Garrison dismissed both Jackson's and Clay's chances to win the electoral votes from Massachusetts. Garrison defined the race in Massachusetts as a battle between Adams and Crawford only and, as he had done with the governor's race a year earlier, a choice between the principles of the Revolution and the actions of a traitor out to destroy the liberties of the people for the benefit of "*office-holders* in the State ... who are fond of *fat salaries*, and of rioting with the people's money." He argued that although the Federalist sentiments of Massachusetts and New England citizens were now a minority view in the nation, they still represented one-quarter of the nation; maintaining their power and influence on a national level required a united front. He urged his fellow Federalists to remain true to "those principles which were promulgated by the Father of his Country, and sanctioned by Jay and Hamilton, and Ames, with a host of other patriots." Despite his support for Crawford, the main thrust of Garrison's plea was decidedly more "anti" Adams than it was "pro" Crawford. Adams was, for Garrison, the traitor who deserted the Federalist Party in the wake of Thomas Jefferson's presidential victory in 1800, who supported the hated Embargo, as well as the "evil administrations of Jefferson and Madison," and who joined with the voices of those who questioned the patriots of the Hartford Convention.

There is little in the "Crisis" series to suggest the older Garrison who would abandon political parties, refuse to vote or participate in the election process in any way, and burn the Constitution as a bargain with the devil. Although he did attack Adams and his supporters with strong and adamant language, the tone of his writing was generally measured and judicious. In the final chapter of the series, however, Garrison defended his rhetoric with words that seem to foreshadow the Garrison who later demanded attention and even the Garrison who denounced politics altogether. He wrote that there "is a time, however, when it becomes the duty of every man to speak and act boldly; when language, strong and forcible, is necessary to command attention; when the voice of liberty should be heard above the ravings of faction."[102] Once again, the voice of the future committed abolitionist, seeker of liberty, and admonisher warning of the crisis that slavery will bring to the nation can be heard clearly. Regardless of Garrison's passion to defeat Adams, Crawford's campaign was in shambles from its beginning when he suffered a stroke and was left partially paralyzed and blind. Crawford won only three states, Virginia, Georgia, and Delaware; he lost Massachusetts (and the presidency) to John Quincy Adams.

This series ended Garrison's early efforts at political commentary. History was not kind to his high-spirited efforts at political prognostication. In a little over two years, from his series on South America to "The Crisis," Garrison predicted that the freedom-seekers in South America might join the United States in one government, that the Russian-Turkish war was about to end, that Harrison Gray Otis would defeat William Eustis for governor, that the name of Timothy Pickering would live in America's memory while the name of John Adams would be forgotten, that American voters would judge Andrew Jackson to be unfit for public office, and that John Quincy Adams would lose Massachusetts and the presidency to William Crawford. Perhaps we can credit the assurance behind these forecasts to youthful extravagance, but the passion with which Garrison defended and explained these choices also reflected his belief in the power of words to shed light on truth and to help shape public policy. If his predictions were found wanting, his commitment to aggressively work to shape public opinion only became stronger.

From a larger perspective, it is possible to recognize that the political commentaries of Garrison's early years were an occasion for the expression of his fundamental beliefs. The printer's apprentice embraced for himself the role of the voice of truth against other voices in the "marketplace of ideas" that public newspapers of the era represented. "There can never be much doubt," Garrison wrote about the situation in South America, "of the result of a contest between those who fight for freedom and independence, and those who oppose them, however unequal the combat may be."[103] In his support for Harrison Gray Otis, he challenged the "democratic papers [which were] pouring forth so liberally their vulgar invectives against" Otis.[104] He apologized to the *Herald*'s readers for his three long essays about the current conditions in Europe but argued that the friends of liberty in Europe and America would suffer along with the Spanish if the "barbarian legions" of the Holy Alliance allow "Despotism [to] triumph over Liberty."[105] In his June 1824 letters to *The Salem Gazette*, Garrison was especially critical of the *National Gazette*, which sacrificed dignity, reason, and justice for the benefit of John Adams, who had deserted the true principles of the revolution "in order to secure the loaves and fishes of office."[106] Finally, the passion which ran through the six parts of "The Crisis" series grew from the "chicanery and deceit" practiced by some influential newspapers in the state which had supported Adams' candidacy. Garrison feared that the citizens of Massachusetts "are willing to be *driven* into blind obedience by such papers as the [*Boston*] *Patriot* and [*Salem*] *Register*."[107] Garrison learned never to be shy about expressing and defending whatever he believed to be just, true, moral, and right. If he can be faulted for his errors of prediction, finding fault with his expression of conviction and morality is hardly possible.

Garrison's next two published essays turned to American literature, revived "An Old Bachelor" and marked his return to the pages of the *Newburyport Herald*. The first of these was quite a substantial effort, titled "American Writers," and covered nearly 80 percent of the *Herald*'s front page.[108] Garrison's essay responded to a series of articles which had appeared in *Blackwood's Magazine*. Published in England and written by an American expatriate named John Neal, the articles critically examined the literary efforts of American writers. Neal was an American novelist, essayist, and literary critic, who was credited with being "a forerunner in utilizing dialect for literary purposes, and ... was among the first to demonstrate that native materials of the colonies and the Revolution may be viable for fiction."[109] In his challenge to Neal's criticism, Garrison acknowledged that American literature was yet in its infancy, but argued that "it remains no longer the subject of doubt, whether we possess the richness of intellect and vigor of thought, of which England ... can boast." English criticism of American literature and art had become muted in recent years and Garrison was particularly offended that, Neal, a former resident of Baltimore, unpatriotically assumed the pose of English critic.

In particular Garrison took up the defense of six American poets: Theophilus Parsons, Joel Barlow, Robert Stevenson Coffin, Richard Henry Dana, Dr. Farmer, and Thomas Green Fessenden. He agreed grudgingly with Neal's assessment of Coffin (also known as the "Boston Bard") but defended the rest, especially Thomas Fessenden.[110] No small part of his defense may have been based on Fessenden's Federalist leanings—he once published a poetic attack on Thomas Jefferson titled *Democracy Unveiled: or Tyranny Stripped of the Garb of Patriotism*.[111] In his closing paragraph, Garrison wrote, "We cannot express sufficiently, our Indignation at this renegade's base attempt to assassinate the reputation of this country," and charged that Neal's attack on American writers was the result of his own "wounded pride" for the "indifference bordering on contempt" his writing received from the American public. Finally, he advised Neal to watch his back if he ever returned to his native land. Garrison had yet to embrace non-resistance.

Neal and Garrison's paths crossed several times in the next forty years, usually with considerable animosity. Not demonstrating any concern about Garrison's warning, Neal returned to his native Maine in 1828 where he became editor of *The Yankee* magazine and continued to write prolifically, while promoting the careers of American authors, including Nathaniel Hawthorne and Edgar Allan Poe. As a vocal supporter of the Colonization Society in Portland, Neal earned several references in *The Liberator* including being called "a notorious religious scoffer and professional blackguard."[112] The two men were reconciled after the Civil War when, at a reception for Garrison in Portland, Neal admitted that with regard to their past differences, "I was wrong ... and Mr. Garrison was right."[113]

His second article on American literature was a book review of a novel, *Resignation: An American Novel, By a Lady*, by Sarah Ann Evans.[114] This article also appeared on the front page of the *Herald* and took up nearly half the page.[115] Garrison began with a brief discussion about the rise in the popularity of the novel, which had created a "mania for this species of reading." He believed that the explosion of novel writing had produced little of merit, or at least little to compare with "the more palatable effusions of *Scott* and *Cooper*." As Garrison was no doubt aware, in the early United States Republic many literary and social critics regarded novel reading as dangerous to the morals of the individual reader. Thus, novelists of the period often claimed that their stories were based on real events and were acceptable because they taught valuable moral lessons. Although the danger commonly associated with novels threatened both young men and young women, current scholarship calls particular attention to the admonition as it affected women's reading habits, how novels often reflected a bias against women's individuality, and how women used the novel as a tool for education and change.[116] Garrison credited the origin of the modern novel to the work of the "Great Unknown" (Sir Walter Scott) who used "historical facts, embellished with the lighter graces of fancy ... [to convey] ... instruction while he captivated the imagination." Garrison also expressed familiarity with and praise for the works of James Fenimore Cooper, Hannah More, Mrs. Opie, and Maria Edgeworth who all used the novel form as a means to "disseminate religious and moral sentiments." The novel, *Resignation*, fell into this category and won Garrison's approval. Although he had some reservations about how Evans developed a few of her minor characters, the novel was "a plain, unadorned tale of Christian suffering and triumph" and consequently worthy of his readers' attention.

Two months later, on December 10, 1825, Garrison's apprenticeship terminated and he moved out into the world to pursue his newspaper career as an adult. As his apprenticeship ended he had not yet begun to focus on the tribulations of the "peculiar institution," but in the deferential world of Federalist Newburyport, he certainly experienced the sting of social exclusion in his own life. His efforts to improve himself were encouraged by reform and improvement societies, but improvement did not lead to acceptance in the elite circles of Newburyport. The pillars of society were men like Caleb Cushing, who advised and encouraged the young printer, but who would not accept his advancement to the refined, intellectual life of a small New England town. As a representative of the Newburyport Debating Club, Cushing delivered the annual Fourth of July oration on several occasions, yet even after the demise of that club, Garrison's Independence Day speech was limited to the members of his own Franklin Debating Society.

Cushing and Garrison became adversaries within a year after Garrison's apprenticeship ended when Garrison actively and very vocally supported Cushing's opponent in the local congressional election of 1826. Garrison was among Cushing's harshest critics in the race and was accused of making "scurrilous attacks on the character of his former benefactor."[117] Garrison returned to Newburyport in September 1830 on his anti-slavery speaking tour of New England which preceded the publication of *The Liberator*. Cushing still resided in town and, although there is no record that he heard Garrison speak, according to Cushing's biographer, "we may be quite sure that he would have found little to approve in the new and radical doctrine which the young abolitionist was expounding."[118] The root of their separation, however, was as much a political disagreement as it was a reflection of Cushing's anger at his treatment by Garrison despite everything Cushing believed he had done for him, as well as Garrison's desire to exert his independence. His accomplishments and experiences as an apprentice clearly influenced Garrison's strident rhetoric and his later passion to "make every single home, press, pulpit, and senate chamber a debating society, with *his* right and wrong for the subject"[119] as certainly as his shocked sensibilities once he fully recognized slavery's horrors.

Three

Political Machinations

At the end of William Lloyd Garrison's apprenticeship in December 1825, three elements formed the foundation for his life: printing, politics, and religion. Late in life, Garrison reminisced about his years in the printing trade and said that he "delighted in nothing more ... than the manipulation of type" and felt blessed to have learned such an important craft.[1] He certainly did not expect everyone was suited to choose printing as a trade; however, politics and religion were, he believed, important elements that did belong in the lives of all citizens. During the next three years, Garrison would attempt to convince the public, when he could address them in the press, about the importance of adopting correct religious and political principles as well as the importance of editorial ethics and integrity. By July of 1829, however, he was fast reaching the point of despair. Not only were the people not listening, but the nation's political and religious institutions, which should have provided clarity and direction for the nation, were leading the people down the wrong path. These institutions were willfully culpable for supporting and encouraging the greatest danger facing the United States at that time: slavery. Out of this frustration and growing sense of despair materialized Garrison's "Park Street Address" on the Fourth of July in 1829. In the address, he described and dissected the problem, called upon the nation's citizens to recognize the dangers the nation faced, and offered the political and religious institutions one final opportunity to lead.

Later in his career, Garrison became notorious for refusing to participate in the political system and for referring to the United States Constitution as a "compact with the devil."[2] Garrison made several comments of this ilk before he publicly burned the Constitution in 1854. His earliest recorded comment was in *The Liberator* on December 29, 1832, when he called it "the most bloody and heaven-daring arrangement ever made by men." He used similar language to condemn the United States Constitution as "null and void" according "to the law of God" during his first trip to England.[3] However, in the years preceding his "Park Street Address" and in his early editorial experiences, Garrison's efforts and practice demonstrated that he had great faith in the American political process and believed that following the correct path in politics was one road to a just and moral life for the individual and the nation.

In December 1825, Garrison was released from his indentures. As a remembrance of this important passage in his life, Garrison commissioned a portrait of himself by William Swain, a local artist.[4] In the portrait, Garrison appears well-dressed with his black hair combed forward to cover a quickly receding hair line, but his steady gaze signaled a young man determined to rise above whatever limitations that might lie before him. Garrison had already succeeded in rising from very humble circumstances to the status of craftsman; he hoped he would soon become a master in his own right, an independent artisan and editor. At the time, as a budding master printer in his own right, Garrison was but a short step away from joining what Sean Wilentz has called the "artisan republicanism" of the early nineteenth century. More than simply being industrious, competent, and productive, the American artisan "exemplified a belief that independent men of relatively small means were both entitled to full citizenship and best equipped to exercise it ... [and] ... would be devoted, not to personal ambition or profit alone, but to the commonwealth."[5] The printer's craft was the underpinning upon which Garrison built his career as a reformer and activist and he took pride in being part of a craft that, he believed, stood above all other crafts. Swain's portrait gives us a glimpse of his determination; now all he needed was the opportunity.

Garrison had learned his lessons "at the case" well and in December 1825 was eager to pursue his craft independently, but without any other opportunities readily available he continued to work as a journeyman in Ephraim Allen's printing office for the next three months. It is not difficult to imagine that as unsatisfying as this situation might have been for Garrison, Allen was probably more than pleased to retain him. After all, he had been a valuable employee who had, for the last three years, completely supervised the printing office while also assuming the editorial duties in Allen's absence.[6] But Allen's fortune was short-lived and, happily, the young master-to-be did not have to wait very long for an opportunity to put the "arts and mysteries" of the printing profession to work for himself.

Allen's *Newburyport Herald* was the voice of the local Federalist party and although the paper's motto boasted "An Independent Press is the Surest Safeguard of Freedom," the local National-Republicans, certainly with some justification, were not convinced of Allen's political independence and countered with a newspaper of their own in 1824 called the *Northern Chronicler*. After the *Chronicler*'s demise as a political organ, Garrison's good friend, fellow apprentice, and future partner, Isaac Knapp, purchased the paper in June 1825 and published it as a non-partisan publication which he called the *Essex Courant*. Knapp's success was limited and in March 1826, he sold the *Courant* to Garrison, who once again renamed the paper, and on March 22, 1826, published the first issue of the Newburyport's newest newspaper, *The Free Press*.[7] Finally, Garrison had an opportunity to pursue "with vigor and zeal" what he called "his favorite avocation." In this first editorial project, in typical Garrisonian fashion, he declared: "As to the political course of the Free Press, it shall be, in the widest extent of the term, *independent*." He also promised that the paper would be "subservient to no party or body of men; and neither the craven fear of loss nor the threats of the disappointed, nor the influence of power, shall awe one single opinion into silence."[8] Strong words indeed, but nothing less than he expected, maybe in youthful enthusiasm, of all editors. In what may seem an unusually generous gesture, he was "kindly aided by Mr. Allen himself" who loaned him the money to purchase the paper.[9] Garrison remembered Allen in an editorial some years later as a man of "integrity, benevolence, and steadfastness of character."[10] Nevertheless, his *Free Press* experience led to several conflicts with his benefactor and provided a valuable lesson for the young master printer: there was cost and consequence attached to political independence, financial dependence, and to the practice of publishing a "free" press.

This reality was something that Allen fully understood, which may help to explain why he kindly assisted his well-trained protégé to enter into competition with him. One reason for Allen's aid was rather straightforward. Competing perspectives about political or social issues stirred readership interest and brought both publications attention and, most importantly, subscribers. Competition among different newspapers in a small town like Newburyport was likely to be good for business for both papers, at least for a while. What was more, there was an additional advantage for the survivor, which Allen no doubt expected would be his *Herald*. Late in 1826, after Garrison's successor at *The Free Press* announced that the paper was ceasing publication, Allen wrote proudly about how he and the *Herald* had, since 1800, weathered thirteen newspaper competitors in Newburyport, and then solicited *The Free Press* subscribers who "wish for a paper in this town, to subscribe for the *Herald*."[11] To the winner belonged the spoils!

In addition to economic considerations, Allen may have believed that the political inclinations of his former apprentice would be useful in light of the changing political environment in Newburyport, in Massachusetts, and in the New England region. Like most newspapers of the time, the *Herald* also claimed independence from political partisanship, but in the early decades of the nineteenth century, as explained earlier, newspapers in the United States had become predominantly political organs for political parties, and Allen's *Herald* was no exception. From the first years of Allen's ownership, the *Herald*'s political affiliation had become, in the words of David Fischer, "decidedly Federalist," although Allen consistently resisted Fischer's label of "electioneering papers," that is, newspapers which were published "not for profit, but only patriotic motives."[12] Allen was decidedly interested in long-term financial success and politics was a useful means to achieve it. The paper which had become Garrison's *Free Press* was originally founded as a National-Republican party paper, and Allen hoped that it would become an organ for an amalgamation of local interests who wanted to replace John Varnum, their Federalist representative to Congress, with Garrison's mentor Caleb Cushing — something which Allen was unwilling to promote at the time.

In his quarter century in Newburyport, Allen had developed and deserved a reputation as a civic-minded businessman, politically astute with cautious good judgment. By 1826 he and other formerly committed Federalists recognized that the old party was dead and they leaned toward supporting the National-Republicans in opposition to the surging Jacksonian Democratic-Republicans.[13] Allen was certainly aware that Garrison had displayed considerable interest in political affairs from the several series of articles he had written for the *Herald* and other local newspapers during his apprenticeship. Perhaps, Allen may have concluded that Garrison's political inclinations would contribute to local political change which he was not yet prepared to fully champion directly in his own paper. For his part, Garrison appreciated the kindnesses Cushing had extended to him and, as Garrison later admitted, "I naturally became one of his admirers in view of his brilliant scholarship and expanding talent."[14] Allen had good reason to expect that Garrison would support Cushing's anticipated effort to replace Varnum. Consequently, Allen's personal interest in supporting the success of his talented and energetic pupil fit nicely with his own economic and political interests.

Even the most casual examination of *The Free Press* reveals the importance that its young editor placed on political issues whether local, statewide, or national. For his part, Garrison wasted little time in stirring political controversy and antagonizing his readers while also demonstrating that he rejected support by or for the National-Republican Party. In his first issue as editor,

March 22, 1826, the lead article carried a bold headline, "Our Claim. No. I," which discussed an old Federalist Party issue that dated to the War of 1812, specifically, that the state of Massachusetts had never been fully reimbursed by the Federal government for the expenses it incurred for defense of the state during the war. The claim was one of those festering issues that troubled the minds and hearts of older hardline Federalists but which younger Federalists, who were beginning to look for ways to cooperate with National-Republicans, had decided was too divisive and should be ignored, at least for the moment. For his part, however, Garrison refused to compromise on what he believed was an important issue. He argued that since the Massachusetts claim was no less justified than the claims of other states, which had been paid promptly, "the people of the Commonwealth have a right to expect, and *do* expect, that ample restitution will be made without further delay."[15]

One week later, a second article about the claim lead the editorial section, "Our Claim No. II." Garrison made it clear that he was unwilling to back down from what he considered to be a simple question of justice. He noted that his remarks in the previous issue about the Massachusetts claim had prompted ten individuals to cancel their subscription but, with dramatic flair, he claimed "that we erase their names from our subscription list *with the same pleasure* that we insert MORE THAN AN EQUAL NUMBER in their place."[16] This was the first time in his editorial career he made a statement like this, but it certainly would not be the last; given a choice between subscribers and editorial freedom, the latter was always preferable. The claim issue remained a focus of *The Free Press* for the entire six months Garrison was editor. "Our Claim No. III." appeared in early April and later in the month he reported on the support the claim received from other newspapers, as well as the support it received from current and former members of Congress from Massachusetts and Maine.[17] He also challenged Daniel Webster, who was then a representative in Congress from Boston, to "stand forth [as] champion of injured merit and impartial justice" and use his powerful voice to support the claim or risk losing the support of the people.[18]

The controversy Garrison encouraged over the Massachusetts claim, the first controversy of a long editorial, was an early indicator of the journalistic temperament for which he became so renowned. There is no doubt that Garrison's was the "other" newspaper in a one-newspaper town, but he was both clever enough and ambitious enough to appreciate the benefit of instigating debate to expand interest in newspapers and readership for both himself and Allen. That cleverness may have contributed to his decision to change the day of publication from Saturday to Thursday, which meant *The Free Press* appeared a day before the *Herald* rather than a day after.[19] He argued that Newburyport was "a large commercial town" that could easily support two papers, welcomed the angry letters that objected to his support for the claim, and at least pretended to take pride in removing the complainers from his subscription list and replacing them with new subscribers who found his arguments just and true.[20] The "claim" was, as he reported, the "first object" of interest to him as editor of *The Free Press*, and as it turned out, it would also be the last. When he sold the paper in September 1826, the closing comments of his final editorial returned to the claim. It was about much more than money, he argued, but was a question of "intentional injustice exercised towards" Massachusetts and a grievance that demanded redress. In words prescient of his bold statement in the first issue of *The Liberator*, it was, he argued, "a question of RIGHT — and it must be heard."[21] From the beginning of his editorial career, Garrison was determined not to be silenced when justice demanded a voice, but in *The Free Press* his voice was principally raised to champion political issues, not reform.

The claim was hardly the only political issue on which Garrison focused during his tenure at *The Free Press*, or even the most important. He often noticed and voiced concern about the changes taking place in the political system, as well as the failure of Massachusetts' citizens to participate sufficiently in elections. In the state elections of April 1826, he expressed dismay about voter turnout and wrote that "a more quiet election never passed over our heads."[22] Garrison became infamous in the late 1830s for his refusal to vote because the political system had become so corrupt. By 1839, Garrison had rejected voting completely; it was a form of cooperation with the slave-power conspiracy, and when challenged at the annual meeting of the American Anti-Slavery Society by Henry Stanton to answer whether he believed it to be a sin to vote, Garrison replied, "Sin for me!"[23] However, in May 1826, he editorialized with great passion about the importance of political participation by all citizens, including exercising the right to vote. What he called the voters' "growing indifference" to elections was a "matter of serious alarm and disquietude" and he suggested that it was a simple political truth that "remissness in this important duty is the first step to slavery." He urged his readers to remember that voting "must be cherished, strengthened, and defended."[24]

In another contrast to his later passions, Garrison's voice was also raised in praise of his country, which was about to celebrate its fiftieth anniversary. Two months ahead of the celebration, Garrison began urging the citizens of Newburyport to prepare "suitable demonstrations of respect and gratitude" in remembrance of the great day.[25] As the day grew closer, he congratulated the organizers of the Newburyport festivities for preparing a celebration that reflected "the highest credit upon the patriotism and munificence of the town" and set about preparing his own special commentary to the public on the great blessings enjoyed by the citizens of the United States.[26] In the issue printed a week before Independence Day, Garrison enumerated those characteristics which made the United States a great nation and voiced high praise for the Constitution, which had kept the nation's political system secure. He offered thanks to God that the days of political factionalism had ended. Furthermore, he expressed special appreciation that the "light of intelligence illuminates every part of our country" and cheered the fact that

> the press is groaning under the weight of intellectual knowledge and general information, and is continually disseminating food for every age and capacity. No American need be *ignorant*: neither poverty nor want of opportunity prevents his attainment of useful learning. Education, that mighty discoverer of man's true dignity and power, is within the reach of all who seek for it.[27]

Clearly Garrison was talking about his own experience, out of which he had emerged to the high position of newspaper editor. The young printer and editor had built for himself a solid foundation and appeared to have a promising future thanks in no small part, in his own estimation, to the special blessings of the American social and political system.

Only one note of caution crept into Garrison's address — a caution that had not been discussed in his Independence Day Address to the Franklin Debating Society two years earlier. As it came to its close, he asked if "there are no dark shades to be seen" in the nation's future? In answer, he called upon Americans to understand that July 4 should be a time for more than "rhapsodies upon the deeds of our fathers" but a time when the nation's "follies and virtues should be skillfully held up to equal light. There is one theme which should be dwelt upon, till our whole country is free from the curse — it is SLAVERY."

The subject of slavery was not a common theme in *The Free Press* during Garrison's editorship and the immediate impetus for this current warning is not known. The potential danger slavery posed for the nation had received some attention in Newburyport a few years earlier in the wake of the Denmark Vesey insurrection in Charleston in 1822. Caleb Cushing was editing the *Herald* at the time and wrote two editorials about slavery in which he expressed concern for the morality of a society in which slavery was commonly accepted, as well as the possible violent rebellions it could inspire.[28] Most of Garrison's fellow citizens in New England likely agreed that slavery was a curse and a cloud that threatened danger in the future for the nation, but were uncertain, as was he, what could be done to rid the nation of the peril. However, what might be more important with regard to this commentary may simply be the fact that the young editor was prepared to turn a light on the nation's faults and misdeeds, and call for change. In a little more than four years, the light became a beacon. It is worth noting that while Ephraim Allen's Independence Day editorial was as full of praise for the nation's founders and called for all citizens to "maintain the rights inherited from our fathers," he did not recognize any faults or flaws that needed modification.[29]

The celebration of the nation's independence was later marred when, soon afterward, word arrived of the deaths of John Adams and Thomas Jefferson, both of whom died on July 4, 1826. The news reached Newburyport within the week, just as both newspapers were filled with reports on the parades, speeches, and toasts that made the day's festivities so memorable and successful.[30] Local reactions to the deaths, especially with regard to Jefferson, led to a serious disagreement with Allen, Garrison's former master and current benefactor, and likely contributed to the eventual loss of his first editorial position.

In his first statement about the deaths, Garrison urged caution about praising either man too highly. "We have neither flattery, nor falsehood, nor hypocrisy, to bedaub the grave of either of these men," he wrote, and he counseled others to "be sparing of our panegyrics." He pointed to the strengths and weaknesses of each man and concluded, "both doubtless were friends to their country — both erred — and both helped to advance the national character" — neither, however, deserved unrestrained praise.[31] Finally, as an example of published newspaper excesses about the two men, Garrison reprinted part of Allen's statement from the *Herald* which he labeled as "bordering on impiety." Indeed, the *Herald* had fantasized about the two men "winging their way" to eternity and being greeted at the throne of the Redeemer by the holy men of old, philosophers, scholars, and heroes of past ages "clustering around them with salutations of joy and voices of welcome; for thou are worthy."[32] Both of the great men had at some time offended Garrison's still strong Federalist leanings and Allen's praise had, in his estimation, simply gone too far.

From this small beginning, a feud between Allen and Garrison developed, although it could have been avoided. In his next issue, Allen gently admonished his "friend of *The Free Press*," admitted that his statement may have been offensive to some, but called upon Garrison to "extend to us his charity and in mercy ponder the old maxim '*de gustibus non*'" ("there is no disputing about taste").[33] Unwilling to let the matter drop, Garrison rather pointedly praised the eulogy of the ex-presidents published by Caleb Cushing, which he said was "but little in sentiment ... and a just estimate of the characters of the deceased," and then he proceeded to sharply attack Allen's inconsistency in his pious reveries about Jefferson. He recalled how Allen had in the past called

Jefferson "the Great Lama of Infidelity" and "the giant who would carry away the gates of Christianity, and open the flood-gates of vice!" Garrison titled this commentary "Sensibility" which may have been intended to infer that Allen's words were more reminiscent of novel writing than journalism — more fiction than fact — the most grievous error any newspaper editor can commit.[34]

In the next several issues of both the *Herald* and *The Free Press*, the two editors jousted back and forth, including what appears to be a not very well-veiled threat in which Allen reminded Garrison that his current position was the consequence of Allen's generosity.[35] But finally, late in the month, Allen ended the war of words with one final defense of his statements about Jefferson and then dismissed Garrison, who he hoped "will excuse us from farther noticing effusions far too precious to be wasted on such unworthy objects as ourselves."[36] Indeed, this appeared to be the case. For the remaining two months that Garrison edited *The Free Press*, Allen neither discussed this issue nor took notice, in the *Herald*, of any news or articles published in Garrison's paper. The next mention of *The Free Press* in the *Herald* appeared in late September when Allen reported, without mentioning Garrison by name, that the paper had been sold to John Harris. Allen wished Harris much success.[37]

In addition to fostering the controversy with Allen, Adams' and Jefferson's deaths also encouraged Garrison to write a series of reflections on the current state of politics in the United States. In his last seven weeks as editor of *The Free Press*, politics took center stage, leading to a final denouement with Allen and a sudden end for Garrison's publishing career in Newburyport. As this period began, Garrison wrote that the animosities of past national political battles had lost power and that it was difficult to find "radical difference between [politicians] in principle and practice." Yet he also expressed regret that this change meant that fewer citizens turned out at the polls and that only a "close observer ... can discriminate between a federal and a republican vote."[38] Later, he warned his readers about the threat faced by the United States as a result of Andrew Jackson's growing popularity; his supporters in many states were busy prejudicing the minds of the people and creating destructive factions.[39] He also published two articles of "political reflections" on the careers of Adams and Jefferson in which he acknowledged the significant contributions of both men and, despite Garrison's deep disdain for Jefferson's religious beliefs and political practices, judged that Jefferson was in fact a better "leader" of a political faction than Adams.[40]

Often without directly naming Allen, Garrison continued to needle him. On several occasions he lavished praise on Caleb Cushing's eulogy of Adams and Jefferson and reprinted portions of both Cushing's and Daniel Webster's eulogies. He clearly seemed to be making the point that it was possible to remember accomplishments of the patriots without the misplaced "sensibility" offered by editors like Allen.[41] As with his Independence Day editorial reflection, he was not beyond believing the United States could become "a more perfect union." Garrison also admonished Allen for his decision to stop publishing a series titled "A View of Greece" that had run for some time in both the *Herald* and *The Free Press*. Like many of his contemporaries, Garrison believed that the struggles for independence going on in the world were in imitation of America's own independence movement in 1776, which had "excited wide interest and sympathy in the United States" around the world.[42] Consequently, on May 4, he began publishing a long series of essays by Estwick Evans of Portsmouth, New Hampshire, about the war for independence in Greece. Allen and many other New England printers soon followed suit; however, the series quickly generated some controversy over its authenticity and accuracy.

By August many newspaper editors elected to stop publishing the series. Soon, Allen announced that he too was discontinuing Evans' series "because they were prolix and tedious, without imparting the desired and promised information."[43] On August 24 Garrison published a lengthy editorial commentary on the decision made by so many of his fellow publishers. While granting that Evans' views were indeed open to criticism, Garrison stood by Evans' claim that he wrote "for the consideration of the public" and that it was on their judgment alone that criticism must stand. Furthermore, he argued, the editor who barred publication of controversial information, simply because it was controversial, did a disservice to his subscribers. Garrison proclaimed that "no class of men in society ... are capable of doing so much good as editors" because "honest printers and writers will ... check the tide of [political] corruption." Finally, he rather pointedly asserted that he wrote for the "exclusive benefit of our brother of the *Herald*. We shall not say one word about *consistency*—but merely apply to him the trite adage, 'If the coat suit,' &c."[44] Allen may have had enough; he did not respond in print.

The need for citizens to be fully informed, involved, and attentive to the actions of their political leaders was a regular message in *The Free Press*. Garrison's analysis of those actions and his implications about his former master's failure in this regard became the last straw in the simmering feud between Allen and Garrison. In early May, Garrison had begun urging his readers to pay attention to the "bargaining in the wind" with regard to the fall elections and alluded to a cabal of "knowing ones" who may be planning to alter the slate of candidates. Later in the month he warned about "knaves and scoundrels [who] will try to direct the reins of government."[45] These warnings persisted throughout the summer, but the final blow came in mid-September when, in an editorial titled "REPRESENTATIVE ELECTION," Garrison declared that a secret plot was underway to replace John Varnum, the current Congressional representative from the Essex North District. He reported that "an organized opposition to the present incumbent is not merely intended, but secretly consolidated." Any opposition to Varnum, Garrison argued, should be based "solely on political grounds ... fairly avowed and as plainly understood." It should not be done in secret by "a set of interested jugglers" seeking to make the "good, honest, substantial yeomanry of Essex North [their] willing puppets."[46] Varnum "had affiliations with the conservative New England Federalists" and was not favored by manufacturing and commercial interests in the district who "were looking about for a younger and bolder nominee." Cushing, of course, was that nominee; he was first urged to run for Congress in July 1825, but withheld his decision and announcement until October 1826, shortly before the election.[47] We cannot know if Ephraim Allen's financial expectations in supporting Garrison's paper were successful, but it appears that his political expectations were not. If Allen had supported Garrison's *Free Press* and a second Newburyport newspaper as a potential political voice in support of Cushing, he had seriously miscalculated; however, he still held the upper hand.

Allen may or may not have been a part of the cabal that schemed to replace Varnum with Cushing, but he certainly admired Cushing and supported the plan once it was revealed. Regardless, exposing the plan evidently cost Garrison his paper. Allen called in the note providing the financial support for *The Free Press* and Garrison was forced to announce the sale of the paper.[48] Garrison attributed the decision to sell to "considerations of importance only to himself." Considering, however, that in the same issue in which he announced the sale of his paper, he celebrated the first six months of its existence and called upon its readers to promptly pay their subscription for the next six months, something extraordinary must have occurred to alter his expectations.[49] Only a few issues earlier, he had advertised for an apprentice, which would seem to indicate his intention to stay in Newburyport and continue publication.[50] The sale announcement has all the appearances of a last minute change, especially in light of Garrison's positive editorial statement regarding the success (and improved subscription list) that *The Free Press* was then enjoying. In any case, the next issue announced the sale of *The Free Press* to John H. Harris. Soon after, Harris and *The Free Press* endorsed Caleb Cushing for the congressional seat.[51]

In his parting editorial, Garrison made no apologies for his initial efforts as a newspaper publisher. He wished Harris success but stipulated that while he was in charge of his press, he had labored only in the support of principles: "principles, which neither fear, nor violence, nor interest, nor policy, has ever shaken, and which have been *independent of everything but* TRUTH." Before closing with one more appeal for the Massachusetts claim, he wrote,

> The Editor who lashes public follies and vices — who strips deception of its borrowed garb, and aims his shafts at corruption, may be accused of arrogance and unchastened zeal — of hatred, and malice, and envy — of an unforgiving, uncharitable, intemperate spirit — but he will hardly be praised for his labors. If the tone of the Free Press has sometimes given offence by its frankness, that frankness has also secured it many friends: if the lash has been occasionally misapplied, it has more frequently scourged the intended victims.

This sounds like the Garrison of later years, but in his first editorial experience at the press, his lash was intended to scourge those engaged, as he wished to be, in the political battles of the day. However, he viewed politics as beneficial, even honorable, only when it was open to all citizens, honest, and rife with debate. For his part, Harris followed Garrison's statement with a promise to restore the paper to its original purpose, support for "republicans," and solicited those who had cancelled their subscriptions to return.[52]

Garrison remained in Newburyport long enough to participate in the November congressional election and to work for Cushing's defeat. In addition to his anger about the secrecy of Cushing's candidacy, Garrison was critical of the tactics Cushing employed in the campaign. A series of letters had appeared in the Boston newspapers extravagantly endorsing Cushing and deprecating Varnum. Eventually it was shown that these letters had been written by Cushing himself. Cushing first denied writing the letters and then later claimed they were written by his wife. Such an outlandish statement so angered Garrison that he wrote several articles against Cushing that appeared "in the Herald and Salem and Haverhill papers to ensure his defeat."[53] Cushing lost the election to Varnum by a vote of 1,399 to 882.[54] While Garrison's animus was strong, it would be wrong to give him alone credit for the loss; many other voices were raised against Cushing. More significantly, Garrison's efforts against Cushing began an estrangement, the result of Garrison's uninvited and "scurrilous attack on the character of his former benefactor" which, according to Cushing's biographer, lasted the rest of their lives.[55] With the election over, his involvement with *The Free Press* resolved, and little local opportunity available, Garrison left Newburyport in December 1826 to seek employment in Boston. Under Harris' editorship, *The Free Press* lasted about one month after the election and ceased publication on December 9, 1826.[56]

There may have been some satisfaction in Cushing's election defeat, but Garrison's first foray into political controversy only seemed to confirm for him that politics was becoming corrupted. What was supposed to be an open and transparent process, in which any interested and educated citizen could participate, was disintegrating. Growing up in a Federalist Party stronghold, Garrison may have grudgingly accepted that an orphaned printer's apprentice would not be welcome into the higher circles of local social and political life. But as an educated and concerned citizen, as a master craftsman and as editor of his own newspaper, certainly he had earned the right, Garrison believed, to participate. He deserved to be at least at the fringes of elite Newburyport society as it determined the political and social course of the town. The secret meetings and secret candidacies shut him, and others, out of the political process; they were undemocratic, and anathema, in Garrison's view, to the principles on which the United States was founded.

In Boston, Garrison first stayed with Thomas Bennett, who had worked for a time in Allen's printing office in Newburyport. Bennett was now printing the *Massachusetts Journal* edited by David Lee Child who, along with Garrison, would be one of the six men to draft the constitution for the New England Anti-Slavery Society in 1831, and which was adopted on January 6, 1832, at the Belknap Street Church.[57] It took Garrison about a month before he found printing work and for the next year he did journeyman's labor at several printing offices in the city, including at Child's *Journal*.[58] Garrison stayed with Bennett only briefly before moving to a boarding house for printers operated by the Reverend William Collier, who was a Baptist city missionary and the founder of the first newspaper in the United States devoted solely to the cause of temperance, the *National Philanthropist*— another printing office at which Garrison worked on occasion.[59]

In addition to fellow printers at Collier's boarding house, Garrison had other friends in the Boston printing community and made use of one of them to re-enter the political fray. Joseph Buckingham was the editor of the *Boston Courier* and when he heard that Garrison had left *The Free Press*, he expressed regret "that any circumstances should occur to induce an editor of such talents, feelings and principles to relinquish his purpose."[60] Barely settled at Bennett's boarding house, Garrison entered the world of Boston politics with a letter published in Buckingham's *Courier* about the upcoming mayoral election. His letter supported the re-election of Josiah Quincy, a sentiment shared by Buckingham who had recently voiced his own support for Quincy in a *Courier* editorial.[61] Quincy had held several political offices including serving as mayor of Boston (1823–1829) and was one of the new school Federalists who embraced the political style and popular practices of the Jeffersonians. Like Garrison, at least in 1826, Quincy remained committed to traditional Federalist beliefs, including the impurity of Jefferson, the unjustness of the War of 1812, and the righteousness of the 1814 Hartford Convention. Even in 1861, Quincy would still identify himself as a Federalist.

Garrison's letter to the *Courier* described his attendance at a party caucus at Faneuil Hall and the shocking accusations some had made about Quincy. Garrison summed them up to be Quincy's belief "that Mr. Jefferson was not immaculate, and that the war [War of 1812] was unjust." Neither of these "offenses" counted for much to Quincy's detriment in Garrison's opinion; rather, they were excellent justification for supporting his candidacy. Quincy's willingness to stand on principle was a great attribute from Garrison's perspective. Win or lose, Quincy could rest reassured, he argued, with the words of the pre-revolutionary political critic known as "Junius":

> Professions of patriotism are become stale and ridiculous. For my own part I claim no merit from endeavoring to do a service to my fellow citizens. I have done it to the best of my understanding. Without looking for the approbation of other men, my conscience is satisfied.[62]

These words, however overstated they might have been on this occasion, are clearly prescient of the kind of devotion and commitment Garrison made when he later embraced the abolitionist cause.[63]

For most of 1827, Garrison's primary concern was finding employment and supporting himself in Boston, yet he also did find time to focus on the condition of national, state, and local politics. In one of his letters in 1827, perhaps disingenuously, he complained, "The hours which should be devoted to labor, Mr. Editor, allow me little time to indulge in newspaper essays" but nevertheless, he did find the time for both essays and controversy.[64] On April 21 and May 7, letters commenting on the upcoming presidential election signed simply by "G" appeared in the *Newburyport Herald*. In the first, Garrison acknowledged that he had supported Crawford over Adams in the 1824 election but that he and many others were converted to the Adams camp because of the "phrensied efforts of the Jackson cabal" to turn Adams out of office by splitting the anti–Jackson forces into several special-interest factions.[65] Similarly, in the second letter, Garrison wrote about the efforts of Jackson supporters to divide and conquer the will of the people of Massachusetts by appealing to "intrigue, chicanery, and falsehood" in order to inflame the passions of the voters about extraneous issues which threatened to undermine the friends of good government.[66] In still another letter to the *Herald*, Garrison addressed the current political controversy created by the "promotion" of Daniel Webster to the United States Senate. Many names had been offered but Garrison believed that the only man who could "amply fill his place" in the House of Representatives was Harrison Gray Otis, a Federalist politician, who had long been a favorite of Garrison and had lost the election for the governorship of Massachusetts in 1823.[67]

Garrison took his support for Otis to a caucus of the Federalist Party that met at the Exchange Coffee House in Boston on July 11 to nominate a successor to Webster, and in doing so became involved in "a brief newspaper controversy" over his actions.[68] For all his political inclinations and his passion for political affairs, Garrison was somewhat behind the times, at least with regard to evolving American politics. He sympathized with what Buckingham called a small cadre of "old Federalists" who did not seem to recognize that the Federalist Party finally died with Adams' election in 1824 and who diligently continued to advocate the election of Federalists like Harrison Gray Otis for several years afterward.[69] Most of the caucus participants had forsaken the Federalist Party and were surprised by Garrison's unexpected address and his entering into nomination a name that had not been part of the planned agenda. In a letter to the *Courier*, Garrison defended his action and expressed chagrin that some of the gentlemen at the meeting resented his suggestion because, he said, he had every intention of supporting whatever candidate "a majority of the party should nominate." For his part, Garrison resented the idea that his participation in the meeting should be considered inappropriate and that the party appeared to be unwilling to listen to the voices of all its members.[70] Other participants, however, supported Garrison's nomination of Otis. The caucus had to be adjourned while a delegation was sent to consult Otis who, as it turned out, was not interested in running for the office. In the next day's paper, Garrison was castigated by "S" for his arrogance in coming "unknown" before the caucus, literally retrieving notes from his hat, and taking the liberty to speak. "S" claimed to have no animosity toward Otis, although he felt Otis had yet to fully explain his position on the tariff, but declared "that it is revolting ... to see a stranger, a man who never paid a tax in our city, and perhaps no where else, to possess the impudence to take the lead, and nominate a candidate."[71]

Defending himself in the next day's paper, Garrison allowed that his address to the caucus may have been "out of place." However, he denied that he had come to the meeting with any intention of causing disruption, but rather only to have the opportunity to express his political ideas publicly. Furthermore, he reminded "S" that his nomination of Otis met with the approval of the majority present at the assembly and suggested that perhaps his anger at Garrison's breach of decorum resulted less from Otis' nomination than from the fact that "S" lost control of the proceedings and had to submit to the will of the majority. In fact, five men were nominated at the caucus. Harrison Gray Otis received 108 votes, Benjamin Gorham 73 and three others a total of 20.

Buckingham, editor of the *Courier*, was secretary of the committee that informed Otis of his selection and reported that he declined the nomination.[72] Garrison also offered to show the gentlemen that he had "paid taxes" in Boston and elsewhere and rather memorably declared:

> It is true that my acquaintance in this city is limited — I have sought for none. Let me assure him, however, that if my life be spared, my name shall one day be known to the world — at least, to such an extent that common inquiry shall be unnecessary. This, I know, will be deemed excessive vanity — but time shall prove it prophetic.[73]

What reason Garrison may have had to express such a grand appraisal of his future, aside from wounded ego, is not easily discernible but few would ever accuse him of temerity in the face of a challenge.

Taking up another hot political topic, in his letter of July 14 Garrison promised "S" that he would make his opinions on the tariff question public and, as promised, another letter from Garrison was published in the *Courier*, about ten days later. In it Garrison supported the tariff and the "American System" but with some caution. He argued that "the danger to be apprehended, then, is, of involving ourselves too deeply in manufacturers, at the expense of the two great interests of our country, — commerce and agriculture." He also believed that the country was blessed with "inexhaustible, unconquerable" natural resources which, if properly used, meant that the United States would not become "dependent on other nations for livelihood, and subject to all the changes and embarrassments of foreign markets." Garrison further asserted his belief that "the affairs of the country are hastening to a crisis." This crisis (which was still not yet slavery) had two causes — both political — the Jacksonian opposition that threatened to divide and destroy the country from within, and an election process that cooperated with that threat by "descending into a *system of pledges*." The election process, Garrison argued, no longer considered "discernment, experience, and integrity" as the most important qualifications for election to office, but rather whether or not the candidate was willing to be the mouthpiece for or representative of "a fraction of the State, and not the whole."[74] In this, and in the Otis affair, Garrison saw the same kind of political elitism and manipulative behavior that had so offended him a year earlier with Caleb Cushing in Newburyport.

The last extant letter written by Garrison in 1827 also dealt with politics. Acting once again as "our correspondent" for the *Herald*, he happily reported the election of Benjamin Gorham to replace Daniel Webster in the House of Representatives. Gorham had been chosen after Otis declined the nomination and Garrison had supported him wholeheartedly because he was "not trammeled by any committals, nor pledged to any interest, nor under the influence of any local prejudices." A much larger portion of this letter, however, was taken up with excoriating Andrew Jackson's political forces in Boston; their support for David Henshaw, Gorham's opponent, came not from honest political evaluation, but from "the hardihood of faction or the recklessness of insanity." Garrison was pleased with Gorham's victory, but a sense of foreboding about the condition of national politics remained, given what Garrison perceived as the disingenuous efforts of the "friends of the National Administration" to employ trickery and deception to enhance the vote for Jackson's candidate.[75]

In January 1828, Garrison's penchant for the political arena became muted (and its focus perhaps re-directed) when he became editor of William Collier's *National Philanthropist*.[76] Even Garrison's children acknowledged that it took "some effort" for him to "keep aloof from party politics."[77] The *Philanthropist* was one of the first newspapers to devote itself to social reform and the first to challenge the "evil ... [of] ... the intemperate use of ardent spirits" which it proudly displayed in its motto, "Moderate Drinking Is the Downhill Road to Intemperance and Drunkenness."[78] Collier used the paper as the organ of the Massachusetts Society for the Suppression of Intemperance. The *National Philanthropist* was first issued on March 4, 1826, and in its prospectus Collier called into action "the mighty powers of the press [and] the pens of our literary and most able writers" to combat intemperance and to communicate the dangers of alcohol and the need for society and government to take action to address those dangers.[79] Garrison's name did not appear on the masthead of the paper until April 1828, when Collier sold the paper to Garrison's friend Nathaniel H. White, but improvements to the layout of the paper in January indicate that there was a new hand at work. Furthermore, his status was confirmed when he resigned his position in July 1828 and both Garrison and White wrote commentaries which indicated that Garrison's editorial role at the newspaper indeed did begin in January 1828.[80]

The *Philanthropist* under Garrison's editorship was well printed, divided each week into several sections, including Intemperance, Health, General Morality, Education, Foreign News, Marriages and Deaths, Poetry, Miscellany and, of course, a section for editorial comment. In keeping with the paper's prospectus, most of the news and information related to the dangers of alcohol, including stories of the terrible consequences that excessive drinking brought to families and society, as well as reports of progress from temperance societies around the nation. The paper also voiced encouragement for social and political action to overcome the great evil of alcohol and its effects on the nation. While continuing that steady drumbeat, Garrison also used his editorial discretion to advocate other reform causes including: abolishing imprisonment for debt, challenging religious infidelity, supporting peace and non-resistance, recognizing women's role in society, promoting reading and education, warning of the potential dangers of novels, advocating sabbatarianism, and opposing slavery.

During the six months that Garrison edited the *Philanthropist*, two of these other reform issues stand out as most prevalent, the latent social and political influence of women in American society, and the critical importance of reading, education, and newspapers, especially for societal reform. While neither was directly political, both had the possibility of becoming powerful political tools and forces for change in society, and Garrison appeared to fully appreciate that potential. Despite their long periods of separation, Garrison's mother had been a vital influence and had significant impact on his life and character. Through her example, he was certainly aware of the ways in which women could become a quiet, but important, social and political force.[81] If Fanny Garrison's guidance and strength were a powerful force in his early life, his experience with women's influence at the *Philanthropist* demonstrated the functional political and very public contributions that women can make; this was later translated to his strong support for women's rights and women's full participation in the abolitionist movement. At first there were only some peripheral comments about women's contributions to society. For instance, in discussing the American response to tragedies associated with the Greek War for Independence, Garrison had special praise for the work of American women who, he told American men, "have more industry, more ardor, and possess a more charming persuasion, than all the males in christendom."[82] He also had praise for some of the writing in "Ladies magazines" although he rather paternalistically reminded women to beware of the dangers associated with novel reading.[83]

Later, Garrison devoted considerably more space to women's role in society and in a three-part series he forcefully editorialized about the "Female Influence" within the temperance movement. In the first part of the series, he argued that women had considerable influence over the lives of men, beginning as mothers, whose job it was to fashion the morals of young boys, and later as wives and mothers, who were directly affected by the consequences of drunken behavior. Considering both their influence and its consequence, Garrison expressed surprise that women's "cooperation in the work of reform, are so unfrequent."[84] In the second of the series, he offered practical suggestions for ways in which women could "concentrate their influence" over the issue of temperance, and in the final part he urged the formation of "Female Temperance Societies" despite objections widely raised in society against women's participation in public issues. Garrison believed the women's organizations had value because, he argued, "private example may influence a household; but public example only can convert a nation."[85] Unaware that some female temperance societies already existed, he offered to encourage their development by promising a free subscription to the *Philanthropist* to each new society.[86] This series and Garrison's decision to welcome the support of women in a public policy issue are an early indication of Garrison's appreciation of women's political influence in reform efforts.

The role of reading, education, and newspapers in everyday life was the second issue that received particularly special attention from Garrison as editor of the *Philanthropist*. Almost seeming to anticipate the sensationalism of the "penny press" that appeared early in the 1830s, Garrison decried the kind of newspapers that were filled with "murders, suicides, prodigies or monstrous births" and consequently contributed little to improving society.[87] Garrison's training and education was centered on the printing trade and his editorial experiences to this point had convinced him of the powerful role the newspaper played in the political process; he discussed that role in depth in an editorial titled "Influence of Moral Reason." As he became increasingly aware of and a participant in the burgeoning reform movements of New England through his editorship at the *Philanthropist*, he also became more convinced of what he called "the utility of moral and religious papers, in influencing the minds and habits of the people." In order for reform to take hold in the United States, "the spirit of inquiry" had to become prevalent in American homes and lives, and it was the obligation of the press to provide the raw material for that inquiry. The first two years of the *Philanthropist*, he argued, seemed to prove his point. It was more common now to read essays about temperance, to hear voices raised against the sin of drunkenness, and to organize or join a temperance society. Success in the battle against this vice was not being won in the courts or the assemblies but by seeking the root of the problem, by educating people to the dangers of alcohol, and by urging communities to act in their own best interest. These changes were accomplished, Garrison claimed, by "that great engine of moral power, THE PRESS."[88] He reiterated this theme a month later when he called the press "the most powerful instrument that can be used in influencing the public mind."[89] Although Garrison had certainly championed the value of newspaper and the press in society before his editorship at the *Philanthropist*, it is not unreasonable to see his experience at the paper as laying the foundation for the organization of his own work in abolition.

Garrison defended newspapers as an integral element of the American press industry and he defined the particular benefits of "a good newspaper" to each member of a family: the father finds "intelligence" on political matters, the mother finds "information" for child rearing and household advice, and the children find the "habit of reading."[90] Later in May, Garrison defended the value of a subscription to a "newspaper of a moral character" against a charge from his old nemesis, John Neal of the Portland *Yankee*, who had written that "newspapers are utterly worthless."[91] Exactly when Neal wrote these words, or whether Garrison was quoting him accurately, is not known, but Neal had written earlier in the spring that "newspaper knowledge" was "the idlest of all knowledge ... the most unsafe, though better than absolute ignorance" and he was known to regularly disparage the value of newspapers in American society.[92] Garrison, of course, did not need to be convinced that the press in general and newspapers in particular were a powerful force in *supporting* public policy. It was a task that newspapers had already performed in the years preceding the American Revolution and in the political environment of the young republic of the United States. He was, however, becoming increasingly more aware of the role it played in the *creation and formation* of public opinion. The *Philanthropist*'s function as a moral regenerator of society's enlightened perception of the dangers of alcohol and the benefits of temperance became a model for *The Liberator*'s effort to change society's perception about slavery, abolition, and emancipation.

Much as he may have tried, Garrison was unable, however, to completely forswear his political predilections in the *Philanthropist*; in fact, his continued interest in politics may have contributed to ending his tenure at the paper. In his very first issue, Garrison editorialized about one of his favorite subjects, the dangers of "party spirit." He warned his readers that it re-directed the attention of both the people and government from "their own common interest ... [and] ... the public good" to a selfish interest in their own benefit.[93] In each of the next six weeks, Garrison used some space to comment directly about various political issues of the day. He wrote, respectively, in defense of Henry Clay; about the "Moral Character of Political Men"; a commentary on Representative John Randolph; and, on the final two occasions, published reprints of political commentaries by Fisher Ames, who was one of the first Federalists to recognize what the Jeffersonians of 1800 already knew, i.e., "the power of the printed word" and newspapers in the political process.[94]

These political comments soon ended and we can speculate that, to solidify his official position as editor of the *Philanthropist*, which was about to be announced, conceivably he was warned about making the paper too political. For whatever reason, for the next three months, Garrison refrained from direct discussion of political topics. Finally, in May, he published an editorial comment under the heading "The New Tariff." The new bill, which became known as the "Tariff of Abominations," had recently been passed in Congress after considerable controversy, not the least because it was supposedly structured to support Andrew Jackson's 1828 presidential campaign by antagonizing northern Yankee manufacturers and pleasing southern slaveholders. In its original form it was unacceptable to New England interests; Senate amendments, however, removed some of the most objectionable provisions and northern manufacturing interests changed their minds, but not without quieting all debate.[95] Following his own comment about the tariff was an extract of Daniel Webster's speech in favor of the bill.[96] Garrison did not support the tariff in its entirety but argued that as a friend of American manufacturers, he believed the country must find some means of reducing its dependence on foreign suppliers. Whether this was accomplished by a tariff or by other means did not matter, he argued, but somehow American industry must be protected. In June Garrison responded to letters from "A Mechanic" who claimed to be a long time subscriber to the *Philanthropist* and who objected that Garrison was "meddl[ing] too much with the politics of the day." In his response, Garrison was typically unrepentant about discussing something that might differ from the views "of many of our readers" and boldly stated that Webster's address could not "reasonably give offense to any man who has rationality or common sense."[97] Restraint and rhetorical temperance were not strong elements of Garrison's character.

Whether Garrison's reentry into political themes was the immediate cause or not, the next issue of the *Philanthropist* announced that he was relinquishing editorial charge of the paper. His withdrawal was not, Garrison claimed, because he had lost zeal for the temperance cause but because "the bent of his inclinations lead him to pursue a different, though perhaps not a more honorable or beneficial employment."[98] This "bent," it might be assumed, was inclined more toward politics rather than reform. Garrison wanted to correct national faults and improve national conditions, but at this point in his life the process for accomplishing these objectives was the nation's political system — faulty though it might be in his analysis. While there is no evidence that Garrison was moving on to another press position, his uncompromising style ended a second editorial post, again after just six months.

Several months before the end of Garrison's second experience as editor, arguably the most important encounter of the future abolitionist's career took place when Garrison met Benjamin Lundy, who quickly inspired his passion for the plight of the slave. They met in March 1828 when Lundy stayed at Collier's boarding house and conducted a meeting with Boston ministers, which Garrison attended, in an effort to gain their support for the anti-slavery cause.[99] Lundy, a peripatetic Quaker abolitionist, was born in New Jersey, had little formal education, served an apprenticeship as a saddler in Wheeling, Virginia, where he saw first-hand the brutality of slavery and decided to devote his life to the anti-slavery cause. After completing his apprenticeship, Lundy married and moved his family to Ohio where he organized a society to assist free blacks. In 1819, he traveled to Missouri to support writing an anti-slavery constitution for a territory aspiring to become a state. In 1821, after assisting in the publication of a Quaker newspaper, he founded his own newspaper, the *Genius of Universal Emancipation,* through which he hoped to appeal to white southern slaveholders to recognize the sinfulness of slavery and begin the process of emancipation. Until his death in 1839, Lundy traveled and delivered anti-slavery lectures to anyone who would listen. Meanwhile, the *Genius* was published, first in Mount Pleasant, Ohio, then in Greeneville, Tennessee, and then in Baltimore, Maryland; later it moved to Washington, D.C. Because of his travels, publication was sometimes monthly, sometimes weekly, and often simply scattered as time and circumstance allowed. Lundy's anti-slavery appeal was clearly more moderate than the radicalism which would describe *The Liberator* of Garrisonian fame, and championed emancipation, whether gradual or immediate, whether with or without colonization.[100] In his obituary for Lundy, Garrison claimed that Lundy was responsible for his abolitionist career and that at that March 1828 meeting his "soul was on fire then, as it is now" to fight the cowardice and obstinacy of those who refuse to recognize and battle the evil that was slavery.[101] This meeting may have contributed to the temporary decline in political rhetoric at the *Philanthropist*, but also may have awakened his political inclinations and faith in the power of the press to create public opinion which in turn would drive political and social change. Furthermore, now there was no more important change that was needed than finding a way to end slavery.

There is some reason to venture that Garrison may have left the *Philanthropist* believing that he would soon join Lundy in publishing the *Genius of Universal Emancipation*. In July 1828, Lundy was on another tour of the New England states looking to build support for his anti-slavery newspaper and was due to return to Boston in early August, where he and Garrison met once again. In a letter to John Neal in August 1828, Garrison claimed that his agreement with Nathanial White, who became owner of the *National Philanthropist* in April 1828, was to be editor on a "temporary" basis and that "I would not oblige myself for a single month."[102] Word of Lundy's imminent visit to Boson may have led Garrison to assume that he was coming to offer the partnership. There is no solid evidence, aside from conjecture, to suggest that Garrison expected Lundy to offer collaboration at that time, and no indication that he did. Regardless, Garrison's patriotism and long-standing belief in the principles of the American system of government took him to Newburyport on July 4 to read the Declaration of Independence at the town's Independence Day celebrations, organized by the local Artillery Company.[103] Fired as he might have been about the evils of slavery, his patriotism and passion for the United States and his nation's social and political ideology remained strong.

Meanwhile, Garrison had to defend himself from charges that he had been "dismissed" from the *Philanthropist*. Longtime adversary, John Neal, was editor of a Portland, New Hampshire, newspaper titled *The Yankee*, established in January 1828. The sniping between Neal and Garrison dated from Garrison's apprenticeship and continued while he edited the *Philanthropist*. In addition to Neal's charge that newspapers were useless, as discussed above, he criticized the abilities and opinions of the editors of both the *Newburyport Herald* and Garrison's *Philanthropist* on at least two occasions.[104] In late July, Neal suggested that Garrison had been dismissed, in part for the political battle he had waged in the *Philanthropist* against Neal.[105] Garrison responded with a letter to Neal accusing Neal of abuse and misrepresentation, and challenged him to correct his error by admitting in print that Neal had not influenced his departure from the *Philanthropist* and that Garrison had not been dismissed. Neal published the letter and let Garrison have his say, but in his accompanying commentary, Neal rather strangely claimed about Garrison that "I had never heard his name before" and that Garrison had repeatedly attacked Neal.[106] The final word was Garrison's. He offered Neal a rather backhanded compliment, stating that his writing showed spirit and talent "when governed by wisdom and moderation ... and when not perverted." But then he repeated the claim he made to "S" just a year earlier and wrote, "If my life be spared, my name shall one day be known extensively," and appended one final statement, *"The task may be yours to write my biography."*[107] Regardless of his reason for leaving the *Philanthropist* in August 1828, with no offer from Lundy, Garrison was once again an unemployed printer in search of a new vehicle for his voice.

A new opportunity appeared from a seemingly unlikely source and from outside Garrison's native Massachusetts. The *Philanthropist* had a fairly broad circulation and Garrison's "crisp style ... attracted favorable comment" in the temperance community in the neighboring state of Vermont.[108] Sometime in August or early September, "a committee of prominent citizens of Bennington," who no doubt were also aware of Garrison's penchant for political matters, came to Boston in order to invite Garrison to undertake the editorship of a newspaper to advocate the re-election of John Quincy Adams. The only newspaper in Bennington at the time was the *Gazette* and it had recently switched its support in the 1828 election from John Quincy Adams to Andrew

Jackson. Since the town and the county were almost unanimous in their support of Adams, the committee believed the current moment was a prime opportunity to begin a second Bennington newspaper.[109] Garrison was not particularly supportive of Adams but had a "well-founded dread" of Jackson and accepted the six-month assignment, but only under the condition that he also be allowed to advocate "Anti-Slavery, Temperance, Peace, and Moral Reform as well."[110] Evidently, politics and reform could mix.

The first issue of Garrison's third newspaper, the *Journal of the Times*, appeared on October 3, 1828, under the motto "Reason Shall Prevail with Us More Than Popular Opinion." The paper was intended to be, in Garrison's estimation, "a singular kind of political newspaper" which would be "in part a political and in part a reformatory paper."[111] His intentions were more clearly spelled out in his comments "TO THE PUBLIC" in the paper's first issue. Of course, the *Journal of the Times* would be, as Garrison invariably claimed, independent and free from partisan influence but, in addition, it would prominently feature several important issues, including, the suppression of intemperance, the gradual emancipation of all slaves, the pursuit of peace, practical education for all, the encouragement of American industry, and, last and seemingly least, the re-election of John Quincy Adams.[112] This was indeed a "singular kind" of electioneering newspaper when the political cause it supported appeared at the bottom of the editor's list of priorities. Under Garrison's editorship, however, the *Journal of the Times* certainly filled the promise of being reform minded. Issue after issue contained news, articles, and information about a wide array of reform issues including temperance, war and peace, morality, religious infidelity, education, Indian rights, sabbatarianism, and of course anti-slavery.

With regard to the *Journal of the Times*, Garrison's failure to use the paper more forcefully to advocate Adams' re-election has often been seen as evidence of his personal distaste for Adams and as evidence that his real concern was not the election, but rather addressing reform issues.[113] However, the truth may be simpler. From several of his own statements, Garrison believed that Adams' re-election was not in doubt. In his first editorial, he argued that within Bennington county "nineteen-twentieths of [the population] are friendly to the re-election" of Adams, but they lacked a newspaper through which their views could be expressed and their voices heard.[114] The widespread support for Adams seemed confirmed, at least in Garrison's estimation, when his subscription list enlarged from not "a single subscriber" to more than "SIX HUNDRED names" within two weeks.[115] Later in the month and shortly before the election he wrote, "the re-election of Mr. Adams is certain," that "no candid, observing man now believes Adams will lose the election," and that "the

Jackson fire is nearly burnt out, and the signs of the times omen a splendid triumph" for Adams. He also reprinted an analysis of the breakdown of the expected Electoral College votes by state which forecast a clear victory for Adams.[116] If Garrison's passion for Adams' election did not burn brightly in October 1828, it is not unreasonable to conclude that it was less a consequence of his unwillingness or reluctance to support Adams and more a consequence of his conviction that Adams could not possibly be defeated.

In the 1828 election, Adams did carry the New England states, including Vermont, but of course lost the presidency to Andrew Jackson. Garrison's prediction for Bennington County, however, was not much of an overestimate; he had predicted 95 percent for Adams, who actually received 81 percent of the county's vote (1664 to 386).[117] Notwithstanding, the loss on the national level was an unexpected and disheartening political disaster from Garrison's perspective. Beginning at the end of November, he wrote and published in the *Journal of the Times* a four-part series titled "The Politician" which revealed the depth of anger and despair Garrison felt after Jackson's victory. In opening the series he wrote, "The great national conflict has terminated in a manner so utterly unexpected and disastrous, as to almost annihilate the hopes of every friend of the country." He described Jackson as ignorant, "incapable of spelling his mother tongue," and clearly unqualified to be president of the United States. He saw "danger to our institutions and national prosperity" in the actions he expected from the new administration. These actions included, in Garrison's opinion, the death of American industry, the breakdown of the moral and physical power of the north, the hostile action of the southern states to dominate all other sections of the country, an infatuation with military glory, and the change in qualifications for office from political wisdom to political ambition. Sectional passion, he wrote, was destroying the United States just as surely as a similar kind of selfishness and factional struggle for power had destroyed the Greek republic of old.[118]

In closing the first part of the series, Garrison held out one small measure of comfort for the nation which "may prove fortunate." Since Jackson's forces, Garrison suggested, had organized "traitorous and disorganizing" factions in all parts of the country, the spark of a close victory for Adams might have set the nation ablaze with violent conflict. Jackson's victory, however, meant that the violent dissolution of the union was, for now, a "distant danger" rather than immediate. "A wise Providence" had given the nation time to redeem itself.[119] Jackson's victory was therefore a wake-up call to Americans, and marked, Garrison hoped, the beginning of renewal for the republic — if only the nation listened and reformed.

Notwithstanding this small glimmer of hope, scorn for Jackson continued in the next part of the series. "The more I reflect," Garrison wrote, "upon the infatuation which has placed an ignorant, guilty, head-strong military chieftain in a civil capacity over this government, the greater is my amazement." He credited Jackson's election principally to his victory at the Battle of New Orleans. The election had subjugated reason and allowed the citizen to prefer a warrior over a statesman for the highest civil office in the land. While granting that throughout the nation many "well-meaning, virtuous citizens" were deluded by emotion into placing "the balance of power ... in the hands of the unskillful and untaught," Garrison was particularly scornful of the "rabble" in the cities and grog-shops of the country whose votes were easily manipulated to help Jackson win. The logic of Jackson's campaign, according to Garrison, was quite simple: Andrew Jackson won the Battle of New Orleans therefore he deserved to be president. In conclusion, he wrote, "the victory of New Orleans has subjugated the virtue of the nation — another such, and it will enslave posterity." Strangely enough, on Jackson, Garrison found himself one with the "impure" Thomas Jefferson, who he quoted with regard to Jackson as having said, "one might as well make a sailor of a cock, or a soldier of a goose, as a President of Andrew Jackson."[120]

In the fourth and final part of the series, Garrison reiterated his contention that faction and self-interest, particularly the self-interest "at the south" was creating "a new system of politics ... in this country." A political system based not on merit but on the ability to acquire power by emotional and numerical force in elections. He warned, "unless better patriotism, and purer virtue, and loftier principles, are found in our National Assembly, we may well despair of the permanency of the Union." Southern interests, Garrison argued, were set upon a path that was inevitably "tyrannous" and the people do not see the danger, do not hear the "voice of warning," and do not comprehend the pending peril for the nation. Most of the citizens who voted in 1828, Garrison continued, had grown up under the Constitution, had participated in or at least witnessed the growth of the country, and seemed to believe that "this government is beyond the reach of change or decay." Such complacency was perilous, seriously misplaced, and, Garrison feared, people "will never discover that they are slaves, till fetters of living iron are fastened upon their limbs and about their necks." The nation was seriously in need of "the real patriot [who] will not despair of a holier change in public sentiment" to stand up and defend the nation against destruction from within.[121] It is unlikely that Garrison considered himself to be that "real patriot"; his role as a journalist was as an auxiliary who contributed to re-fashioning public opinion as part of the process of political change. He was, however, determined to do his part and fulfill his obligations. As 1828 came to a close, Garrison reflected on his

Three: Political Machinations

twenty-fourth birthday as well as purpose in his life. He wrote that he would be wrong to "remain an idler here, or a passive spectator of the context between right and wrong — virtue and vice — truth and error — which must continue to the end of time."[122] He would continue to look for a "real patriot" but meanwhile was not, if he ever was, willing to be inactive or passive.

Jackson's victory in November 1828 was only the first of two great political defeats and disappointments for Garrison while he edited the *Journal of the Times*. The second resulted from his success in circulating and collecting signatures for a petition to Congress to abolish the slave trade in Washington and the failure of Congress to take any meaningful action on the subject. In addition to advocating Adams' election, Garrison, of course, had come to Bennington to advocate reform, including an end to slavery, and he took up the cause immediately and often. An important first step, he believed, was to present Congress with petitions from across New England to remove the disgraceful presence of active slave trading from the streets of the nation's capital. The right "to petition the Government for a redress of grievances" is one of the five rights protected by the First Amendment to the U.S. Constitution and was frequently used in the early republic for a variety of issues. Antislavery petitions or petitions to end the slave trade in the District of Columbia were often delivered to Congress between 1790 and the 1830s but routinely "southerners convinced their congressional colleagues to restrict or prevent discussion" or debate.[123] A renewed call for the circulation of these anti-slavery petitions was one positive result of Benjamin Lundy's August 1828 meeting in Boston with Garrison and others. Garrison wrote enthusiastically in the *Journal of the Times* about petitions circulating throughout the towns of Massachusetts, although in reality only one petition signed by some Boston residents resulted.[124] Nevertheless, Garrison's Vermont petition was part of a region-wide movement in 1828-29, as well as the largest of the petitions submitted to Congress at that time.[125]

In the second issue of the *Journal of the Times*, Garrison called for a meeting in Bennington to plan Vermont's participation in this effort.[126] He organized several meetings in the town with regard to the petition and editorialized about its importance, explaining that it was an immediate step the people of New England could take to "remove the evils of slavery." He also carefully explained that, however regrettable, Congress did not have the power to end slavery throughout the nation, but it did have the power to abolish it in the District of Columbia.[127] In early November, at a meeting at the Bennington Academy, a petition addressed to the Senate and the House of Representatives, written and read by Garrison, was adopted and approved for distribution. It was hardly a radical or harsh document. It rather innocuously called slavery "detrimental" to the nation, acknowledged that as regards slavery Congress had no power to act beyond the District of Columbia, and requested that slavery in the District be ended as soon as "interest and welfare shall demand."[128]

The petition was to be sent to Vermont towns to collect citizens' signatures by taking advantage of the local postmasters' "franking" privilege.[129] The petition circulated through the towns of the state and shortly after the beginning of the new year, Garrison proudly reported that the petition signed by 2,352 residents of Vermont had been transmitted to Congress.[130] In the next issue he reported that the petition which was, he believed, "by far the most important subject presented for the consideration of Congress" had been received in Congress and that he had reason "to anticipate a favorable reception." He also reported that similar petitions were pouring into Congress and suggested that it only remained to be seen "whether the majesty of public opinion will be treated with contempt, or whether it will give liberty to the captive." Furthermore, Garrison anticipated little opposition since the petition did not call for release of the slave "to-day or to-morrow, or next month or next year" but only for a "speedy and equitable provision" for emancipation in D.C. sometime soon.[131]

Notwithstanding Garrison's optimism, which was likely overstated, Congress dismissed the petitions as both inexpedient and harmful. The Congressional Committee Report on the petitions rejected them as detrimental because the petitions opened the subject of slavery "to an acrimonious debate" on the floor of the House. Memory of that and other debates as well as the continued submission of anti-slavery petitions eventually contributed to the establishment of the "Gag Rule" of 1836–44, which tabled all anti-slavery petitions without any debate.[132] Once again, in 1829, the American political system, which Garrison believed in so strongly, failed him and, he believed, the nation.

In March, Garrison reported that the petitions were rejected by Congress. The idea of ending the slave trade, if only in the nation's capital, according to the report from the Committee on the District of Columbia, raised the specter of "serious mischief, if not danger, to the peace and harmony of the Union." Garrison quite naturally refuted the arguments presented by the Committee against the petition which claimed that slavery would slowly disappear, that meddling on the subject only makes the slaves restless and insubordinate, and that the citizens of the District of Columbia are already "lenient and kind in the treatment of their slaves." None of these arguments justified Congress' intransigence for Garrison and he rather ominously warned that without immediate action, slavery may someday end, "but not peaceably, not without breaking up the foundations of the republic — through an ocean of blood." As if to underscore his point and to emphasize the evil, he followed his comments with a reprint of an advertisement from a Washington paper. The ad offered a *"Negro Girl for Sale ...* for cash ... to satisfy house-rent!!"[133] Slavery mingled with prostitution as these activities, both of which Garrison believed were sinful, increasingly became "directed by economic and market forces."[134] This advertisement represented the true character of the system of slavery. The refusal of the nation's political leaders to begin to address that evil was, for Garrison, beyond prudence or reason and a clear failure of the nation's political will.

Garrison's report in the *Journal of the Times* about the Committee's action ended with a promise that his comments would be continued in the next issue of the paper, but this was not to be. Rather, the next issue contained his "VALEDICTION" and only a cryptic note stating that his report on the petitions to Congress would be finished "through another medium." Once again, after six months as editor, Garrison announced his sudden departure. This time he wrote, "I am invited to occupy a broader field, and engage in a higher enterprise: that field embraces the whole country — that enterprise is in behalf of the slave population." He was pleased with the efforts he had made to bring attention to reforms in Vermont but argued that "the weight of public sentiment has been against me" and that the "recent triumph of the sword over the pen" clearly demonstrated that fact. His final comment as editor also expressed his continuing hope for the American political system. Garrison encouraged his readers to examine a recent speech by Henry Clay which was very critical of Andrew Jackson, and then with great fanfare Garrison nominated "HENRY CLAY of Kentucky" for the presidency in 1832. With confidence he wrote, "nothing but death can prevent his election."[135] Despite the setbacks he had experienced in Bennington, Garrison hardly seemed prepared to give up on American politics.

While his departure from the *Journal of the Times* may have been somewhat sudden, it is not altogether inexplicable. The paper was an "electioneering" paper for Adams and the election was over. In addition, Benjamin Lundy had come to Bennington early in the year and proposed a "merger of talents" with Garrison in the publication of the *Genius of Universal Emancipation* in Baltimore. Lundy's paper would be enlarged and published weekly instead of monthly; Garrison would become the resident editor while Lundy traveled to deliver anti-slavery lectures and to promote subscriptions.[136] During the winter of 1828-1829, Lundy had written to abolitionist friends in Philadelphia that he expected to have a partner by next summer, which would allow him to expand and improve the paper.[137] Garrison did not take long to accept Lundy's offer "because," as he wrote later, "the path of duty appeared very plain."[138] At the moment, however, Lundy was on a mission to Haiti and would not return for some time. Garrison might have stayed longer in Bennington, but his six-month agreement with Henry Hull had expired and he had no desire to extend the agreement for another six months and apparently no regret about leaving Vermont. In a letter to a friend, Stephen Foster, written just three days after his final issue of the *Journal of the Times*, Garrison complained that Hull had become abusive and demanding. Moreover he had reneged on their original financial arrangements and, Garrison wrote, "I would not stay with him six months longer for the wealth of the State."[139] If Hull mistreated Garrison he was nonetheless full of praise for Garrison's "industry and talent" in editing the *Journal,* expressed regret at his leaving, and wished him well in his new endeavor on behalf of the slave.[140]

In his experiences as a young editor, Garrison had learned several valuable lessons about the convoluted nature of the relationship between the press and political action. While apparently still convinced of their interdependence, *The Free Press* taught him that the editor's voice could be silenced by financial dependence, the *Philanthropist* taught him something about the extent of reform that was needed in American society, and at the *Journal of the Times*, the strength of a corrupted, but not yet irredeemable, political process taught the need for him to redouble his efforts to re-channel the political will of the nation's citizen. He did not yet despair that the political process in the United States was too broken or too corrupt to address and resolve difficult problems, including slavery. As with Jackson's election, the danger was still distant rather than immediate, but the voice of change — the voice of a free, fair, and truthful press — could not be ignored much longer.

Four

Religious Apathy

IN JULY 1829, just as he was not yet ready to abandon hope in the national political institutions, neither was Garrison prepared to completely forsake the authority and influence of the nation's churches or the churches' ministers as a consequence of their failure to adequately address the issue of slavery and emancipation. He still hoped for their assistance and participation, although they had given him more than sufficient reason to doubt their commitment. He would not, however, remain that sanguine for long. Late in his life, Garrison responded to an inquiry about his religious beliefs and wrote:

> I discard all human authority in matters of religious beliefs and practice, and maintain it is the right and the duty of everyone to judge and decide for himself what is truth and what error ... that no book, or day, or institution possesses any inherent sacredness; that the worst heresy is a slavish conformity to what happens to be the orthodox standard of the hour.[1]

This statement hardly reflected his attitude in 1829 or the religion that Garrison experienced in his youth, although it does express the concept of "priesthood of all believers" that has been identified with Martin Luther.[2] It does, however, also represent the culmination of his long-term experience as both a participant and a leader of various moral reform movements during the antebellum reform era.

To a significant degree, Garrison, like many others in the antebellum reform movements, was initially inspired to participate in reform activity as a result of his religious beliefs and convictions.[3] Alexis de Tocqueville, during his travels in America, observed the influence religion played on American society in the early antebellum years. It cannot be said, de Tocqueville wrote, "that in the United States religion influences the laws or political opinions in detail, but it does direct mores, and by regulating domestic life it helps to regulate the state."[4] Garrison certainly accepted this role for religion and in July 1829 he hoped to arouse that religious influence and those "mores" to champion the effort to abolish slavery. Unfortunately, he eventually came to the conclusion that, as with political institutions, most religious institutions were not prepared or willing to cooperate.

Garrison's religious convictions and moral intensity were nourished in his youth by his mother, Fanny Lloyd Garrison. As a child, Fanny Lloyd witnessed the excitement of religious revival as it swept through her home in Nova Scotia. Along with several of her girlfriends, Fanny secretly attended the local camp meetings where Baptists spread the word of the possibility of salvation through a "new birth" in a personal commitment to Jesus Christ. Before attending these meetings, she was among many in her community who ridiculed the Baptists as they preached their message; she did not expect to succumb to it, but soon did. Her parents were members of the Episcopal church and extremely bigoted against the itinerant Baptists. When Fanny announced her conversion, they threatened to banish her from their home if she was baptized, but feeling God's call in her life, Fanny believed that she had no choice. After she was baptized, her parents carried through with their threat and Fanny was forced to find refuge for several years with a sympathetic uncle. Fanny's willingness to take a firm moral position and endure the consequences was a lesson that her son Lloyd (as she called William) learned well. In 1834, he described Fanny to his future wife, Helen Benson, as not only a passionately caring mother, but also as a "masterpiece of womankind" who had a mind "of the first order — clear, vigorous, creative, and lustrous, and sanctified by an ever-glowing piety."[5] Fanny's passion and piety provided a foundation for Garrison's own moral rigidity.

Fanny remained committed to her Baptist faith after meeting and marrying Abijah Garrison in 1798, and during the difficult years of their marriage. Abijah was a seaman and he moved his family several times before settling in 1805 in the prosperous seaport town of Newburyport; for some time he experienced success. The success disappeared suddenly when Jefferson's Embargo of 1807 effectively shut down commercial shipping throughout the region.[6] Much to Fanny's alarm, first at sea and then also at home during the long lulls in employment, Abijah surrendered to alcohol — often in excess. He regularly felt the bite of Fanny's moral indignation over his refusal to abandon the habit and she never relented in her efforts to convince Abijah to accompany her to her Baptist church and seek help from the Lord for his weaknesses. After an incident in which Fanny banished Abijah and his drinking companions from her house and destroyed their bottles, Abijah deserted Fanny and their three small children.[7]

Life quickly became even more difficult, but it was Fanny's Baptist faith, she believed, which gave her strength to persevere. Her strength was further aided by her close relationship with her landlady, Martha Farnham. "Aunt" Martha, as Garrison remembered her, was also an ardent Baptist and both she and Fanny were members of the First Baptist Church in Newburyport. Young William Lloyd also joined the church, although he was never baptized. He attended services regularly and, like his mother, became a member of the choir where he began a life-long fondness for sacred hymns, which he retained even as he lost respect for the religious organizations. According to his children, on the night before he died, he was unable to speak but the family gathered around his bed to sing his favorite hymns while he beat time "both with his hands and feet."[8] James Garrison, his eldest brother, who followed his father's path to sea and to intemperance, attested to their mother's firm and active religious faith in his memoirs, written shortly before he died in 1841. Before he left home, his mother rescued James from several difficult scrapes caused by his appetite for strong drink. Each time she prayed with him to find the power to overcome his sinful ways.[9] Fanny's religious faith, however, obviously had more direct and lasting effect on William than it had on James.

After leaving Baltimore in the fall of 1816, Lloyd only saw his mother once more before her death in September 1823, yet that did not prevent her from imposing a strong spiritual influence in his life.[10] Despite several relocations and family separations, William's religious training continued with or without his mother present. While living away from her in Newburyport and before his apprenticeship at the *Herald*, he was left either in the care of "Aunt" Martha or with Deacon Ezekiel Bartlett of the Baptist Church.[11] Additionally, regardless the distance, a series of motherly letters prodded her son to avoid the "temptation of this evil world," reminded him that God will bless his good behavior, and that "you have a Mother ... that loves you with tenderness."[12] They continued to correspond during his apprenticeship and when the young apprentice had several of his letters anonymously published in Allen's *Herald*, Fanny was the only person to whom Lloyd revealed the secret of his authorship and his pseudonym, "An Old Bachelor" or "A.O.B." He was proud of his efforts and she offered some tepid encouragement. "If Mr. Allen approves of it," then he might continue, but she teased him as well by requesting a sample of his work so she might judge "whether you are A.O.B., as A may stand for Ass, and O for Oaf, and B for Blockhead."[13] In response to her request, he sent copies of his three part series "Our Next Governor," written in support of the election of Harrison Gray Otis in the spring of 1823.

Fanny's last letter to her son before she died directly addressed his journalistic efforts, and scolded him for spending his time writing about political matters. True to her concern about building a connection with God, she urged her son to spend his time "searching the scriptures for truth, and praying for direction of the holy spirit to lead your mind in the path of holiness."[14] Keeping her son focused on his spiritual health was never far from Fanny's mind and fostered a similar inclination in the nascent adult; he may have taken his mother's advice to heart, at least temporarily. He did not write anything for publication in the next year; although, when he did return to print he once again wrote primarily about political matters. Nevertheless, while Garrison's renewed published commentary focused primarily on politics, the thrust of his messages often decried the absence of morality in the national or local political arena. His mother would have approved. This was especially apparent in his six part series, titled "The Crisis," that appeared in *The Salem Gazette* between August and October 1824.[15]

Before fully embracing the abolitionist agenda, Garrison did not abandon his perspective on the power and importance of religion in his life and all peoples' lives. God's work in the world was an important theme of his July 4 "Address to the Debating Club" in 1824. Garrison argued that the Declaration of Independence in 1776 had stimulated a desire for liberty which, he believed, was now changing many nations. This desire appealed to God for assistance and was supported by "the deafening roar of heaven's artillery."[16] The last significant article Garrison wrote before his apprenticeship ended at the *Herald* also had significant religious overtones. In his book review of *Resignation: An American Novel. By a Lady,* Garrison argued that the role of the novel was to teach religious sentiments and he praised the author of *Resignation* for telling an appealing story about the triumph of Christian values.[17] Garrison also encouraged his friend Tobias Miller, who published the *Journal of Literature and Politics* in Portsmouth, New Hampshire, to reprint his book review of *Resignation* "for the hope of drawing the public attention to this excellent work, and of encouraging *christian genius.*"[18] Fanny Garrison's influence and her devotion to the role of religion in his daily life may have become subdued in favor of political analysis, but did not completely vanish from her son's consideration.

Several months later when Garrison became editor of *The Free Press*, his commentary focused primarily on politics and political affairs. In his inaugural editorial, he defined the "political course" of the paper, which he intended to be "subservient to no party or body of men."[19] For the next six months, as has already been discussed, Garrison devoted his attention to local, regional, and national political issues, such as the Massachusetts claim, the importance of voting, his concern about citizens' failure to participate in the political process, the celebration of Independence Day, the political contributions of Jefferson and Adams, and the political machinations of Caleb Cushing. Despite the lack of direct attention, Garrison was not able to (nor was he willing to) divorce religious and moral considerations completely from his discussion of public affairs. His commentary on Independence Day in 1826 once again acknowledged God's role in the creation of the United States and in overcoming the "bitter spirit of party" which threatened to destroy the country.[20] Also, Garrison's religious disposition was clearly offended by the "impiety" of Ephraim Allen's panegyric to Thomas Jefferson after his death. At Allen's printing office and in a New England town, the young editor had been fully engulfed in Federalist rhetoric about Jefferson's infidelity to orthodox Christian teaching. Flowery words about heaven's gates opening and "choirs of the just" welcoming the deist bordered on sacrilege for the young editor.[21] Garrison's own commentary on Jefferson, which found cause to both praise and criticize the great man, hardly touched upon his "infidelity" but was principally devoted to a discussion of his political accomplishments and errors. Nevertheless, for Allen to completely ignore Jefferson's religious apostasy was simply unacceptable.

Arguably, the issue that most affected Garrison's religious and moral sensibilities, and the one which ended his editorial career in Newburyport, was the controversy involving Caleb Cushing's campaign for election to Congress in 1826. Garrison had been mentored by Cushing; he looked to Cushing as a leader in local society, and had praised him profusely in *The Free Press* for the brilliance of his eulogies of both Adams and Jefferson. Therefore, he was greatly disappointed to find out that Cushing was chief among the "knot of politicians" who, for the benefit of their own interests and power, sought to unseat Newburyport's current representative in Congress. While the issue was certainly political in origin, Garrison was most troubled by what he perceived to be Cushing's efforts to aggrandize himself and maliciously libel his opponent, John Varnum. Late in his life, Garrison wrote to his son about the incident and explained that he was less offended by Cushing's political maneuvering than by the puffery in the letters Cushing wrote to the Boston newspapers. Those letters, Garrison claimed, praised Cushing "in the most extravagant terms" while "greatly depreciating" Varnum, and, as a result, "outraged my sense of moral rectitude." Written after Cushing's death, Garrison had yet to recover from his anger over the incident or forgive Cushing for his transgressions, and told his son that Cushing "seemed to have been born without a moral sense."[22] Nevertheless, while he remained in Newburyport, Garrison seemed to have generally put aside his mother's admonition that he should search the scriptures, rather than political philosophy, to find the "path to holiness."

In December 1826, after editing *The Free Press* for six months and settling his affairs in Newburyport, Garrison left his hometown for Boston.[23] He stayed briefly with Thomas Bennett, whom Garrison had met at Allen's printing office, but he soon moved into a boarding house at 30 Federal Street run by the Reverend William Collier. Except for six months in Bennington while he edited the *Journal of the Times*, Collier's house remained Garrison's home until he left to begin his partnership with Benjamin Lundy in Baltimore in August 1829.[24] In addition, when he returned from Baltimore and his work at the *Genius of Universal Emancipation* in 1830, Garrison returned to Collier's house briefly before he and Isaac Knapp began publishing *The Liberator*.[25] Other printers residing with Collier offered Garrison the company of fellow craftsmen as well as information about employment possibilities.[26]

Garrison may have been directed to Collier's house by the minister of his Baptist Church in Newburyport, the Reverend John Peak. Both Peak and Collier were disciples of the Reverend Dr. Baldwin and, after retiring in 1828, Peak also moved to Boston where he worked with Collier in serving the city's underprivileged. In 1829, Peak and Collier shared duties in ministering to the Black Baptists in the Belknap Street Church (or the African Church as it was also known), after their pastor of over a quarter century, the Reverend Thomas Paul, retired.[27] In addition to providing Garrison with a place to live and opportunities for employment, Collier played a significant role in re-directing Garrison's printing career from an inclination for political affairs to an inclination for reform by capitalizing on his already well developed, if partially dormant, religious and moral inclinations.

William Collier became a Baptist as a young man and then studied theology at Rhode Island College (later Brown University) before being ordained a minister. He served as the pastor of churches in New York and Massachusetts but resigned his last pastorate in Charlestown in 1820 to practice as a city missionary in Boston. During his career Collier actively ministered to the poor and less fortunate in society, including the prisoners at the Charlestown Penitentiary, where he served as chaplain. Following his move to Boston and until he died, according to a brief biography published after his death in 1842, Collier served the spiritual needs of the Female Society for Missionary Purposes, and "he visited the sick and dying in places seldom trodden by christian feet ... [and] ... he rescued from the haunts of infamy not a few who were on the frontiers of perdition."[28]

Furthermore, and perhaps most significantly for Garrison's career, Collier had long shown an interest in using the printing press as a means of spreading the ideals of Christianity. Early in his clerical career, he authored and published several collections of hymns as well as collections of sermons and inspirational essays both for adults and for use in schools. He was also an early temperance advocate and, while still serving in Charlestown, he re-published articles by Dr. Benjamin Rush on the harmful effects of alcohol. In March 1826, Collier began publication of the *National Philanthropist*, one of the first newspapers in the United States devoted to social reform and the first devoted exclusively to temperance. Published for the Massachusetts Society for the Suppression of Intemperance, the paper's prospectus called for all temperance societies to employ the "mighty powers of the press" to overcome the intemperate use of "ardent spirits."[29] The *Philanthropist* was the first and most successful of a series of reform-minded newspapers that Collier published. He also edited or published at least four monthlies: from October 1827 to August 1830 *The Baptist Preacher*, and in 1828 *The Anti-Masonic Tract*, *The American Manufacturer*, and *The Medical Advisor*, all three of which lasted only a few months.[30] At Collier's boarding house in Boston, Garrison found not only the companionship of fellow printers, but he was also nurtured by Collier in the potential of the press and newspapers to counter licentiousness and bring about a reformation of modern American society. Given Garrison's already well-developed appreciation for the importance of the press, newspapers in particular, to mold public opinion, he was certainly prepared to embrace the concept.

Collier's activities reflected his part in the burgeoning realization by religious organizations and tract societies during the first several decades of the nineteenth century about the power of the printing press to spread their message nationwide. David Paul Nord has written that Bible and Tract societies in the early decades of the century "helped to lay the foundation for mass media in America" when they organized and executed plans to distribute "the same printed message to everyone in America." They created several publishing houses, helped to finance the first paper-making machinery in the United States, were among the first to install modern steam-powered printing presses, and organized extensive systems for distribution of their product. By 1827 they were prepared to put upwards of twelve million tracts per year into people's hands countrywide, and by 1829 believed they had the capacity to print half a million Bibles.[31] Collier's efforts were on the periphery of this extraordinary operation but his ideas about the power of the printing press were unquestionably representative of the phenomenon — a phenomenon with which Garrison was already familiar.

There were other aspects of life in the busy city of Boston which appealed to Garrison's religious inclinations. Soon after his arrival, Garrison learned to appreciate and enjoy the benefits and advantages of city life with its diversity of opportunity, particularly with regard to religion. While at the time he remained committed to his Baptist faith, he attended a variety of churches, including the Hanover Street Church of Lyman Beecher, the Federal Street Church of William Ellery Channing, and the Hollis Street Church of John Peirpont. He was most comfortable with the orthodox teachings of Beecher but, although he did not always agree with the teachings of the latter two ministers, Garrison had "unbounded admiration for their intellectual ability, and profound respect for their personal character."[32]

For most of 1827, aside from attending church, Garrison was busy searching for work, had limited time for writing and, except for one letter, his correspondence focused on political matters rather than religious or moral issues. The exception was a letter about a lottery bill before the House of Representatives. He wrote the letter "as a friend to the poor, as a lover of morality, and an enemy to vice" and as one who hoped that the bill would not pass because lotteries have a tendency to "make men vicious and [are] injurious to public morals." Then he argued that the social costs of a lottery were devastating, including its potential to drive men to crime in order to acquire the money to participate, to deprive children of food and shelter, and to force cold and hungry women to pawn their meager possessions to raise the funds to participate. In closing, he contended that legislatures must find a way to raise public funds without corrupting public morals.[33] It is possible, however, that his passion in this instance may be a little suspect, since the particular lottery in question was intended to raise funds for the benefit of the Jefferson family.[34]

Nevertheless, once he took on editorship at the *Philanthropist* in January 1828, there can be no mistaking the resurgence in Garrison's commitment to the moral reformation of society and to the potential influence of newspapers in forming and reforming society. He began by bringing a new level of energy and printing professionalism to the paper. In his first issue as editor, the paper was enlarged from sixteen to twenty columns, its appearance improved with better and sharper typeface for easier reading, and articles were re-organized by sections devoted to specific topics. As noted earlier, Garrison may have had some difficulty in restraining himself from discussion of political issues but, nonetheless, he addressed a variety of moral and religious questions with sincerity and vigor, while not abandoning politics altogether. In addition to temperance, the paper's principal focus, regular attention was also given to a variety of reform issues: education, lotteries, imprisonment for debt, desecration of the Sabbath, slavery, treatment of the Indians, and women's influence in society.

Most importantly, however, as editor of the *Philanthropist*, Garrison not only displayed a growing interest in reform issues, but he persuasively articulated the importance of morality in people's lives, while also emphasizing the influential role that newspapers performed in informing and inculcating that morality. In this, Garrison was a precursor to the journalistic practice later associated with Horace Greeley and his *New York Tribune*, which began publication in 1841. Greeley believed that the journalist should provide information "to enlighten and lead the public, rather than merely divert and possibly seduce it"[35] and he intended the *Tribune* to be "nothing less than an evangelical mission on behalf of virtue and decorum."[36] In 1828 at the *Philanthropist*, with the memory of both the Cushing affair in Newburyport and the Otis affair in Boston still fresh, Garrison reminded his readers of the importance of examining the "moral qualifications of the men they vote for in elections" as closely as they examined their political deeds.[37] Likewise, in offering support for William Ladd's peace movement, Garrison noted that changing the world could only be accomplished "through the instrumentality of Christian example and enterprise."[38] Above all, Garrison argued, information and inquiry were required before any reform could succeed and "to aid its extension should be the dominant motive of the conductors of the press."[39] The power of the press to advise and promote moral behavior, and the responsibilities of editors to conduct newspapers accordingly was, of course, a topic Garrison addressed regularly.[40]

Editorship of the *Philanthropist* was at least in part responsible for reawakening Garrison's religious convictions, but undoubtedly the most important event during his editorship, and one of the most definitive events of Garrison's life, was Benjamin Lundy's visit to Boston in March 1828. It fully reawakened and revitalized his religious convictions. Lundy was a member of the Society of Friends; he, like many Quakers, had embraced the anti-slavery struggle and had become active in promoting the anti-slavery movement more than ten years earlier. Since 1821, Lundy had been struggling to publish his anti-slavery newspaper, the *Genius of Universal Emancipation*. It was a lonely and difficult endeavor and, when bankruptcy threatened in early 1828, Lundy traveled to the northeast states to seek support from that region of the nation for the first time. Previously his efforts for support had been directed principally toward those who expressed anti-slavery sentiment in the slave states—in an era when such sentiments had yet to be completely silenced. His journey north had three purposes: first, to encourage the organization of anti-slavery societies; second, to organize petition campaigns to end slavery in the District of Columbia; and third, to find new subscribers for his newspaper.[41] Garrison was certainly familiar with the *Genius* since it was one of many exchange papers he read as editor of the *Philanthropist*. In his tribute to Lundy after his death, Garrison described the *Genius* as "a dingy monthly periodical" but one that he credited with enlightening his ignorance on the subject of slavery.[42]

Boston was one of the final stops on Lundy's journey, and by the time he reached Boston, his appeals to the Northeastern states had met with little success.[43] In New York Lundy had called upon the wealthy reform-minded philanthropist, Arthur Tappan, who was, just yet, unwilling to commit more than sympathy to the anti-slavery cause. According to Bertram Wyatt-Brown, Lundy was one of many "earnest mendicants" who approached Tappan for financial support and, in March 1828, Tappan "politely refused him."[44] In Providence, Lundy had found one receptive ear in the person of William Goodell, who edited the *Investigator and General Intelligencer*, and was already involved in many reform issues.[45] But after leaving Providence, Lundy was harshly attacked in the press by Sylvester Southwick, editor of the *Literary Cadet*. Southwick accused Lundy of secretly working to destroy the American Colonization Society by supporting anti-southern political interests in a plan that was "wild and extravagant ... [and which] ... can never be accomplished." Southwick also charged "that Mr. Lundy, whilst engaged in this business, has an eye to his own personal gain, and is as fond of the world as others are."[46] Thus far, success in the North for Lundy had been as elusive as success in the South.

Without achieving any of his goals in New York or Providence, Lundy proceeded to Boston where he hoped to muster the support of the city's clergy to his cause. In Boston, Lundy stayed at Collier's boarding house, where he believed "he would be close to men whose access to the inner circles of Boston reform would assure the prosperity of his own efforts"—most especially with the clergy in the religious capitol of the nation.[47] Unfortunately, Lundy's goals found little more success in Boston than had been found in New York or Providence. Nevertheless, at Collier's house, Lundy met Garrison and, quite unexpectedly, Lundy found a new associate and Garrison found a new passion.

On March 17, eight Boston ministers came to Collier's to hear Lundy's plea for the formation of a local anti-slavery society; unfortunately, the ministers' names were not recorded. Lundy hoped to convince them to become the nucleus of anti-slavery leadership in New England, to form a strong foundation for moral opposition to slavery, and to begin planning a peaceful demise for the "peculiar institution." Garrison attended the meeting and was impressed by Lundy's ideas. The ministers, however, did not share his enthusiasm. They "were unwilling to initiate any active movement or to take part in the formation of an anti-slavery committee" and agreed only to sign a paper "recommending the *Genius* to the patronage of the public."[48]

The immediate effect Lundy's visit had on Garrison can be found in the next issue of the *National Philanthropist*. Garrison briefly reported on the ministers' meeting with Lundy without providing any details about their reticence to support Lundy's goals. He recommended Lundy's *Genius* to all "lovers of liberty, virtue, and happiness," and also published a lengthy editorial comment titled "Progress of Public Opinion, Against Intemperance, Slavery and War." As was fitting for the editor of a temperance newspaper, Garrison first acknowledged the successes of the "anti-intemperance societies" both in the minds of the public as well as in the opinions of the medical community. He also wrote about the formation of Peace Societies and the hope these societies inspire "peace [to rule] all nations," despite "the sneers of derision" by their enemies. But the largest portion of the editorial was reserved for the issue of slavery. The nation, he reported, could now boast over one hundred and thirty anti-slavery societies, and the American Colonization Society had transported thousands to Liberia and Haiti. Although these thousands were obviously a small number compared to the millions of slaves in the United States, he called it a "good beginning" and certainly beneficial to those who were freed — Garrison had yet to see the flaws in the colonization scheme. The public, he argued, had been awakened to the "curse of slavery" and had begun to realize that neither slavery nor its inevitable insurrections could be ignored. What was more, it was now apparent that more people knew that "emancipation alone will preserve the life of the republic."[49] Despite the failure of the ministers to respond positively to Lundy's appeal, Garrison was hopeful that public awareness about slavery, which editors like himself provided, would lead to ministerial action.

Given the disappointing results of Lundy's meeting with the Boston ministers, the enthusiasm and fervor of Garrison's editorial seems somewhat problematic. But if Garrison's optimism about the potential for progress in reform did not truly reflect the reality in Boston, it does reflect his personal perspective and his deepening commitment to the cause of reform, especially, anti-slavery agitation.[50] For Garrison, the "moral revolution" had begun, and in closing his commentary, he admonished the *Philanthropist*'s readers,

> We ought to exult that the "signs of the times" are so auspicious. Let the desponding take courage — the fainting gather strength — the listless be inspired; for though the victory be not won, we shall not lose it if we persevere. The struggle is full of sublimity — the conquest embraces the world.

Garrison was now prepared, if necessary, to embrace the struggle — with or without the Boston clergy.

Lundy's visit in March 1828 exposed, at least to Garrison, the apathy and indifference of the Boston clergy as well as their unwillingness to use the power of the church to combat what was so clearly, for Garrison, a moral and spiritual crisis in American society. The ministers' recalcitrance became even more apparent when Lundy returned just five months later, in August 1828, as part of another effort to build support for anti-slavery activity and find new subscribers for the *Genius*. Henry Mayer claimed that in March 1828 Lundy promised that after a few months in Baltimore he would return to Boston and "resume, perhaps with Garrison's help, his canvas of the northeast."[51] According to Merton Dillon, Lundy's journey was a "*tour de force*" effort to accomplish what he had failed to do earlier in 1828. He traveled mostly by foot, covering as much as forty-five miles in one day, gave forty-three lectures, often to Quakers but also to many other denominations and local community forums, including those in Brooklyn (Connecticut), Providence, Nantucket, Portland, and Portsmouth, and met with numerous religious leaders. Once again, however, evidence of success is scant, although Dillon suggests that because Lundy spoke to so many who "already saw slavery as a grievous national problem," the true effect of his efforts simply cannot be known with any certainty, except with regard to his continued influence on Garrison.[52]

By the time Lundy reached Boston in August 1828, Garrison no longer edited the *Philanthropist* and although some have speculated that he resigned the paper in order to assist Lundy's anti-slavery campaign, that idea lacks clear confirmation. Garrison's comments in his final editorial for the *Philanthropist* on July 4 might be interpreted to indicate that he had some expectation or specific plans; however, no direct evidence supports the idea that he and Lundy were about to begin any kind of partnership at that time. Lundy had some difficulty finding a venue in Boston for a public meeting on anti-slavery action, but was finally able to arrange for the use of the Reverend Howard Malcom's Federal Street Baptist Church and a meeting was held on the evening of August 7, 1828.[53] Several days later, Garrison sent two letters to the *Boston Courier*, both signed with his familiar pseudonym "A.O.B." and both of which reported on the meeting and the disheartening public and ministerial response to Lundy's proposals.

In the first letter, Garrison summarized Lundy's presentation and his call for action in New England in the anti-slavery struggle. "A.O.B." described how Lundy assured his listeners that the majority of southerners, including most slaveholders, were anxious to have slavery abolished, both because of the threat it represented to security and because they understood it to be wrong. Although anti-slavery sentiment in Southern society during the colonial and early national period was not unusual, by the time Lundy spoke in 1828, these assurances were overly hopeful. Pro-slavery arguments which declared slavery a "positive good" were in ascendancy by this time and would become dominant after Nat Turner's revolt in 1831.[54] Nevertheless, Lundy argued that the small minority who supported slavery did not depend on the Bible to support the system, but primarily on the brute force of their own whips and on "*your arms and physical force at the north*" in case of insurrection.[55] In other words, for Lundy, slavery in 1828 was dependent on two principal factors, southern violence and northern power in support of that violence. His northern listeners were complicit in the maintenance and security of American slavery and therefore, those in the north had an obligation to participate in the process of bringing it to an end.

As he had done at his meeting with the ministers in March, Lundy also spoke of the various measures that were already in place to work for the abolition of slavery, including southern anti-slavery societies and the American Colonization Society, but he also argued that these were not enough. To believe that colonization alone could liberate all the slaves was "in the highest degree fallacious." A more "rational system" was needed — a plan that would "unite the moral strength of the country ... till the shackles of the oppressed are broken by the will, not by the wealth, of the people." For slavery to end, Lundy reasoned, the people of the northern states and New England had to disengage themselves from the notion that they had "no interest in the matter ... and should let their voice be heard." In closing his address, Lundy offered a way to begin. He encouraged his listeners to organize anti-slavery societies and to participate in the efforts to send petitions to Congress for the removal of slavery from the District of Columbia. Garrison, of course, fully supported these ideas, but deferred further comments about anti-slavery petitions and discussion about the disappointing and disparaging comments made by the Reverend Malcom after Lundy finished until the next day's communication.

The next day's letter began by reiterating Lundy's call for the formation of New England anti-slavery societies, "in conjunction with the people of the south," with an initial objective of petitioning to end slavery in Washington. However, as soon as Lundy finished, the Reverend Malcom rose and forcefully argued that it was both unnecessary and unwise for the people of Boston to organize anti-slavery societies. Malcom asserted that "in consequence of the briskness of the slave market" throughout the South, the work of emancipation had already begun; as slavery moved into the deep south, slaves in the District of Columbia, Maryland, and Virginia would be emancipated. "Upon the whole," as Garrison reported Malcom's words, "the practice was not so *very* bad, as it forwarded the work of emancipation quite as fast, perhaps, as could be desirable." According to Malcom, as a result of an active slave trade, slaves "would, ere long, unquestionably free themselves" without any interference from New England; emancipation had already begun without any help from the north! Garrison recounted the audience's shock and indignation at the

Reverend's comments, but Malcom gave them no opportunity to respond because he "immediately dismiss[ed] the assembly"—an action Garrison deemed to be very "unfair conduct."[56]

Malcom defended himself several years later in a letter printed in *The Liberator*. The letter was in reaction to an article from a week earlier about a supposedly pro-slavery gathering at Faneuil Hall which was endorsed with the signatures of over fifteen hundred people, including one minister, the Reverend Howard Malcom. Garrison used it as an opportunity to remind his readers about Malcom's comments after Lundy's meeting in 1828 which Malcom declared "that the north had nothing whatever to do with southern slavery, and ought not to meddle with it in any shape."[57] For his part, Malcom wanted to set the record straight; he asserted that he hospitably opened his church's door to Lundy and provided a forum for his lecture when others would not. After Lundy spoke, Malcom claimed that he did not want to subvert Lundy's plans, but to suggest that God may allow evil, like slavery, to exist in order to achieve some "ultimate good." Thus, the slave trade in Kentucky, Virginia, and Maryland would eventually turn them into free states; the process would continue in Tennessee and North Carolina and so on until we "see the evil greatly circumscribed."[58] Garrison did not comment about the letter; none was necessary. Malcom's rationalization only confirmed the extent of ministerial intransigence about anti-slavery efforts—we cannot end slavery but must wait for it to disappear in God's own time. This was hardly acceptable for Garrison in 1828, much less in 1835.

Without recourse to challenge Malcom at the public meeting in 1828, Garrison asked him, in his second letter to the *Courier*, to produce some statistical evidence to support his supposition that the number of slaves in any southern state was declining. In addition, Garrison argued, whatever inducements which may have existed to sell or transfer slaves only aided in creating a "perpetual barter" system with no foreseeable end. Furthermore, such a system created inducements for Virginians and others to continue using their female slaves to propagate new slaves for the market. The consequence of this "inhuman traffic" would not produce, as Malcom claimed, an end to slavery, but rather, in Garrison's opinion, only a continuation of a slave trade that "consolidates oppression, and renders the liability of insurrections still more formidable." In closing, Garrison maintained that he had no intention of questioning the minister's philanthropy or the "goodness of his heart" but that, in spite of Malcom's objections, an anti-slavery society would be formed in Boston and a petition campaign organized shortly.[59] However, once again it appeared to Garrison that if anti-slavery action was to take place in Boston, it would be without the backing or assistance of Boston's clergy.

The results of the August 1828 meeting were hardly the success that Garrison had predicted in the *Courier*. Another meeting was organized at which an anti-slavery committee of twenty was formed, including Garrison, and they immediately called for the circulation of petitions in every town in the Commonwealth. The committee, however, never formed an anti-slavery society and, in the end, only one petition from Massachusetts, described as "almost apologetically worded," was submitted to Congress.[60] Lundy's efforts in his second pilgrimage to the Northern states had inspired little success; Boston churches did not readily open their doors to hear his plea and clerical support for anti-slavery organization and agitation did not materialize.

While we do not know if the famous Unitarian minister, William Ellery Channing, was among the eight ministers who met Lundy at Collier's boarding house in March (or at Lundy's address in August), his reaction to Lundy's visit was likely representative. In a letter to Daniel Webster in May 1828, Channing described the purpose of Lundy's visit as an effort "to stir us up to the work of abolishing slavery at the South." While he believed ending slavery was a worthy goal, Channing was more concerned about the hostility and misapprehensions such activity would create among "our Southern brethren." In place of anti-slavery agitation, Channing believed that the Northern states must first convince the South of their friendship, their sympathy, and willingness to share the burden and expense of finding a way to abolish slavery. Even the moderate entreaties of a pacifist Quaker like Benjamin Lundy, "by rousing sectional pride and passion," threatened, Channing believed, to "break the country into two great parties" and precipitate a great civil war. Channing hoped that Webster would use his position and influence to find a means to a safe and beneficial solution, and a way to save the nation from "the rashness of enthusiasts, and from the perils to which our very virtue expose us."[61] To describe Benjamin Lundy as someone given to "rash" enthusiasm is to not truly understand the quiet, although no doubt persistent, Quaker. Yet, this representation of anti-slavery and pro-slavery arguments as somehow equivalently dangerous was typical of the reaction Lundy received in the northern states, which were supposedly sympathetic to anti-slavery sentiment.

In his obituary for Lundy in 1839, titled "THE PIONEER FALLEN," Garrison further elaborated on his own reaction to the two meetings. He disclosed the personal effect of Lundy's visits and reported that he found new insight and passion for the plight of the American slave. Lundy had, Garrison wrote, increased his "interest in the cause of the oppressed and [enkindled] a zeal which I trust will never be extinguished until the chain of the last bondsman is severed." His soul was set "on fire" then and remained on fire still. But, he also discussed Lundy's failure to win the support of the clergy and wrote, with some passion, that Lundy

> might as well have argued the stones in the streets to cry out in behalf of the perishing captives. O the moral cowardice, the chilling apathy, the criminal unbelief, the cruel skepticism, that were revealed on that memorable occasion.

If Garrison's soul was set "on fire," it was as much because of the timidity and apathy of the ministers as it was because of the strength of Lundy's appeal. Lundy's first meeting with Boston's clergy marks a fixed starting point for Garrison's recognition that the infidelity which he decried at the personal and political level of American society was present in the religious leaders and religious institutions of the nation as well.[62]

Garrison's recollection of Lundy's efforts in Boston in 1828 clearly reflected Channing's sentiments. With regard to the second meeting, Garrison wrote:

> Every soul in the room was heartily opposed to slavery — but — it would terribly alarm and enrage the South to know that an anti-slavery society existed in Boston! But — it would do harm, rather than good, openly to agitate the subject! But — we had nothing to do with the question, and the less we meddled with it, the better! But — perhaps a select committee might be formed, to be called by some name that would neither give offense, nor excite suspicion as to its real design. One or two only were for bold and decisive action; but as they had neither station nor influence, and did not rank among the wise and prudent, their opinions did not weigh very heavily, and the project was abandoned.

As Garrison implied, this kind of dismissive response from religious leaders of Boston on an issue that he believed was morally unambiguous was simply unacceptable. Nevertheless, this was the reality for anti-slavery activists in the northern, and slave-free, part of the United States, even those as mild and peaceful as Benjamin Lundy. Much to Garrison's chagrin, the clergy and other local leaders argued that anti-slavery activity "would do harm rather than good," that they would be meddling in an issue that was not their concern and that to be aggressive on the issue would only give offence without effecting any real opportunity for change. Lundy's appeals were completely rejected by these eminent clergymen whose aid, Garrison charged, "he had a right to expect."[63]

Lundy returned to Baltimore after visiting several more cities, especially towns in the "Burned-Over" district of New York. Meanwhile, as Garrison prepared to move to Bennington to begin publishing a political newspaper (the *Journal of the Times*) there was scant evidence of a burgeoning abolitionist movement in New England. But if the clergy were not prepared to stand up for abolition, Lundy had reason not to consider the effort a complete failure.[64]

Lundy had found a convert and disciple in Garrison. In early October, in a letter to Garrison, Lundy wrote, "I am now strengthened in the hope, that I shall not only find a valuable coadjutor in the person of my friend Garrison, but that the '*ice is broken*'" in his effort to encourage New England to join the anti-slavery struggle. Furthermore, while admonishing Garrison not to expect too much too soon, Lundy reminded him, "You have now girded on a holy warfare. Lay not down your weapons, until *honorable* terms are obtained."[65] By the time Garrison received this letter, he had opened his printing office in Bennington; however, from the start he never expected it to be more than a temporary assignment. Roused by Lundy to the horrors of slavery and galvanized by the ministers' failure to act on behalf of the enslaved, Garrison's future lay beyond the editorship of a small town political newspaper in southern Vermont.

The *Journal of the Times* was, as Garrison intended, a "singular kind of political paper" but from its inception it reflected the editor's commitment to moral and religious themes as well. In a brief article, separate from his first editorial, Garrison indicated that his paper would be "strictly moral" in its tone. "The day is at hand," he argued, " when all newspapers will find it a matter of necessity, if not of choice to combine in their contents religious and moral topics, with secular concerns" and it was the duty of all editors to "inculcate religious instruction" for the benefit of the nation.[66] Indeed, an important element of Garrison's vitriolic opposition to Andrew Jackson in the upcoming election was the threat Jackson posed to the nation's moral character. "His ultimate triumph," Garrison wrote,

> would do violence to every virtuous sentiment, to every christian desire, and to every moral excellence. Before God we declare, that we view this struggle as involving the religious as well as the secular prosperity of our country.

After the presidential election, Garrison could not, and did not, abandon politics completely, but his paper was filled, as he promised, with advocacy for a variety of reform issues, especially temperance, anti-slavery, and non-resistance. In addition, he engaged in a running editorial controversy with the *Salem Courier* and John Neal's Portland *Yankee* over the efforts of "orthodox and devout men" and "Tract, and Bible, and Education Societies" to improve the moral character of society. *The Yankee*'s "hostility to the great religious measures of the day" was simply the work of a "blockhead," and Neal was a poorly educated "infidel."[67]

In spite of Jackson's election, Garrison did not contend in the *Journal of the Times* that the triumph over religious and moral values was complete. At the beginning of the new year Garrison reviewed the events of the past year.

The most disastrous occurrence was, of course, the election of Andrew Jackson which, according to Garrison, augured impending evil for the nation unless God "by his special providence" intervened. Overall, however, Garrison believed the year had been beneficial from "a religious and moral point of view" because a "new impulse has been given to the energies of the friends of religion." This new impulse was the work being done by temperance societies to dry up "an ocean of ardent spirits," by anti-slavery societies to stir the nation's sympathy for the condition of the slave population, by the Colonization Society's efforts to liberate and transport freed slaves, and by the effort currently underway to "free the District of Columbia from the reproach of slavery."[68] Considering the repeated failure of the Boston clergy to respond to Lundy's appeals, one can speculate that, in private, Garrison's optimism about a new impulse in society must have been somewhat subdued, at least with regard to anti-slavery activity, but publically the editor expressed more confidence. In addition, he must have been somewhat skeptical about the extent to which the ministers of the churches could be considered "friends of religion."

Undoubtedly, however, Garrison was feeling particularly pleased when he wrote his review of 1828 in early January, because in December 1828 he had been visited once again by Lundy, who came from Baltimore to discuss the possibility of a collaboration.[69] Legend has it that Lundy walked from Baltimore to meet with Garrison, but the truth is that he traveled from New York to Albany by steamboat and only walked the final leg of his journey, from Albany to Bennington.[70] Lundy held no public meetings in Bennington, but in his private meeting with Garrison, he supposedly proposed that the *Genius* be enlarged, changed from a monthly to a weekly newspaper, and that Garrison act as resident editor while Lundy traveled the country lecturing and obtaining new subscribers.[71] For the moment, however, the plans were kept private, at least in part because Lundy apparently still may have had some reservations about a partnership with Garrison.

Lundy's reservations were conspicuous in an editorial comment in the *Genius*, shortly after their meeting in Bennington, about Garrison's *Journal of the Times*. Lundy commended the paper and praised Garrison for his commitment to "the claims of the poor distressed *African*." He then expressed his hope that Garrison would not be like so many others who came to the cause of abolition with vigor and passion, only to abandon it nearly as quickly as they embraced it.[72] For his part, Garrison readily welcomed the collaboration; to reassure Lundy that he was not like the "luke-warm reformer" of Lundy's *Genius* commentary, he publicly declared in the *Journal*:

> Before God and our country, we give our pledge, that the liberation of the enslaved Africans shall always be uppermost in our pursuits. The people of

New-England are interested in this matter, and they must be aroused from their lethargy as by a trumpet-call. They shall not quietly slumber, while we have the arrangement of a press, or strength to hold our pen.[73]

However, the collaboration could not begin until after Garrison had finished his six-month assignment in Bennington, and it was then delayed further by Lundy's decision to travel to Haiti with some recently emancipated slaves; a Maryland slaveholder agreed to emancipate twelve of his slaves, but only on the condition that Lundy accompanied them to Haiti.[74] Meanwhile, in the *Journal of the Times*, Garrison continued to unite religion, politics, and the press in support of reform.

In addition, he returned to an issue dear to his heart and emphatically promoted the positive role printers and newspapers should play in reforming society — including in ending slavery. He believed that editors had to make it a priority in all publications to provide information that allowed the public to make correct moral and political choices. Because he believed this priority was so important, Garrison had, since the first issue of the *Journal of the Times*, seen fit to pass judgment on those newspapers which did or did not fulfill that obligation. For example, he charged that the *Salem Courier* was "avowedly hostile to the great religious measures of the day" and that its editors intended to undermine "the hope of reform" in the country.[75] In February Garrison assailed the *Literary Subaltern* published in Providence, Rhode Island, by Sylvester Southworth, who had publicly attacked Lundy during his trip to New England in March 1828.[76] Southworth was, Garrison charged, "depraved, with a heart like a lump of ice, on which the sunshine of humanity or a ray of goodness seems never to have fallen" and he was intent on destroying any enterprise for public improvement.[77] A month later, Garrison dismissed the *New Hampshire Patriot* as "eminently malignant and uniformly base" and its editor, Isaac Hill, as interested solely in his own political power and not what benefits the citizens of his state.[78] "The spirit of infidelity," in Garrison's estimation, "is artfully striving to poison the public virtue through the medium of the press" and these newspapers supported that effort.[79]

Several other newspapers were criticized, but many were likewise praised for their commitment to reform, including, of course, Lundy's *Genius*, Collier's *American Manufacturer* and William Ladd's *Harbinger of Peace*, but also the *Vermont Chronicle*, the *Journal of Commerce*, the *New England Inquirer*, and the *Williamstown Advocate*.[80] These newspapers taught "sound morality and sterling truth" and should, Garrison believed, be welcomed into "every virtuous home."[81] In his valedictory statement when he left Bennington, Garrison continued this theme and proudly suggested that the position of newspaper editor had developed into a new and higher calling. Editorship of a newspaper could no longer be entrusted to "a political adventurer, or a loose moralist." He, and others like him, he maintained, were part of a "new race of editors" who "will sustain every moral enterprise, and diffuse a healthful influence far and wide, and fearlessly maintain the truth."[82] Plainly, Garrison now envisioned the printing and editing of a newspaper as more than a livelihood, more than a means to influence political affairs, and more than an advocate for moral or religious sentiment, but as a means to change the world.

By early April, Garrison had returned to Boston, was again lodging at William Collier's boarding house, and began looking for temporary work as a journeyman printer to tide him over until it was time to move to Baltimore and apply the lessons he had learned since December 1825.[83] During these few months, he became better acquainted with William Goodell, who was now editing Garrison's old paper, the *National Philanthropist*; he tried to help Garrison find work in Boston while Garrison awaited Lundy's return from Haiti. Goodell had also been converted to anti-slavery activity by Lundy when he met with him in Providence during his early 1828 New England pilgrimage. Goodell and Garrison spent many hours together, walking through the streets of Boston discussing anti-slavery issues. Together they also visited many "prominent ministers" and attempted "to secure their cooperation in the cause."[84] He and Garrison, despite the two unsuccessful efforts by Lundy in 1828, nevertheless saw no reason to expect anything but their cooperation and assistance in the immediate future.

Goodell later wrote that, at the time, their "expectations of important assistance from [the ministers] were ... very sanguine." Once again, unfortunately, the expected cooperation of the ministers did not materialize. The ministers' failure to join in their crusade was not, as Goodell argued later, because they supported the continuation of slavery or because they believed that Garrison and Goodell were "fanatics" or "incendiaries." Rather, in early 1829, the ministers opposed any "agitation of the subject" which, they believed, threatened, as Channing had also suggested, to "break the country into two great parties." Had the churches joined the movement in the summer of 1829, "as they should have done," Goodell asserted, they could have saved themselves from being forced to oppose a more radical and aggressive abolitionism in the 1830s. In addition, he wrote that the churches of America have long been split between "progressive" and "conservative" parties, and that at the time in New England, the latter party was dominant.[85] This perspective was little comfort for Garrison; his experience in 1829 with Goodell was the third time in a little more than a year that he had participated in an effort to secure cooperation and assistance from the clergy of Boston and for the third time, his hope for support from the leaders of the institutional churches of Boston was rejected.

Nevertheless, just as with his frustration regarding the political institutions of the nation, Garrison was not yet prepared to dismiss the power and influence of the nation's religious institutions as lost. Together they were the primary instruments for instigating change in the American republic, but if the press must act to inform public opinion in order to stimulate these institutions to create moral and just public policy, he looked forward to the opportunity to help make that happen. Onward to Baltimore!

Five

A Change of Heart

WHILE GARRISON AWAITED WORD from Lundy before traveling to Baltimore, he was invited to deliver a speech about slavery at the Fourth of July services jointly held by the Boston Congregationalist Churches at the Park Street Church. Although not directly supported by the American Colonization Society, the service was an annual event at which a collection was taken up for the benefit of the society.[1] Garrison accepted and immediately began preparing what became a long and impassioned plea to begin the process of emancipation by bringing the powers of both politics and pulpit to address what he considered not only the greatest evil facing the nation's salvation but the greatest threat facing the nation's liberty as well: slavery. A week before the speech was to be delivered, Garrison wrote a friend, Jacob Horton, in Newburyport. He told Horton that after July 4, barring a call from Baltimore, if he could not secure work as a journeyman in Boston, he would return to Newburyport and "dig on at the case for Mr. Allen." The letter also expressed some concern about the speech's length, which was "a little over an hour," its tone, which "will offend some," and his own nervousness about addressing so large a crowd.[2] But these concerns were not about to deter the messenger.

His speech represented something of an evolution in Garrison's experience with Independence Day speeches. The first one extant was delivered to his friends in the Franklin Debating Society in 1824 while still an apprentice and is likely his first public address on any subject. Filled with patriotic fervor, Garrison glorified the father of the nation, George Washington, celebrated the "truths" of equality and the rights defined by Thomas Jefferson's Declaration, examined the failures of other nations (South America, Spain, Greece, and France) to follow our revolutionary example, and marveled at the "blessings of freedom and independence" that all United States citizens enjoyed.³ A year later, the July 4 celebrations in Newburyport were without "a formal celebration in the customary style" perhaps especially on account of heavy rains during most of the day. An address was delivered at the Presbyterian Church by the "Reverend Mr. Williams" who praised the efforts at gradual elimination of slavery. Afterward a collection was taken up for the American Colonization Society.⁴ There is no record that Garrison participated in any celebrations in 1825, but the next year, as editor of *The Free Press* for the 50th anniversary of the Declaration, he wrote a fervent commentary about the event. With somewhat less nationalistic homage then two years earlier, the commentary examined most closely the contemporary conditions in the country rather than recalling the patriotic contributions of the founders, as he had done two years earlier. It was nonetheless filled with praise for the day and for the Constitution, but emphasized the expansion in education, knowledge, and opportunity for all citizens, while concluding with a warning: Americans must look beyond their blessing and accomplishments and recognize the faults which remain yet to be corrected — particularly "the curse" of slavery.⁵ In 1827, Garrison was busy looking for work in Boston, but a year later on July 4, 1828, as the final issue of his editorship of the *Philanthropist* was issued, with no mention of the holiday, Garrison had made his way to Newburyport. There he read the Declaration of Independence at one of two celebrations in town. Interestingly enough at the other celebration, Caleb Cushing also read the Declaration; whether this represented some level of ongoing competition between the two adversaries is not known.⁶ In 1829, Garrison did begin his address with a brief section offering praise for the liberties which the day's celebration represented but, unlike either 1824 or 1826, he quickly turned to a detailed examination not only of slavery but the "Dangers of the Nation," the title of his speech.⁷

More than half the speech was a well-organized and direct assault on the American system of slavery and the rationalizations which supported its continuation. With great clarity and precision he asserted four "distinct and defensible propositions" about slavery. First, slaves in the United States have as great a claim to "redress" of their grievances as the Americans had in 1776 or in 1812. Using a structure reminiscent of the Declaration of Independence, Garrison proposed a similar slave declaration with a long list of grievances, including: the malicious invasion of their countries and villages, forced sales to distant shores and within those shores, subjection to unrelenting labor and brutal whipping, destruction of family both in Africa and in America, and denial of knowledge about true Christian beliefs — just as a start. If the patriots of 1776 had justification for rebellion, American slaves did as well — if not more so. Second, the free-states are as complicit in the evil as the slave-states, but are denied or resist their obligations to participate in "the overthrow of slavery." Biblical injunctions support such an obligation: "whatsoever ye would that men should do to you, do ye even so to them." Furthermore, the people of the North are a majority in the nation, must treat others in the nation as they would treat their own family, and must no longer tolerate the "monstrous inequality" of unequal representation, as imposed by a Constitution which denies the free-states "their just influence in the councils of the nation." Third, objections to freedom for the enslaved based on beliefs which suggest that blacks are incapable of appreciating the benefits of freedom, or that their condition in American is "preferable to that of blacks in Africa," or that their treatment is actually not harsh and coercive but rather is kind and generous, or that the laws in slave states cannot be easily or safely changed, simply do not hold up to scrutiny or logic. The fourth and final proposition asserted that freedom and education will "qualify our colored population for self-government, and elevate them to a proper rank in the scale of being." Any who might declare that a black skin denotes a lack of intelligence or lack of a human soul, Garrison dismissed outright: "evidence of their own humanity is more doubtful than that of the blacks." The ancient history of Africa and the current success of former slaves in Haiti and Liberia are clear evidence of their talents and skills.

Swift change to slavery, he acknowledged, should not be expected, but to those who might argue that the nation must wait for a more propitious time, Garrison warned: "If we cannot safely unloose *two millions* of slaves now, how shall we bind upwards of TWENTY MILLIONS, at the close of the present century?" He also granted that emancipation of "all the slaves" in the current generation was "out of the question" and that it may be many years before the process is complete, but the time to begin is now — or else the "terrible judgments of an incensed God will complete the catastrophe of republican America." Finally, he called upon the nation's churches to "lead in this great enterprise"; upon the women of New England, whose benevolence is far greater than men's, to form associations to relieve the slaves' misery; upon on all citizens to join colonization associations; upon the "great body of newspaper editors" to publicize the issue regularly and build public sentiment for emancipation; and finally upon the American people to elect representatives who are "not too ignorant to know, too blind to see, nor too timid to perform their duty." The nation must either face the issue immediately or face millions of armed and dangerous men in the future.

As much as he extorted his listeners to concede the realities and jeopardy associated with the continuation of slavery in the United States, the heart of Garrison's address was the twin "Dangers" currently plaguing the country, namely "the prevalence of infidelity in our land," which Garrison had experienced in both his and Lundy's dealing with Boston's clergy, and "that our politics are rotten to the core," which Garrison had seen first-hand during his editorial experiences, from Newburyport's *Free Press* to Bennington's *Journal of the Times*. It was these "dangers" which made the nation unable to respond adequately to the great evil of slavery. Garrison revisited the current political system in the nation as he perceived it, and the ills within that system which he had been railing against for several years from his various editorial outposts.

Considering his experience with Caleb Cushing in Newburyport and Harrison Gray Otis in Boston, Garrison argued that citizens had given away their freedom by allowing "unprincipled jugglers" to control the political process; furthermore, citizens abused their liberty by going to the polls "without carefully investigating the merits of candidates." Throughout the nation, he declared, we were becoming citizens governed by our "passions [and] led by our ears, not by our understandings." Recalling his recent effort in Vermont, he argued that the "humble petitions for relief" emanating from the people for redress of grievances were not only rejected but treated as the source of "the most horrible spectres and injurious apprehensions." And mindful of the recent presidential election, he charged that "a good moral character" is no longer "an indispensable qualification" for political candidates from "a Town Clerk to a President of the United States."

These political deficiencies threatened America with succumbing to the power of what Garrison called an "aristocratic monster" in the form of southern power and slavery apologists who argued that the "free States" had no right to advocate "the overthrow of slavery" across the country. This "monster" was given its power by the Constitution, Garrison asserted, which because of the "Three-Fifths Compromise" allowed the South more representation than it statistically deserved based on the actual distribution of the free population. In what is supposed to be a democratic republic, a Southern free-white minority had effective control over a Northern free-white majority. Consequently, he argued, if the South permitted the North to share in the guilt of slavery through the Constitution, then the South cannot also insist that the free-states of the North had "no interest" in slavery and "no right" to advocate its demise.

Garrison's passion for political issues was tempered with fears about the cabals and conspiracies to either hide the real issues or undermine the voice of the people. From the local elite in Newburyport, who secretly planned Caleb Cushing's campaign for Congress, to the Boston politicians who had already decided without consulting interested party members on Daniel Webster's replacement, to the national campaign of the Jacksonians whose primary interest, at least in Garrison's opinion, was the accumulation of power and not the good of the commonwealth, to the power of southern interests who decided which issues would be allowed redress in Congress, politics had become, for Garrison, tinged with a sense of foreboding and potential corruption. Only later would that corruption become fully realized with the adamant refusal on the part of any mainstream American political organization to oppose slavery or pro-slavery interests. When Garrison abandoned politics completely in the 1840s it was only after he became convinced that the American political system had already abandoned its ideological foundations—it had abandoned him, not he it. The political system of the United States was flawed and corrupt in July 1829, but Garrison was not yet prepared to declare it to be "a terrible curse to the land" as he did thirteen years later.[8]

Adding to his concern about the immediate danger to the nation, for Garrison, however, there was something still more troubling. Not only were the political institutions of the United States abandoning their ideological foundations, but the religious institutions were doing so as well. Both institutions, which should have formed the centerpiece of protection for the nation's welfare and morality, were neglecting what Garrison argued was an imminent threat: slavery. Rather than working to resolve that threat, they were fast becoming part of the problem. While politicians embraced the principle that "all men are created equal" on the Fourth of July and ministers proclaimed the unity of all mankind at Sunday service, slavery was simply accepted in both settings as an evil beyond the power of either to challenge—much less abolish.

The celebration of Independence Day was a duty, Garrison maintained, for both "Christians and Patriots" who must give thanksgiving to God for the blessings He has given the nation. However, in 1829, in Garrison's opinion, the patriotic spirit had degenerated into indulgence and the great day had become an excuse for inebriation and excess. No true patriot of the current day, he charged, would "be caught at a religious celebration of our national anniversary"—God and His gifts to the nation were ignored. Furthermore, after fifty-three years of independence, many citizens have come to believe the "fatal delusion" that "the republic is immortal" and ignore the signs of danger that have destroyed other nations and now threatened the "stability of our Union." The "prevalence of infidelity in our land" was not the violent bloody renunciation of God, clergy, and religion that terrorized Europe during the French Revolution but, rather, it appeared mild and restrained. The "God of Reason" had pervaded American Christian society, Garrison warned, and had made men blind to "the clear light of truth" while also accepting "vain philosophy for sound morality, licentiousness for liberty." In many and various ways, Americans regularly denied the nation's "accountability to God," including for example, the desecration of the Sabbath, the exclusion of men imbued with religious and moral principles from holding political office, and the excessive use of alcohol. He also condemned the "profligacy of the press" which with notable exceptions regularly denounced benevolent enterprises and moral associations, while the press itself received profit and support from the corruption that benevolence sought to destroy.

But the most serious failure of accountability for the nation's churches was slavery. Garrison asked, "What has Christianity done ... for our slave population?" The answer, he asserted, was simple: nothing. While the churches searched the world to evangelize, they ignored "a multitude of miserable beings at home" and while charitable societies spread their benevolence to the legions of those in need, they "bring no sustenance to the perishing slave." Just as the ministers who had heard pleas for aid from Lundy, Garrison, and Goodell and could offer only sympathy but no action, so too, the clanking of the slave's chains rang in the Christian's ears, "but they cannot penetrate her heart." Furthermore, since "slavery [was] strictly a national sin" in which the money and ships of New England had participated and profited as surely as the plantation owners had, New England must also participate in bringing slavery to an end. He called upon the "ambassadors of Christ everywhere" to proclaim "liberty to the captives" and the "Churches of the living God" to take the lead in the effort. Just as the churches had united their members' efforts in support of other benevolent enterprises, they must now allow the anti-slavery effort to "stand uppermost" in the appeal for humanitarian reform. On slavery, Garrison insisted, "Christians have been asleep: let them shake off their slumbers, and arm for the holy contest." Despite his rhetoric, as with his assessment of the failings of the political institutions in the United States, Garrison was not yet willing to abandon the nation's religious institutions as beyond redemption. Clearly, however, he had deep concerns that moral and religious truths were being ignored by both politics and the pulpit.

The address was aggressive, challenging, and hardly the kind of Independence Day speech most would expect on a day set aside for the celebration of national ideology and pride. As Garrison had written to Jacob Horton, he did have reason to worry that he would "offend some," but while there was criticism, it was hardly a torrent — perhaps especially not the torrent Garrison may have sought. Two Boston newspapers, the *Boston Commercial Gazette* and the *Boston Recorder*, did little more than report his address as one of several during the day.[9] One other paper provided a bit more detail and also published a letter scathing in its criticism.

Three days afterward, a report of Garrison's speech appeared in the Boston

American Traveller. The article reported on several addresses given that day throughout Boston, made light of Garrison's "youthful appearance," the suit he wore for the occasion, and commented less on the content of the speech than on the speaker's abilities. His opening comments were "rendered inaudible by the feebleness of his utterance" although as he continued, he became more confident and "his earnestness became perceptible." It stated that the address was intended to "establish four positions in relation to the colonization of blacks," provided several short quotes from the address, but failed to provide any substantive analysis of Garrison's arguments, aside from reporting his concern about "infidelity" and that politics were "wrotten."[10] The paper's article was, Garrison believed, so "meager and imperfect" regarding the content of his address that he felt compelled to respond.[11] In the *Boston Courier* he wrote that his youthful appearance was "the fault of Time's not mine" and suggested that the *Traveller* should have been "more interested in the performance than in the performer." His message was not difficult to understand, he wrote, "the moral and political tendency of this nation is downward" and then corrected several misquotes of the speech which had appeared in the *Traveller*'s original report. Furthermore, Garrison wanted to be certain that his message was clear: the nation's tendency may be downward but was not yet unsalvageable.[12]

Five days later, a long letter signed "Junio" appeared in the *Traveller*. The correspondent excoriated Garrison's "violent tirade," deprecated his clothing and appearance, accused him of slandering American institutions, and blackening the name of "good and great men of former generations ... whose deeds have rendered their names immortal." He had delivered "one of the most injudicious, intemperate productions ever written."[13] Garrison did not comment himself, but a spirited defense was printed in Allen's *Herald* a week later. While acknowledging the speaker's "great ardor of sentiment" and that he might have "committed some slight indiscretions," "Honestus" warmly embraced most of Garrison's arguments and called "Junio" one of his "little enemies" who might benefit from following Garrison's example.[14] There were a few subsequent editorial attacks on Garrison in the *Traveller* but he took little notice. Within a few days of the address, he had left Boston to visit Newburyport before leaving to join Lundy in Baltimore. Garrison had faith that the printing press was the engine which could move the church and state into action, and convince them to embrace the struggle to end slavery. At the *Genius of Universal Emancipation* in Baltimore, he planned to stoke that engine and propel change in both institutions.

By 1829, William Lloyd Garrison believed that despite his reservations about politics and the nation's churches, the country was on the verge of significant change with regard to slavery. Aggressive action by a few publishers and editors, like himself, could provide the needed motivation. In the first issue of the year, the *Journal of the Times* reported on the religious triumphs of the previous year and confidently forecast that "a splendid triumph is near."[15] Later in the month he reprinted Benjamin Lundy's comments about the petitions to abolish slavery in the District of Columbia, sent to the United States Congress from several states, including Maryland, Delaware, New Jersey, and, of course, Vermont. "Thus we perceive," Lundy wrote, "that a moving of the waters has taken place. The moral eyes of the nation are opening."[16] In his Park Street Address in July, Garrison had explained the dangers that faced the nation and, at that time, he called upon politicians, religious leaders, and ordinary citizens to join the struggle to end slavery. Lundy and Garrison both hoped that the tide was turning in support of emancipation, and Garrison was determined to fan the flames and find new fuel to drive his engine for change — the printing press. In Baltimore, Garrison expected to engage the power of the press in a full-scale effort to support religious institutions and politics as the battle against the pro-slavery opposition accelerated.

Garrison arrived in Baltimore sometime in August 1829 after a fifteen-day voyage at sea. Rather than the expensive and fast steamboat connection from Boston, he had opted for more economical travel by sail; consequently he spent many days in misery "becalmed, day after day, on the bosom of the sea ... and a hot sun blazing down." Perhaps this allowed time for him to reflect on his new editorial project, but it also left Garrison resolved to "trudge on foot" rather than endure such inconvenience ever again.[17] The *Genius* was the most well-known anti-slavery publication at the time, and the city of Baltimore provided an ideal venue for the voice of anti-slavery to be heard — near the boundary separating the free North and the slave South. In 1804, New Jersey had become the last Northern state to pass a gradual emancipation law; it freed the children of slaves born after the law passed at age twenty-five for boys and twenty-one for girls. Consequently, by 1810, "about three-quarters of all Northern blacks were free, and within a generation virtually all would be."[18] Slavery did not end in Maryland, of course, until the Civil War, but in 1829, the state of Maryland and the city of Baltimore in particular represented a unique confluence between slave and free that had significant influence on Garrison's abolitionism.

In his new endeavor, Garrison expected to employ his years of training and experience as a printer to publish a resurgent and aggressive *Genius* in a new and much enlarged format. The paper, which Lundy had suspended on January 3, 1829, had been a small, three-column, four-page weekly, which was cleanly but rather plainly printed. He promised that when it returned with his new co-editor, it would be "enlarged and improved."[19] Under Garrison's direction, the new *Genius* was noticeably enhanced: larger, four columns, eight pages, well printed, and divided neatly into several sections — with the last page printed in French for the *Genius*'s subscribers in Haiti. It included a "Ladies Repository" written "By A Lady," although this was not Garrison's idea, but had been arranged by Lundy. Elizabeth Margaret Chandler was a Philadelphia Quaker who had previously written essays for the *Genius*; she agreed to edit the "Ladies Repository" in the new paper on condition of strict anonymity.[20] Garrison quickly learned to appreciate her commitment and energy for the anti-slavery cause; several years later he recalled her as "a prodigy of moral worth and intellectual endowment."[21] The new banner featured an impressive woodcut of an American eagle in flight above the paper's motto: "We hold these truths to be self-evident: that all men are created equal, and endowed by their Creator with certain unalienable rights, that among these are life, liberty and the pursuit of happiness." Furthermore, for the first time in his printing career, Garrison did not have to set type and physically print the newspaper he was editing. Lundy had arranged for the paper to be printed by contract.[22] Freed from these regular chores, and as managing editor, Garrison had more time to read, write, and instigate. From this foundation, Garrison hoped to launch a printer's assault on slavery.

This assault began with a new approach to emancipation — at least it was new for Garrison. In the interim between his Fourth of July speech and his arrival in Baltimore, he had made a momentous decision and had decided on a new strategy in his effort to invigorate the anti-slavery movement. Garrison met with Lundy immediately after his arrival and appraised him about his intent to lay "the axe at the root of the tree and [demand] immediate emancipation."[23] Advocating immediate emancipation was an unexpected change in Garrison's anti-slavery ideology. Just weeks earlier, in his "Park Street Address," Garrison had said, "immediate and complete emancipation is not desirable. No rational man cherishes so wild a vision." Emancipation could only be accomplished, he asserted, over time and "must be taken away brick by brick, and foot by foot, till it is reduced so low that it may be overturned without burying the nation in ruins. Years may elapse before the completion of the achievement; generations of blacks may go down to the grave manacled and lacerated, without a hope for their children." But the effort to end slavery must begin, though it may require a "desperate struggle of a thousand years."[24] Considering Lundy's gentle Quaker personality and his undoubted familiarity with Garrison's July address, it is not hard to envision his shock, and possibly some anxiety, at Garrison's announcement. On the other hand, given the aggressive tone of his "Park Street Address" this change of heart is really not all that surprising. Just as the patriots of 1776, who declared that independence could no longer be deferred, American slaves in 1829 were as arguably entitled to claim the same immediacy. Lundy was not prepared to espouse what was widely viewed as a radical idea, but wanted the partnership to move forward; he agreed to allow both of their voices a place in the *Genius,* and he reportedly told Garrison, "thee may put thy initials to thy articles, and I will put my initials to mine, and each will bear his own burden."[25] Unfortunately, it did not quite work this easily for Lundy who could not avoid some of the burden for Garrison's immediatism or for his aggressive, critical and libelous accusations.

In his opening editorial, "To The Public," in the newly formatted *Genius,* Garrison was lavish in his praise for Lundy's anti-slavery efforts and said it was "my highest ambition" to be "assistant editor of this paper." He then announced his rejection of gradual emancipation and defended immediatism as right, wise, and just. Since his address in Boston, he wrote, "on mature reflection no valid excuse can be given for the continuance of the evil a single hour." He had long been known as a strident opponent of slavery, but considering this extraordinary change, he thought it was necessary to explain his current perspective. First, he wrote, to hold slaves even one day longer in bondage was "both tyrannical and unnecessary." Second, expediency or convenience cannot be an excuse to delay what was right and that "it is not for those who tyrannise to say when they may safely break the chains of their subjects." Third, colonizing newly-freed slaves to Africa, Haiti, or other areas abroad was a delusion that had worked with only limited success to date and would not, Garrison believed, work any more successfully in the future, although he did not reject continuing colonization efforts. It was safer and wiser to free the slaves and to educate two million freedmen today, rather than four million in twenty-five years. Liberation would remove all threat of revolt, while employment and religious training would turn the freedmen into productive and peaceful citizens.[26]

The concept of immediate emancipation certainly was not introduced to the anti-slavery struggle by Garrison. It was at least implied in anti-slavery writings during the eighteenth century and had been directly or indirectly discussed in anti-slavery circles, especially in Great Britain, for some time. When it entered public debate in the early nineteenth century, most considered it to be an impractical and exceedingly radical idea, but in time, it eventually reshaped the antebellum anti-slavery movement.[27] One of the earliest books directly advocating immediate emancipation was written by George Bourne, an English Presbyterian minister who had come to America and, after several years in Baltimore, settled in western Virginia. In 1816, he published *The Book and Slavery Irreconcilable* in which he argued that slavery was not only against the laws of God but against the laws of man as well. He wrote,

Every man who holds slaves and pretends to be a Christian or a Republican, is either an incurable Idiot who cannot distinguish good from evil, or an obdurate sinner who resolutely defies every social, moral and divine requisition. Evangelical charity induces the hope that he is an ignoramus.[28]

Furthermore, he attacked the churches for their cooperation with slavery and he rejected colonization. For many years before he published *The Book*, Bourne had vigorously expressed his hostility to slavery and slaveholders, and his anger at the complicity of the Presbyterian Church, which refused to condemn slavery. This eventually led to his removal from the ministry by the General Assembly of the Presbyterian Church in 1818.[29] David Brion Davis called Bourne's book "the most radical abolitionist tract yet to appear in America" but also suggested that the increasing attractiveness of colonization around the same time resulted in an "exodus of potential abolitionist leaders" in the mid–1810s, including Bourne.[30] This "exodus" contributed to the transitory success of his message, until Garrison embraced it as his own. In 1824, Bourne was restored to his ministry after he expressed contrition "for whatever may have been ecclesiastically irregular or morally wrong in his deportment." Nevertheless, he did not abandon his position against slavery but rather acknowledged only that his combative conduct was wrong.[31] William Lloyd Garrison, of course, would not be so conciliatory.

After Bourne, the next major document espousing immediatism was a pamphlet titled *Immediate, Not Gradual Abolition*, published in England in 1824 by a Quaker named Elizabeth Coltman Heyrick. Her arguments were primarily focused on the distinctive problems of West Indian slavery; however, her belief that gradual emancipation was ineffective and that immediate emancipation was the only morally justifiable stance resonated with some in the American anti-slavery community. Quakers in Philadelphia arranged for an American edition in 1825 and Lundy serialized the pamphlet in the *Genius* during the winter of 1825-26. The pamphlet was widely available by the end of the decade.[32]

Despite the availability of information and literature on immediate emancipation, throughout his life, Garrison maintained that he had seen neither Bourne's book nor Heyrick's pamphlet prior to his time in Baltimore. How and why Garrison suddenly embraced it and the reasons why Garrison chose his co-editorship of the *Genius* as the right moment to advocate immediate emancipation are a mystery. Ralph Korngold suggested that during July 1829 Garrison "picked up a copy of Bourne's pamphlet on some Boston bookstall" and after reading it he decided to adopt immediate emancipation as his platform, but offers no evidence to support this theory.[33] Christie and Dumond accuse Garrison of being "shamefully negligent" in not acknowledging Bourne's influence on his decision. This certainly is not an unreasonable theory, but again they can offer only conjecture regarding Garrison's decision.[34] In a like manner, Russel Nye suggested that in discussions with William Goodell before Garrison left Boston for Baltimore he changed his mind about "gradual *versus* immediate emancipation" and that immediatism was "in the air." Nye does so, however, without providing any solid evidence.[35]

As for Garrison's own testimony on the subject, at the celebration of the sixtieth anniversary of his apprenticeship in 1878, he explained that "on revolving the matter in my mind" he had simply decided that if it was justified to hold a person in slavery for one hour, then lifetime slavery could be justified as well. Therefore, he decided, the only morally justifiable position to take was to demand "immediate and unconditional emancipation."[36] In *The Liberator* in 1832, Garrison praised Bourne, who at the time was editor of a New York City newspaper *The Protestant* and whose commentary regularly appeared in *The Liberator*, for his tireless moral leadership and the longstanding influence of his book on anti-slavery activity. "Next to the Bible," Garrison wrote, "we are indebted to this work for our views of the system of slavery.... The more we read it, the higher does our admiration of its author rise."[37] Again in August Garrison offered effusive praise both for the Bourne's newspaper and the abuse he endured in consequence of his early advocacy for immediate emancipation; however, Garrison does not indicate when Bourne's book first came to his attention.[38]

Other evidence also suggests that Heyrick's pamphlet did not induce Garrison's resolve to advocate immediate emancipation. Given that Heyrick's pamphlet was reprinted by Lundy while Garrison was engaged with *The Free Press*, at which he was most focused on political affairs and not in exchange with the *Genius*; it is at least plausible that he was unaware of her work. In addition, after passage of the Thirteenth Amendment and after Garrison had discontinued publication of *The Liberator*, he wrote regularly for *The Independent*, a New York City newspaper edited, until 1870, by Theodore Tilton. In an editorial comment in 1868, Tilton discussed Garrison's stance as an "immediatist." With regard to Heyrick's pamphlet, Tilton wrote that "we have the highest authority for saying that Mr. Garrison never saw it or heard of it until a considerable time after he had raised the banner of immediate and unconditional emancipation." Rather, he continued, Garrison "cipher[ed] out the doctrine in his own mind as a moral duty and a logical necessity."[39] Nevertheless, if Garrison's immediatism did not arise from reading either Bourne or Heyrick, it is logical to conclude that neither did it emerge in isolation.

Writing several decades after the fact and a year after Garrison's death, Oliver Johnson credited the Reverend Lyman Beecher with teaching Garrison the "doctrine of immediatism." When Garrison was in Boston in 1828, according to Johnson, he enjoyed listening to Beecher's sermons. A prominent part of Beecher's preaching was "the duty of every sinner to repent instantly and give his heart to Christ." However, Johnson noted, while Beecher was willing to apply that practice to most sins, his "moral blindness" left him unwilling to apply it to the sin of slavery.[40] Garrison's involvement in the temperance movement, most prominently as editor of the *National Philanthropist*, also exposed him to an absolutist approach to temperance reform consistent with immediatism in anti-slavery. In the early decades of the nineteenth century, the "United States was an alcohol-soaked culture" and public drinking and drunkenness had become a significant social problem which threatened, temperance advocates argued, the moral character of the nation and the virtue of the republic.[41] The answer to this threat was not moderation, but rather total abstinence, or, as the motto of the *National Philanthropist* proclaimed, "Moderate Drinking is the Downhill Road to Intemperance and Drunkenness." Here again the influence of the Reverend Beecher may have been important. Until the mid-1820s, most temperance advocates opposed only distilled spirits and not fermented spirits like cider, beer, and wine. In the fall of 1825, Beecher delivered a series of sermons in which he rejected the use of alcohol in any form, no matter how moderate and no matter what quantity. For Beecher, there was no middle ground and he envisioned a future which included "banishment of ardent spirits from the list of lawful articles of commerce." In response to Beecher's call, the American Society for the Promotion of Temperance was founded in 1826.[42] Influenced by these changes, Garrison advocated immediate and complete abstinence from all types of alcohol in the *Journal of the Times*. Teetotaling, he contended, had become "the universal creed of sober men" everywhere.[43] While it is certainly likely that religion and temperance ideals influenced Garrison's inclination toward immediatism in abolition, the free blacks of Boston may have been even more influential in opening Garrison's eyes to the inconsistency of a gradual approach to the abolition of slavery.

    The black population of Boston in 1830 was only about 1,875 (3 percent of the city's total population of 61,000) and they were heavily concentrated in the four "Negro" wards of the city.[44] Within those wards in 1806, the Reverend Thomas Paul became minister of the African Baptist Church. Also known as the African Church or the Belknap Street Church, it was the first of four black churches, two Baptist and two Methodist, established in Boston between 1805 and 1848; it was officially organized in August 1805.[45] Paul was an extraordinary leader for the community and under his ministry the church extended its influence not only among the city's blacks but in missionary outreach beyond the state, to New York City and even Haiti.[46] As mentioned earlier, on Paul's retirement in 1829, Garrison's old Newburyport minister, John Peak, and his fellow editor, William Collier, ministered to the congregation until a new black minister could be found.[47] Paul left because of long-term health issues and died two years later. Garrison's familiarity with the Reverend Paul was on display in the obituary published in *The Liberator*. He expressed high praise for Paul's character, dignity, piety, and intelligence; he wrote that "his influence was as beneficial as extensive" and "his eloquence charmed the ear."[48] We can only presume that one of those charmed ears was Garrison's.

Boston's black community can trace its institutional promotion of political and social benefit for fellow-blacks to the end of the nineteenth century and the Massachusetts court decision in the case of *Commonwealth of Massachusetts v. Jennison* in 1781 which declared slavery as unconstitutional within the state. No small part of the agitation which led to this ruling were initiatives taken by Massachusetts and Boston slaves themselves; they challenged slavery in light of not only the state's constitution but the ideology of the American Revolution itself. What followed was a coalescing of black residents in Boston to work together for the benefit of their own community; they knew that no one else was prepared to help them. In this effort, for instance, the African Society was created in 1796 to provide, among other things, social-welfare benefits for those less fortunate in their own community. The Society reflected community values which were "typical of nineteenth-century American society. Moral living, temperance, self-improvement, and education" were commonly discussed at meetings of black leaders and in publications which circulated in black communities.[49] Each of these values would have registered positively with Garrison. Until around 1830 and the founding of *The Liberator* and emergence of a Garrisonian-led group of white citizens willing to work side-by-side with black citizens, the black organizations had worked primarily within their own community and with their own people. Black leaders in Boston were optimistic about this change because the "merger did not involve a white displacement of black leadership" and many black-only organizations became more integrated.[50] During his years in Boston before *The Liberator* began, and especially as the result of his association with Reverends Peak, Collier, and Paul at the Belknap Street Church, Garrison undoubtedly became familiar with black citizens in Boston, sympathetic with their position in American society, and likely influenced by their perspective on the anti-slavery struggle. Their influence in his decision for immediate emancipation, however, has never been definitively established.

Some evidence of their influence, nevertheless, can be gleaned from an article Garrison wrote in his inaugural issue of the *Genius*. Writing as "An Observer," Garrison reported on an "African Celebration in Boston" which he had attended ten days after his Park Street Address. The event celebrated the anniversary of the end of the slave trade in Great Britain in 1807 and was an annual event in black Boston at the time.[51] Garrison was impressed with the dignified manner in which the black community commemorated the day. Unlike the way "our *white* countrymen" celebrate their independence, there was no drinking to inebriation, no profane language, no bullying and no fighting. A neat procession of the African Abolition Society marched to the Belknap Street Church where they sang, listened to a reading of the Society's Constitution, and "a discourse was delivered by a clergyman of the city."

The speaker initially caused some discontent among the audience for speaking about the "importance of good moral and religious character." This was not what they came to hear and many got up to leave; however, the disruption was quieted by "a colored clergyman" who counseled patience and urged the audience not to pass judgment about the speaker's message in haste. The speaker continued; he denounced the degradation and suffering endured by his listeners and by the millions of their brethren in slavery, but he exhorted them not to seek revenge or change through violent means. Instead he suggested that a better way to break the chains of oppression was "for the free colored people of Boston, and elsewhere, to show by their conduct, that they were capable of self-government." Their industriousness and peacefulness in Boston would be seen by the whole nation as evidence of their "sobriety and intelligence." With his concluding words, the speaker proclaimed a certain result: "In a few years, you will take the white men's places. They will go down, and you will rise up." This was the message they had wanted to hear and for which they had already been working for several decades.

However, before this successful conclusion to the address, there was another incident that particularly impressed Garrison. This incident, he wrote, "showed that the spirit of liberty was not confined exclusively to whites" and may have significantly contributed to his reassessment of immediate emancipation, which he had rejected as "too radical" only a few days earlier. A minister and an agent of the American Colonization Society, who were also present, endeavored to assert that the liberation of two million slaves "in their present condition" was not beneficial to the slaves, not safe for the country, and not possible at the moment. If freed immediately, the slaves, the two men explained, had no land to cultivate, were "degraded in mind and morals," and would be entirely dependent on others until they could be properly prepared for freedom. The audience, Garrison reported, audibly murmured as the minister presented these arguments and the murmur became "more earnest and decisive" as the colonization agent attempted to support the minister. The audience rejected the arguments and Garrison speculated that if he were in their position, "I too would growl my disapprobation." Suppose, he argued, that two million white Americans were forcefully oppressed and degraded in the same manner as America's black slaves and then were told that their oppression was justified because of their degradation. "Who," he asked, "would not be indignant at the insult?" These black citizens of Boston were expressing, he believed, the essence of liberty and in doing so "it gave me a higher opinion of this body of men." Black slaves had committed no crime and deserved no punishment. What then justified depriving "them of their liberties?" For Garrison, neither Bourne nor Heyrick could make a better argument for immediate emancipation than the instinctive reaction of this audience of black Bostonians.[52]

Whatever the source of Garrison's decision to advocate immediate emancipation, we cannot doubt the sincerity of his belief. It became the fundamental doctrine of Garrisonian abolition and of the American Anti-Slavery Society (AASS). From September 1829 until the passage of the Thirteenth Amendment, for Garrison, immediate emancipation was more than a "radical slogan," and if he did not expect it to become a reality at once, he did believe that anything less was unjustifiable.[53] In an 1853 speech, Garrison argued that the one vital principle of the AASS was "that immediate emancipation is the right of the slave and the duty of the master."[54] There were many different forces in his life which could have led him in August 1829 to choose to advocate what he had only recently considered to be irrational. It cannot be denied, however, that in the final analysis, his decision may also have been one of expediency, and consciously made to provoke confrontation and spur discussion and debate. If that was part of his motive, then he did not have to wait long for reactions to surface.

Before the end of September, Garrison reported in the *Genius* some of the responses to his demand for immediate emancipation. The *Christian Register*, a Boston newspaper edited by David Reed and which declared itself "devoted to Unitarian Christianity," editorialized strongly against Garrison's immediatism. The newspaper characterized his ideas as "hasty and violent proposals and crude suggestions." Reed supported gradual emancipation which was required, he argued, for the safety of the national community. Just as criminals, "lunatics," and children are "deprived of their natural liberty" for either their own safety or the safety of society, so too slaves must remain bound until some undefined but appropriate time for emancipation. He questioned whether Garrison was truly serious, and suggested that immediate emancipation would only delay abolition because it was "offensive to the white population" of the southern states.⁵⁵ Whether it was the right thing to do from a Christian perspective was not part of this "Christian" paper's discussion, which must have been especially frustrating for Garrison.

Garrison also reported receiving a letter from "one of my best friends" who likewise questioned whether he honestly meant to advocate "immediate and complete emancipation of the slaves," and reminded him that such a policy had dangerous consequences and was doomed to failure. To both commentaries Garrison responded that he was indeed serious, and made it clear that he fully intended to create controversy. "That [immediate emancipation] will create much opposition," he wrote, "I cannot doubt; that *therefore* [it] should be abandoned, I cannot admit." Furthermore, he argued that it was not a dangerous policy but in fact ultimately beneficial for the nation, and expressed gratification that his advocacy of immediatism was bringing public attention to the plight of the slave. Garrison wanted the *Genius* to shine the light of inquiry on the issue of emancipation in the struggle "to undermine the huge fabric of slavery." If his advocacy of immediatism provoked discussion and debate, then he was accomplishing his purpose. To both the editor of the *Christian Register* and his correspondent he issued a challenge, "Let us all begin to talk, and interrogate, and plan; and depend upon it, something noble will be done — and not till then."⁵⁶ In other words, immediate emancipation had to be part of the marketplace of ideas that a free press nourished in order for change to take place.

Again in October, Garrison printed parts of letters he had received regarding his plea for immediate emancipation and responded to both. One came from a correspondent in Pennsylvania who acknowledged that immediate emancipation was required by justice, but argued that its implementation would only bring misery to the slaves who were unprepared for freedom. As "friends of Africans," the correspondent contended, the abolitionists must insist on programs of education and training for the slaves before emancipation, which could only occur at some time in the future, but certainly not immediately. Garrison countered that "talk of *expediency*" only allowed the crime to persist and was tantamount to embracing the immoral idea that one could "do evil, that good may come." The second letter came from a minister in Massachusetts who urged Garrison to adopt "a tone more calculated to secure sympathy and an exhibition of principles less liable to the charge of extravagance," and expressed concern for the damage Garrison could do to the anti-slavery cause. In reply, Garrison likened the Reverend's comments to a trial in which the jurors claim a willingness to dispense justice, but are unwilling to listen to the testimony that will result in a guilty verdict. He, however, was unwilling to limit his prosecution when the law was explicit, the evidence overwhelming, and "the guilt of the culprit ... self-evident."⁵⁷ Whatever else had influenced Garrison's decision to support immediate emancipation, it was, as Merton Dillon argued, "designed to arouse complacent persons to their duty with respect to slavery."⁵⁸ In making the concept of immediate emancipation essential to the abolitionist movement, at least in his editorial contributions in the *Genius*, Garrison intended to provoke those uncommitted to anti-slavery, to arouse those who were moderate abolitionists, to inflame those who supported and defended the "peculiar institution"—whether in the North or South—and to make "every single home, press, pulpit, and senate chamber a debating society, with *his* right and wrong for the subject."⁵⁹

Given Garrison's dramatic turnaround regarding emancipation, it seems somewhat problematic that he was not yet finally prepared to dismiss the colonization movement, as he had dismissed gradual emancipation, as a false answer for the anti-slavery movement. His address at the Park Street Church on July 4 was in part a fund-raising effort for the American Colonization Society although he barely mentioned their efforts in his speech. In its closing he called upon all to "assist in establishing auxiliary colonization societies" around the country, encouraged support of the "parent society," and he offered encomiums for the accomplishments in Haiti and Liberia, where many former slaves had traveled as a result of colonization.⁶⁰ In his "To The Public" editorial in the *Genius*, Garrison argued that since "a very large proportion" of slaves were born "on American soil," no one had the right to coerce their removal; however, he was not ready to eschew colonization altogether. This may reflect his respect for Lundy who was still strongly committed to the work of colonization, at least in Haiti, if not in Africa. Nevertheless, for Garrison, colonization should now be viewed as merely an "auxiliary" to abolition, not the ultimate remedy, which was "the eternal principles of justice," that is, immediate emancipation. His own enlightenment about colonization took some time, but developed more maturity in a large part as a result of his brief stay in Baltimore. As with his change of heart on immediate emancipation, his change of heart on colonization was strongly influenced by his interaction with another black community.

Blacks in Boston had become part of what Benjamin Quarles called "Abolition's New Breed" and had come together in their opposition to colonization. Opposition was first voiced in Philadelphia in January 1817, less than a year after the formation of the American Colonization Society. By the late 1820s, opposition to colonization schemes and the threat of exile, the implication of black inferiority, and the belief that blacks could not compete successfully in a free society had succeeded in uniting freed blacks in many cities throughout the North.⁶¹ This was certainly as true, and conceivably even more valid, in the border state of Maryland and in the city of Baltimore's black community. Garrison's "colored friends" in Baltimore were, according to his children, the first to show him the "dangerous character and tendency" of the colonization society.[62] It is likely, however, that he had already heard as much in Boston, but his brief time with the blacks in Baltimore confirmed, personalized and enhanced this perspective.

The growth of free black labor in Baltimore, and white reaction to that growth, had been underway for some time before 1829. Slavery had spread into the city of Baltimore roughly between 1770 and 1815, and Maryland black slaves had played an important role in establishing Baltimore as one of the nation's prominent ports. However, between 1800 and 1830, slave labor in the city was increasingly supplanted by free black labor. Hard work, self-purchase, and manumission agreements (such as "delayed manumission" which freed a slave after a number of years of loyal service) allowed blacks in Baltimore to become freed much faster than in the rest of the state. The need for reliable labor among employers in Baltimore created opportunities for slaves to seek manumission, which masters used as a means of maintaining control while blacks used it as a means to obtain freedom. By 1830, 80 percent of Baltimore's blacks were free, in contrast to approximately 25 percent in the rest of the state.[63] Free black households in Baltimore, which had represented about 1.3 percent of the city's population in 1790, had grown to represent 15 percent in 1830.[64] As a result of this change, and despite continuing economic deprivation that left the city's free black community overwhelmingly poor, a strong and multifaceted black community developed within the city. "Communal organization and group solidarity," wrote Christopher Phillips, "allowed Baltimore's black people to create a mature community, one that looked within for identification"—much in the same fashion as in Boston—although, Baltimore emerged from a more recent and continuing connection with chattel slavery. This identification was formed by black-organized and black-run benevolent associations, fraternal organizations, churches, schools, and other social institutions.[65]

By the late 1820s, some white Baltimoreans were beginning to believe that they had lost control of their black population and were looking for ways to reassert their power. Free blacks had become competitors for day-wage laboring jobs, but they still lacked any social or political rights, which, naturally, resulted in significant legal discrimination against them. Beginning around 1825, state laws were passed requiring unemployed free blacks to give security for their good behavior or else leave the state. Furthermore, free blacks convicted of crimes were required to leave the state once their jail sentences were complete.[66] In addition, blacks were routinely disparaged and depicted as naturally prone to violence and crime. White city constables sought out black suspects for petty crimes, and the rate of incarcerated blacks far exceeded the proportion of free blacks in the population.[67] Garrison noted this increasingly hostile attitude in the *Genius* when he commented on the tendency within the city, "to traduce the habits and morals of our free blacks. The most scandalous exaggerations in regard to their condition are circulated by a thousand mischievous tongues."[68]

The growth of the free black community in Baltimore was also instrumental during the 1820s in redirecting and bolstering white support for colonization. Increasingly, white citizens of the city were encouraged to believe that in addition to their supposed criminal tendencies, free blacks were routinely accomplices to runaway slaves. In 1821, a Baltimore attorney, Joseph D. Learned, proposed a plan to forcibly remove all free blacks in the United States to trans–Mississippi Missouri, where "in isolation, they would develop social and trade skills" which would allow them to compete with white settlers once they came into the area.[69] Later in the decade, other Baltimoreans tried to convince the state legislature to provide funding for colonization plans.[70] In addition, some effort was made, supported by at least some city black leaders, to convince free blacks in Baltimore that colonization was beneficial. One of the most vocal in opposition to colonization was William Watkins, a teacher and part-time minister, who urged blacks to reject colonization, to "die in Maryland," and over the years convinced many freed blacks to abandon their plans to emigrate. He is considered to have been more influential than anyone else in convincing Garrison to reassess his support, as tepid as in was in 1829, for colonization.[71]

Watkins was born in Baltimore around 1803 and for most of his life was associated with the Sharp Street Methodist Church. His father was a trustee of the Church and Watkins attended a school at the church run by Daniel Crocker. He was a good student, a quick learner, and started teaching at the school in 1820; when Crocker emigrated to Liberia two years later, he took on full responsibility for operating the school. Primarily self-taught after learning the basics under Crocker, Watkins was acclaimed among the city's freed blacks, as well as many in the white community, as an excellent academic and strict disciplinarian who dispensed a first-class education to his students. The school became known as Watkins Academy; he taught a wide range of subjects, including history, geography, mathematics, philosophy, Greek, Latin, music, English and rhetoric until 1852 when he emigrated to Toronto, Canada. He was especially accomplished at writing and the sophistication and grace of his works astonished Baltimore's white citizens who were shocked by a black man's linguistic skills. Much as he encouraged and cajoled his students to seek the benefits of education, he did likewise for himself. He was founder of the Black Literary Society which met regularly to debate literature and politics, became a minister at the Sharp Street Church around 1825, taught himself enough medicine to practice within the community, and became a regular newspaper correspondent. Finally, he was not afraid to challenge those in power or confront local social, political, or religious leadership. He advocated abolitionism and helped to publish as well as distribute Lundy's *Genius* and, later, Garrison's *Liberator* in the face of increasing public disapproval of both publications. Consequently, his life was threatened several times.[72] After Garrison arrived in Baltimore, he and Lundy "boarded with two Quaker ladies ... who lived as 135 Market Street" and their circle of friends included other Quakers and "some of the more intelligent colored people of the city," including William Watkins.[73] Given Watkins' passion for education and to educate, his strength of character, and his willingness to advocate unpopular ideas, it is not difficult to appreciate his appeal for Garrison and the ways in which Watkins could influence and even alter Garrison's anti-slavery ideology.

The efforts to convince blacks in the mid–1820s in Baltimore about the benefits of colonization were most responsible for Watkins' engagement with newspapers and began in earnest after two December 1826 meetings about colonization, one held at the Bethel Church and the other at Watkins' own Sharp Street Church. Watkins attended the December 11 meeting at Sharp Street and was joined by an estimated "two-thirds of the blacks" in attendance in opposition to the idea; he was not necessarily against people deciding to emigrate to Africa, but was clearly opposed to the use of intimidation, whether subtle or blatant, to force blacks to emigrate. Despite their opposition, after the meetings a pro-colonization memorial, signed by black leaders, William Cornish and Robert Cowley for the Bethel Church, and James Deaver and Remus Harvey for the Sharp Street Church, but which was actually written by two white men, Charles Harper and John H.B. Latrobe, was published in the local press in order to demonstrate support for colonization among leading members of the city's black community.[74]

"Memorial of the Free People of Colour" acknowledged "the efforts of the wise and philanthropic on our behalf." Furthermore, it recognized that Baltimore free blacks were strangers among the "freest people" of the world, yet on account of their condition, skin color, and natural prejudices could never be allowed to "mingle with you ... in the benefits of citizenship." Citizens of the United States, it claimed, had been unwillingly saddled with slavery by Great Britain and, after independence was achieved, made great efforts to end the slave trade and find ways for the eventual extermination of "the evil" (i.e., slavery). In addition, since republican principles are undermined by the presence of a people who can never participate in the system and who take jobs from "the whites — your fellow-citizens," it was reasonable for the white citizens to desire that those black residents who were willing to do so should be encouraged to remove themselves. Meanwhile, as much as great benefit would accrue to whites as a result of removal, which they certainly were unwilling to demand, even greater would be the rewards for blacks. Because of their status in the United States, it will never be possible for blacks to develop the full abilities with which God has endowed them; however, in Africa, they would be able to work more successfully to bring liberty to all brethren currently in bondage and prevent bondage in the future. Therefore, "of the many schemes that have been proposed, we most approve of that of *Africa Colonization.*" In conclusion, the memorial thanked Americans for the "kind concern" extended to them and wished that, as a result of this program, Americans would be blessed with "the riddance of the stain and evil of slavery, the extension of civilization and the Gospel, and the blessing of our common Creator."[75] Needless to say, this memorial did not reflect William Watkins' sentiments.

Spurred by the tone of the "Memorial," which did not speak either for him or for, he believed, most blacks in Baltimore, Watkins penned the first of a long collection of newspaper correspondence and articles under the pseudonym "A COLOURED BALTIMOREAN." He began by identifying himself as one of those "whose degraded condition" was to be a recipient of the benevolence of the "good and wise of our country"; however, he then quickly turned to question both that wisdom and that benevolence. The fact that the most distinguished members of the American Colonization Society were slaveholders was, he thought, rather puzzling. Their benevolence and philanthropic care for the freed blacks, whom they had never met, did not seem consistent with their lack of concern for the "degraded condition" of those "directly under their observation." This led him to conclude that a "philanthropic slaveholder is as great a solecism as a sober drunkard." From here Watkins launched into a series of questions about the features of the plan of colonization which seemed, he implied, more tailored to the desires of the slaveholder than the freed black or the former slave. Was it not anti–Christian to argue that blacks could not receive justice in "this land of civilization and gospel light"? How can blacks not be entitled to the unalienable rights which belong to all men in the "land of the free and home of the brave"? What is it, other than the color of our skin that makes us a "nuisance" which can only be resolved by sending us to a distant, foreign, and inhospitable land? Why are the principles, which drive the American Colonization Society, not subject to examination or discussion? Where is the benevolence in a society which forces a people to move while still mired in "ignorance and depravity" (according to whites' own representations) and without the preparation necessary, especially education, to enable them to carry civilization, law, and liberty to the land of their forefathers? In closing, Watkins simply requested a dialogue about colonization; despite his questions, he conceded the sincerity and honesty behind their perspective, expected the same of them regarding his objections and agree, "after mature deliberation" to abide by the results of those deliberations, "as long as I believe them right."[76] It was a masterful response which clearly demonstrated not only Watkins' intelligence and erudition, but the manipulative and unscrupulous nature of the colonization scheme.

For the better part of the next three decades, the writings of "THE COLOURED BALTIMOREAN" (or "THE COLOURED CANADIAN" after Watkins moved to Toronto) were periodically found in many newspapers, including *Freedom's Journal* in New York City, the *Genius of Universal Emancipation* in Baltimore, *The Liberator* in Boston, *The Colored American* in Baltimore, and *Frederick Douglass Paper* in Rochester, New York. His subject most often was opposition to colonization but he also discussed the failure of the American churches to agitate more strongly against slavery and for true Christianity, abolition, the treatment of the American Indian, and justice for all people regardless of skin color. Few colonization supporters likely gave much credence to anything appearing in the black or abolitionist press and fewer would have been interested in a dialogue or debate with a black man, even one who was educated and articulate. However, they may not have been Watkins' target audience; more likely he wanted to reach anti-slavery advocates and abolitionists like Garrison, who still needed to be convinced of the duplicity of the colonizationists' arguments.

Whether Garrison was aware of Watkins' letters before coming to Baltimore is not known for certain, but from his interactions with free blacks in Boston, doubtlessly he was at least familiar with their opposition to the colonization movement. Yet, when he arrived in Baltimore, he still maintained some level of support for it. At the Park Street Church in July 1829, he encouraged citizens to provide "liberal patronage" for colonization. In his first editorial at the *Genius* three months later, he acknowledged that the American Colonization Society was a good "auxiliary," although not the final solution; his support could hardly be called robust. In the months he stayed in Baltimore, his viewpoint was changed and in the second issue of *The Liberator*, he wrote that the "American Colonization Society is wrong in principle and impotent in design."[77] No small part of the change of heart was his relationship with the freed black community of Baltimore in the slave state of Maryland. Advocates like William Watkins and others like him were closer to the realities of slavery than the free blacks in Boston and, unlike their fellow blacks to the north, they were under direct assault from slaveholding interests on account of their numbers and increasing influence within the city. These facts not only made the adversarial relationship between planters and freed blacks more obvious but made the dishonesty of colonizationists' motives more clear and visible.

On June 4, 1831, another letter from "A COLORED BALTIMOREAN" was published under the headline "AN ABLE REPLY" in *The Liberator*. The letter once again dismissed the latest "selfish policies" of colonizationists and asserted that "we would rather die in Maryland" under cruel and unjust laws than be exiled to the infectious environment of Africa. Coincidentally or not, it was published just at Garrison was leaving to deliver an address in Philadelphia at the First Annual Convention of the Free People of Color in the United States.[78] At the convention, he exhorted the attendees to respect themselves, to stand up for their rights, and to not despair as what was likely to be a long struggle continued. Further he told them to "Abandon all thoughts of colonizing," and that anyone who did leave "ought to be considered as a traitor to your cause." At considerable length, he fully explained the false promises, lies, and evil intentions of the colonization societies.[79] On his return from the convention, he wrote to his distant cousin, Ebenezer Dole, who had written Garrison to announce his own resolution to oppose colonization. Garrison congratulated him for the decision and admitted that for some time he had been deceived about the society, but "after the most candid and prayerful investigation ... my judgment tells me they are abhorrent."[80] William Watkins could not have said it better.

If Garrison liked to consider himself to be the "original disturber of the peace," Watkins' rhetorical style demonstrated a comparable inclination, but there were other similarities which suggest good reason to believe Garrison would have found Watkins a useful and appealing confidant. They were close in age, both considered themselves to be self-made men, both relished the importance of education, both challenged their respective communities to embrace new ideas, both vilified the recalcitrance of American churches to oppose slavery, both expounded on the importance of the press in shaping public opinion, and both men valued discussion and debate. Furthermore, their bond reached to another generation. Watkins' son, William J. Watkins, moved to Boston for several years in the 1840s and early 1850s, contributed regularly to *The Liberator* and became respected member of Garrison's pool of antislavery lecturers before moving to Rochester to become assistant editor for Frederick Douglass' newspaper.[81] While clearly following in his father's footsteps, the son credited a visit from Garrison immediately after he was released from jail for libel in Baltimore for advice about his future. Then just five years old, at his father's house, Garrison told him to be "always an abolitionist"; he continued to be faithful to that admonition and became a well-known and strong advocate in his own right.[82]

In the months following his Park Street Address, William Lloyd Garrison, who was already considered a radical, aggressive, and destabilizing voice in the marketplace of ideas that was early nineteenth-century newspapers, experienced a remarkable transformation. Gradual emancipation was no longer justifiable. A good Christian did not withdraw from sin slowly but must do so without delay; no greater sin was part of American society than slavery and its end must be immediate. The reasonable hope that colonization could aid in this process was also no longer acceptable. Garrison himself was a first-generation American; most slaves had been in America for many more generations and no more should be required to leave than he. Colonization flew in the face of Christian and republican principles. An extraordinary change of heart forced Garrison to move in new directions. This change was certainly spurred by his own study and reflection, but it was also influenced significantly by his association with the black communities in Boston and Baltimore.

Six

On Trial in Baltimore

As critical as abolition was for Garrison, he did not limit his efforts at provocation to advocacy for immediate emancipation, or even to other reform issues such as temperance or imprisonment for debt, although these issues were often examined and discussed. In a long article in the third issue of the co-edited *Genius of Universal Emancipation*, Garrison dismissed the militia system in the country as designed essentially *"to make men skillful murderers"* and declared that he "will never obey any order to bear arms."[1] The plight of the American Indians was also frequently the subject of commentary, especially in light of Georgia's repeated attempts to remove Native Americans from the state, and Andrew Jackson's support for the removal policy. Government treatment of the Indian was another sign that the United States was a "nation of tyrants, and the bent of our legislation is oppressive." Just as with government policy toward the oppressed African slave, Garrison argued, Indian policy was driven by expediency and the desire for land when it should have been driven by justice.[2]

Political affairs received regular attention as well. Ironically, in fact, one conceivable influence on Garrison's clarion call for all Americans to embrace the right moral choices in social and political life was the inauguration of Andrew Jackson as president of the United States, just six months before the first issue of Garrison's co-editorship. He was still stinging from the election of someone he believed to be completely unfit for the office of president, as he had proclaimed in Bennington. Additionally, like many New Englanders, he had long been a supporter of the "American System" and after Jackson attacked the National Bank as unconstitutional and inexpedient in his first address to Congress, Garrison warned his readers of the ominous consequences.[3] Destruction of the bank, Garrison argued, would be "more dangerous to the liberties of the people than a standing army of one hundred thousand men." Furthermore, the economic harm would be most felt by "widows and orphans" and those least capable of bearing the burden.[4] Under Jackson, the tariff was also threatened with repeal. The tariff was not perfect, in Garrison's opinion, but its opponents, the most vociferous being Southern white cotton plantation owners who supported Jackson, were intent on destroying its benefits and not repairing its faults.[5] Garrison also drew attention to the plan of some in the south to purchase and annex Texas to the Union. He called it a "dangerous and desperate project" which was only intended to create more slave states and therefore increase southern power in Congress.[6] Lundy agreed, but was willing to consider an annexed Texas where slavery was prohibited, as it was under Mexican law, because it would be a suitable place for freed slaves to emigrate.[7] This, of course, was not what Texas and southern cotton interests wanted or were even willing to consider.

Despite his fears about Jackson's influence, Garrison had yet to despair of the potential for the political system to provide a path to justice for all and to promote change that was necessary in society — including finding a way to abolish slavery. In October, a *Genius* editorial strongly endorsed the election of Daniel Raymond to the Maryland House of Delegates. Raymond was a lawyer, political economist, president of the Maryland Abolition Society and one of the leading anti-slavery advocates in Baltimore during the 1820s. He had been defeated for election to the Baltimore City Council in 1825 and 1828. In the minds of Maryland planters, who strongly opposed his candidacy, Raymond and his anti-slavery activism represented the debilitating effects of life in an urban environment like Baltimore. The "foundations on which slavery was built in Maryland" were rural and did not reflect the free labor inclinations of the city's white mechanics, who had provided much of Raymond's support in his failed campaigns.[8] The editorial called for citizens to support candidates in all elections, federal or state, who did not "blindly pursue a party," but in particular, it called for voters to elect Raymond to the Maryland legislature. Raymond was described in glowing details as a patriot, philanthropist, supporter of the "American System," of unimpeachable moral character, and "unbiased by party considerations." Baltimore citizens were urged to "PULL ALTOGETHER, for the friend of public improvement and general reform."[9] This editorial was signed by neither "L" nor "G" to indicate authorship. This may indicate that it was a joint editorial; however, Lundy was out of town at the time and according to another editorial comment on that day, the paper was "under the direction of the junior editor." In any case, while the endorsement of Raymond may have been shared, the language of the editorial sounded distinctly like it came from Garrison's pen.

Six: On Trial in Baltimore

The next week's *Genius* reported the results of the election; Raymond was defeated by an enormous margin. He came in last of six candidates and received only 186 votes, or about 1.3 percent of all votes cast. The two candidates who won election to the House of Delegates were both Democratic supporters of Andrew Jackson and each received over 4,000 votes. Garrison expressed great disappointment and blamed Raymond's loss on the failure of "the sober reflecting portion of our citizens" to turn out to vote. They despaired of winning the election — a feeling Garrison shared — but were unwilling, even with their votes, to offer resistance to "a popular fanaticism" that threatened to destroy citizens' liberties along with "the sublime superstructure which our fathers erected." Raymond lost, in Garrison's evaluation, because he came before the citizens of Baltimore as an independent man, uncommitted to any particular party's platform. Garrison included himself as a member of a small group of individuals who "profess to acknowledge not one political leader, to be controlled by no party machinery, to regard only moral and intellectual worth in the selection of candidates." Accordingly, he considered Raymond's 186 votes a greater victory than the 4,000 received by the victors, which represented "appeals to the passions and prejudices of men." Their votes were a victory for "party"; Raymond's were a victory for "principle."[10] As convoluted as was Garrison's argument, it at least demonstrated that he had not yet lost confidence altogether in the American political system.

Garrison also harbored hope for a change in the political power structure as the result of the Virginia Constitutional Convention, which met from October 1829 to January 1830. The convention was called to address the unequal distribution of statewide political power. State legislators in Virginia were apportioned by a formula which combined white population and property value, including, of course, the value of slaves as property. Consequently, the formula gave greater representation to the larger slaveholding eastern districts than the lesser slaveholding western districts. After lengthy debate, a more egalitarian, but hardly more democratic, basis was eventually agreed upon. The property portion of the formula was abolished but the eastern elite remained in power by requiring apportionment based on the 1820 census, with no future re-apportionment allowed. Political power was thus permanently frozen in favor of the eastern elites.[11] Nevertheless, as the convention began, in October 1829, Garrison held out great hope that it would begin the process of ending slavery in the southern states. He praised the "array of talent" present; they represented the "most experienced legislators, and [Virginia] may safely rely on their integrity." He urged the convention to demonstrate that Virginia was "in truth the advocate of equal rights, and anxious to blot out the foul stain of oppression upon her escutcheon."[12] His articles about the convention appeared regularly in the *Genius* over the next few months; they discussed the convention and anticipated that substantive changes in Virginia's Constitution would presage change in other southern states.[13]

Garrison's optimism about the convention was misplaced; however, his faith in the political process was bent but not yet broken. He called the results of the convention an improvement, but tempered this assessment and suggested that "this constitution is neither so aristocratical as the old one, nor so republican as it ought to be."[14] Although the slaveholding elite in Tidewater Virginia had made some concessions to the trans–Allegheny farmers, they retained effective control over the state legislature both in the present and in the future. Slaves as property were no longer part of the formula for apportioning legislative power in Virginia, but governance in Virginia remained primarily the prerogative of slaveholders.

With regard to politics, the greatest hope for the future of the nation, in Garrison's estimation, rested in the career of Henry Clay. In March 1829, he had predicted in the *Journal of the Times* that only death could prevent Clay from being elected president in 1832, and he reasserted this prediction in January 1830, even as he severely criticized Clay, in that same issue of the *Genius*, for his continuing support of colonization as the only viable solution to the evil of slavery.[15] Although Clay was a citizen and representative of a slaveholding state, Garrison admitted that he "cherish[ed] the highest regard" for him. Clay was, in Garrison's estimation, the champion of the "only policy which I believe will raise this country from a state of abject dependence to a state of independent superiority."[16] That policy was, of course, the so-called "American System" which was closely associated with Clay throughout his political career. The "American System" was a form of economic nationalism which sought to use governmental authority to assist and improve all sectors of the economy: industry, agriculture, and commerce — creating an interdependent relationship beneficial to the whole nation.[17] Despite Clay's antipathy toward free blacks, he was, Garrison believed, a politician with integrity who placed the good of the country above self-interest, a statesman with the capacity to lead the nation, a public servant who "has done more for the prosperity of the Union than almost any other man living," and as a leader in the American Colonization Society, a "friend to the cause of emancipation."[18]

As had Thomas Jefferson, a young Henry Clay clerked and read law for several years under the tutelage of George Wythe, who is generally credited with introducing Clay to the inconsistency present in a nation founded on "liberty for all" while dependent on bound labor.[19] Colonization would become, for Clay, the only means for resolving this incongruity. As a political neophyte in 1799, Clay had supported a proposal for gradual emancipation in Kentucky only to be treated as radical agitator by the more seasoned political veterans, and slaveholders, in the state. He lost in that effort while learning, perhaps, an important political lesson and developing a more nuanced (and arguably for the time, more enlightened) attitude about emancipation and colonization than others in southern states. In December 1816, Clay delivered a speech and presided at the meeting which founded the American Colonization Society, and for the rest of his life remained strongly committed to colonization as the best long-term solution to slavery in the United States. Clay believed that slavery was evil and was not afraid to say so in public; he asserted that if it did not already exist in Kentucky he would use "all the force and energy in my power" to prevent its introduction. Clay's support for the American Colonization Society, however, was not founded on the racism that was prevalent among many slaveholders, but on his perception of the real-life experiences of freed blacks in the United States. Like Jefferson, Clay believed that free blacks could not succeed in American society; whites and blacks could not co-exist peacefully. Those freedmen might be nominally free according to the law, but prejudice denied them the privileges that freedom should have provided. Thus, Clay "believed that only colonization would give [freed slaves] a chance to live as free men with dignity."[20] All things considered, however, Garrison's support for Clay may have emerged more from his hatred of Andrew Jackson than his approval of Clay's politics, but his support for Clay was strong, if not consistent with Garrison's abolitionist ideology. In any case, in 1830 Garrison still believed Clay had the potential to redeem the American political system from the corruption threatened by the presidency of Andrew Jackson.

Clay once again repeated his fundamental message about slavery and colonization in an address he delivered to the Kentucky Colonization Society in December 1829, which Garrison reprinted in the *Genius* in January 1830.[21] Garrison then responded to Clay's address in a three part series. He began by again declaring his high regard for Clay and admitting that few people "look forward to his ultimate elevation to the Presidency with more satisfaction than I do." Nevertheless, Garrison did not withhold his criticism for Clay's willingness to condemn slavery as evil while he was unwilling to support its quick destruction. What was worse, Clay did not truly support even gradual emancipation; rather, he accepted conditions that, in Garrison's estimation, "would make slavery eternal." For instance, Clay had argued in his speech that, without either removal or colonization, neither gradual nor immediate emancipation was a wise choice. This was, of course, completely unacceptable for Garrison, but in light of his continued political support for Clay, he granted the Kentucky senator astonishing leeway by suggesting that it was "morally impossible for a slaveholder to reason correctly on the subject of slavery."[22]

Regardless of Clay's continued support of colonization and his apparent blindness with regard to justice for the slave, Garrison still hoped that Clay's political ascent would be accompanied by a personal and national revival. Especially in light of Garrison's withering criticism of President Jackson, he waxed eloquent in the first of his three-part series about Clay: "men of principle ... look up to Mr. Clay as the champion who is destined to save this country from anarchy, corruption and ruin." Furthermore, as a journalist he believed the political system required the nation's newspapers to inform the public opinion which ultimately shaped the political state of the republic. Whether at the local or national levels, even in 1830 Garrison did not regard the political system of the nation as totally debased and beyond redemption; in fact he appeared to see redemption in the near future in the political career of Henry Clay.

Likewise, Garrison did not despair that religion and the churches might yet join and fully participate in the abolitionist struggle. As has already been explained, Garrison believed that religious institutions in the United States were failing to deliver the leadership that they should have provided for the anti-slavery struggle, but he seldom addressed the clergy directly. The *Genius* certainly examined political issues, such as the Virginian Convention, the annexation of Texas, the removal of the Indians, the tariff, local and national political campaigns, as well as temperance and other reform movements with much greater frequency than religion. Nevertheless, Garrison did not lose sight of the critical message churches and religious leaders had a responsibility to assert in the anti-slavery struggle. In several articles he challenged the failure of those who claimed to be religious, yet who were not consistently following the teaching of Christ. For instance, in his first month at the *Genius*, he took the *Christian Register*, a paper "Devoted to Unitarian Christianity" to task for deprecating Garrison's support for immediate emancipation. In December he urged "ye lukewarm, timorous *Christians*" to protest a South Carolina effort to criminalize the practice of teaching slaves to read and write. A few months later, Garrison wondered if a slaveholder could be a Christian. "The two characters differ so widely," he contended, "that I know not how they can unite in one man."[23]

At least twice, however, Garrison vehemently and directly attacked the nation's religious establishments' complicity in slavery. Responding to a letter to the *Genius* about the sexual transgressions of slaveholders, Garrison angrily asked, "What sort of religion is now extant among us?" This was not the religion that Jesus Christ had founded, but rather

> it is a religion, which complacently tolerates open adultery, oppression, robbery, and murder! seldom or never lifting up a warning voice or note of remonstrance

... a religion which is graduated by the corrupt, defective laws of the State, and not the pure, perfect laws of God! ... a religion which has no courage, no faithfulness, no self-denial, deeming it better to give heed unto men than unto God![24]

A month later, for reasons that are not clear, the unforgiving, tempestuous, and aggressive language, which would become Garrison's hallmark, was again on display and targeted those "false ministers of Jesus Christ" who owned slaves themselves. In an article titled "STRANGE INCONSISTENCY," Garrison vigorously railed against the "hair-splitting moralists," especially the "professed follower of a crucified Redeemer" who nevertheless consented "to call the creatures of God *his property*." In particular, Garrison condemned ministers who owned slaves yet continued to "mock heaven with thy much fasting, and thy long prayers, and thy insincere services." They use the Bible, Garrison charged, to claim authority for their actions, but they are none the less "GREAT ROBBERS AND GREAT TYRANTS."[25] Articles about religion as unyielding and implacable as these were not routine, but neither did Garrison apologize for his severe language. Generally, however, he cajoled rather than condemned, hoping conceivably, as with Henry Clay, that a change of heart and a return to right moral teaching was imminent if only they would listen to his pleas.

Meanwhile, if a nationwide change of heart about slavery was going to occur in politics and religion, Garrison behaved as if he believed that the editors, newspapers, and the printing press would point the political and religious leaders of the nation in the right direction. In the *Genius*, Garrison continued to emphasize the important function that newspapers and editors were required to exercise in re-ordering and reforming society. Almost every issue of the *Genius* contained a notice of a new publication or a worthy already-established paper which deserved the attention of the public — especially newspapers that were, in Garrison's opinion, politically or morally correct. Newspapers and magazines for different religious denominations or for particular occupations (such as sailors or firemen), journals of health and literature, and papers for a wide variety of reform issues were recognized, encouraged, and recommended to the public for their enlightenment and benefit.

For instance, the inaugural issue of the *Genius* regretted the departure of John Greenleaf Whittier from the editorship of William Collier's *Boston Manufacturer*, but strongly recommended the paper to those who, like Garrison, were interested in promoting the "American System."[26] William Ladd's *Harbinger of Peace* and the *National Philanthropist*, now edited by William Goodell, often were a source of information for the *Genius* and Garrison regularly commended the value provided and praised their editors. In late September, Garrison wrote brief comments on eight publications which, he believed, deserved the attention of his readers. These papers were variously "very useful and promising," "politically and morally right," "full of promise," "constantly ... enriching [their] readers," filled with "rich treasures," and generally deserving of "notice and patronage" by all. He welcomed these, encouraged others to begin an exchange with the *Genius*, and let all know that he was "ready to interchange civilities, or, if need be, to exercise cudgels with our ancient and honorable fraternity."[27] In the next issue, another group of newspapers were reviewed and complimented, and in future issues Garrison continued to advise his readers that right-minded reform publications were available and should be supported.

In early 1830, Garrison wrote that so many new publications were appearing that he had "half resolved" not to praise them until they had lasted six months. However, he could not withhold immediate praise for the first issue of the *Lynn Record* published by Alonzo Lewis, who was "a rigid moralist ... and an uncompromising enemy of slavery."[28] Even when Garrison published his final edition as co-editor of the *Genius*, he used its columns to acclaim the *New England Review* as it entered its third year, and the reformist *Free Press* of Oswego, New York, as it began its first.[29] During the early decades of the nineteenth century, the vast majority of newspapers "predominantly supported, promoted, and aided political parties," rather than addressing reform issues.[30] As much as this remained largely true and that the political newspapers of the era strongly appealed to political party regulars, in a comparable fashion Garrison was attempting to call together a press community of moralists and reformers. He believed that readers of like-minded reform newspapers and magazines could and should create a communication network to enlighten, inform, and energize American citizens to reform and improve society.

As much as he praised right-minded editors and their publications, neither did Garrison withhold his censure for newspapers that failed either to follow proper editorial policy or to support proper moral strictures. For this reason, in addition to re-printing articles taken from newspaper "exchanges" without comment, Garrison routinely scrutinized, analyzed, re-printed, and commented on exchange articles and editorials from a variety of sources. As did most newspaper publishers of the era, Garrison "exchanged" papers with other editors and publishers across the country. For most of the nineteenth century printers continued a practice begun in the 1700s and were able to exchange their newspapers postage-free via the United States mail system. This was a convenient and effective means of transmitting information across the nation in an era before telegraph and news services.[31] In the same issue in which he reviewed the eight papers discussed above, Garrison took as much space to reprimand the editor of the *Catskill Recorder*, and charged that "his political notions are most offensive to our judgment."[32] He admonished the editor of the *American Traveller* of Boston for being "as hopeless a blockhead as ever ... entered a printing office" and for slandering Garrison as "a libeler of the Declaration of Independence."[33] This was the newspaper which had been rather dismissive about Garrison's Park Street Address four months earlier. For additional impact, Garrison re-printed what he likely expected his readers would believe were shocking and scandalous articles from Southern pro-slavery newspapers accompanied by his own commentary. For instance, an article in the *Columbia* (S.C.) *Telescope* opposed any education for slaves, and the *Augusta Chronicle* condemned "the teaching of negroes the art of setting type"[34] — something to which Garrison would have been particularly sensitive, since setting type was essentially the means of his own education and in a very real sense, for Garrison, the instrument to change the nation.

Beyond the content of newspapers, Garrison also addressed the moral obligations of editors in the conduct of their press. He frequently copied ads about runaways and the rewards posted for their return to additionally underscore the horror of the institution. Special ire was reserved for those editors and publishers, who, Garrison believed, were "ostensibly opposed to slavery," but who nevertheless accepted money to advertise slave sales, such as the *Baltimore American*.[35] In October, Garrison admonished newspaper editors for accepting advertisements for runaway slaves or for slave traders, like Austin Woolfolk. Woolfolk was a notorious and influential slave trader in Baltimore who Garrison frequently targeted for censure. The reason for this special attention on Woolfolk was not only his participation in the slave trade, but also because he had accosted and severely beaten Benjamin Lundy in 1827 for allegedly libeling him in the *Genius*. Woolfolk was found guilty of assault, but fined only one dollar plus costs because Judge Nicholas Brice (the same judge who would preside over Garrison's libel trial in 1830) ruled that Lundy's words had egregiously provoked the attack.[36]

In this particular article, he chastised three newspapers which had each published Woolfolk ads for slavery sales: the *Republican*, *Patriot*, and *Chronicle*. Garrison defended his right to invoke judgment on the actions of his fellow editors as part of his duty (and the duty of all men) "to keep a perpetual supervision over the public press; to applaud what is meritorious, and to condemn what is unjust or licentious." Continuing, Garrison also singled out for especial chastisement the editor of the *Republican*; he was, Garrison charged, a "son of New-England" but nonetheless he regularly published advertisements for slave sales, and then attempted to justify the advertisements by suggesting that some slaves escaped harsh masters as a consequence of their sale. He challenged the editor to "tell me how many victims" had benefited. Nothing justified participation in the slave market and, by Garrison's assessment, editors who accepted slave trade advertisements were no different or better than Woolfolk himself. Both the slave trader and the editors engaged in and cooperated with the slave trade for financial gain, therefore, "both must receive a similar condemnation." Evidently, Garrison's comments found their target when Woolfolk reacted and again accused Lundy of libel. In the next issue, Garrison took Woolfolk to task for his renewed "curses and ... threats to the senior editor of this paper for the insertion of a paragraph which was written by another." He chided the slave trader and asked, "Has he forgotten his alphabet?" and if he could not distinguish between the "L" and the "G" at the end of editorial comments in the *Genius*. Garrison assured Woolfolk that he was not intimidated by his threats and to be certain that there was no confusion defiantly signed the article "W.L.G."[37] Perhaps not knowing that Garrison was as committed to non-violence as the pacifist Quaker, Woolfolk did not attempt to confront or accost him.

Again, a month later, Garrison wondered if all newspaper editors "were so impoverished, that they will do violence to all their notions of equity and republicanism, for the sake of a small recompense." The particular object of his wrath this time was the editor of the *National Intelligencer,* Joseph Gales, who was also a politician, the mayor of Washington, and active in the American Colonization Society. The paper was a leading Whig Party newspaper which had supported John Quincy Adams' administration.[38] To Garrison, however, he was a "specious hypocrite" who dishonored the editorial fraternity.[39] At the other end of the spectrum, in January, Garrison praised the editors of the *Village Record* and *Rochester Observer* for "rare exhibitions of moral principle" because they refused to accept advertisements for local lotteries. They were among the few, Garrison claimed, who understood "the moral responsibility which rests upon their station."[40] The role of the editor in maintaining the nation's morality and righteousness was an exacting and demanding responsibility, which Garrison was unafraid to bear for himself and unyieldingly to demand from others. Since his days at *The Free Press* in Newburyport through all his editorial experiences before the *Genius* and now in Baltimore, Garrison's advocacy of the editor's ethical and moral responsibilities to society was a frequent and consistent message. In early 1830, however, as demanding as an editor must be, Garrison still remained a voice calling the political and religious institutions, which were responsible for defining and defending social morality, to step up to the task, and not the source of that morality itself.

These commentaries about newspaper content and editorial obligations were sometimes part of the *Genius*'s editorial section, sometimes part of a separate section titled "NEWSPAPERS" or "NOTICE OF PERIODICALS," but most often these items were found in the "BLACK LIST" section of the paper. Lundy had begun this special column in 1821 and used it occasionally to report some of the horrors of slavery, although by 1829 he appeared to have largely abandoned its use. The column did not appear in the *Genius* at all for the entire year of 1828. While Lundy was not averse to using strong language and shining a light on the realities of slave life, he was, according to Merton Dillon, more interested in finding a way to end slavery than "in merely condemning it or arousing hatred of slaveholders."[41] Consequently, the potential incitement triggered by the column did not appeal to his Quaker temperament, although he did certainly contribute to the column on occasion. Garrison, on the other hand, was less inclined to avoid provocation and the "Black List" section in the *Genius* certainly cohered with his perceived obligation to render judgment regarding editorial responsibility and morality. As a result, the column was revived with the first co-edited issue of the *Genius*. To further draw attention to it, the column was headed by a woodcut of a nearly naked black man in shackles, on one knee, as if he was appealing for mercy, and encircled above with the caption "AM I NOT A MAN AND A BROTHER?" This image originally appeared in china made by Joseph Wedgewood in England in 1787, became very popular in the anti-slavery movement, and was duplicated on pottery, jewelry and needlework, which was sold to raise money for the anti-slavery cause.[42] The precise nature of the column was broadcast beneath the image, "HORRIBLE NEWS — DOMESTIC AND FOREIGN." Each item found in the section was intended to alarm his regular readers, to incite reaction among the enemies of abolition, and to stimulate resolve among abolition's supporters to continue the struggle.

The focus of the "BLACK LIST" column generally highlighted the horrible crimes of southern slavery or castigated the unscrupulous behavior of anyone who supported the slave trade in any fashion. For instance, in late September the column questioned the effectiveness of new regulations in New Orleans to restrict the international slave trade while the trade was "carried on briskly" according to newspaper reports; described the hanging of slaves accused of engaging in an insurrection; reprinted "verbatim" an advertisement for a runaway slave written by his obviously illiterate white owner; and published a poem written about a chain-gang of slaves seen being driven through a Virginia town. In October, the "Black List" included a story about a Georgian state plan to purchase a few dozen men and women slaves and use them and "their increase" as a long term project to maintain the state's roads; a report of cannibalism on a slave ship captured by a Dutch war-sloop; and several advertisements from southern newspapers about slave families which could "be sold together ... [or] ... *separate*, to suit the purchasers."[43]

Without doubt, however, the most famous incident associated with the "Black List" column during Garrison's stay in Baltimore came from an unlikely source — his own home town of Newburyport. In early November, Garrison led the column with news about the domestic slave trade, which "continues to be pursued with unabated alacrity," especially between the ports of Baltimore and New Orleans. He promised more information on one ship in particular in the next issue; that ship was owned by Newburyport native, Francis Todd — "So much for New-England principle!"[44] In the next issue of the *Genius*, Garrison expanded on the incident, as promised. He expressed shock, not because slaves were being transported to the Deep South, but because they were transported by a New Englander. Shippers clearly had the legal right to carry whatever cargo they liked, including slaves, within American waters; but, for Garrison, carrying slaves was nefarious business whether it occurred along the coast of Africa or along the coast of the United States. He called Todd and the ship's captain, Nicholas Brown, "enemies of their own species — highway robbers and murderers," who should be sentenced to solitary confinement for life. He also insinuated that Todd routinely carried slave cargo and wrote, "It was always a mystery in Newburyport how Mr. Todd contrived to make profitable voyages to New Orleans." He claimed that the ship "carried off *seventy-five* slaves, chained in a narrow space between decks" and would have taken another seventy-five more but "another hard-hearted shipmaster underbid him in the price of passage." Finally, he requested that his old master, Ephraim Allen, reprint this information in the *Newburyport Herald*, not, Garrison asserted, to demean Todd, but "to enlighten the public mind in that quarter" about the internal traffic in slaves.[45]

Allen did not re-print the article, and did not comment on the affair for six months. A passing reference to the incident appeared in April 1830 when Allen quoted a brief notice from the *United States Gazette*. The notice discussed the "discontinuance" of the *Genius of Universal Emancipation* as a weekly newspaper and its expected emergence as a monthly pamphlet. In addition, it reported that "Mr. Garrison has been in the hands of the law, for certain freedom of expression in the paper, touching treatment of slaves" and concluded with praise for Garrison as "a gentleman of talents, a vigorous writer, and ardently attached to the true cause of freedom."[46] Allen did not add any words of his own at the time. A month later, using well over a full column of print, Allen finally commented. He praised his former apprentice for fighting both slavery and the internal traffic in slaves, which he agreed deserved "the reprobation of every man who dares call himself free, just, or humane."

Notwithstanding this praise, he took Garrison to task for an "act of rashness and indiscretion" against "the character and conduct of a merchant of this town." Without naming Todd, Allen reprimanded Garrison for slandering the reputation of a man who was "not, and would never be guilty of joining in [the slave trade]" and suggested that Todd's willingness to challenge the accusation in court was evidence that he was "just and benevolent." Allen also acknowledged that he had been requested to re-print "the obnoxious publication" but he refrained on account of fear of his own prosecution.[47]

The threat of prosecution, however, had not been a concern in Garrison's decision to publish the article about Todd's transportation of slaves. He believed that he had only written the facts of the case as was his duty, nothing more or less. Todd disagreed, and he accused both Garrison and Lundy of libeling him in an effort to destroy his good reputation. In January, a short notice in the *Genius* reported that the editors of the paper were being sued for $5,000 for an "alleged libel published in our Black List Department." Garrison summarily dismissed the suit with a Latin proverb "Qui non vetat peccare cum possit, jubet" ("He who does not prevent a crime when he can, encourages it").[48] But Todd was just as serious about the justice of his legal action, and the case was sent to the Baltimore grand jury for indictment in February.[49]

Without doubt, the change in tone and the more aggressive style that Garrison brought to the *Genius* contributed to Todd's decision to seek legal redress. Garrison had quickly succeeded in his effort to stimulate controversy. Lundy had been tolerated in Baltimore, according to Oliver Johnson, because of his mild tone. That toleration had begun to weaken before Garrison arrived principally as a consequence of increased white fear about the influence of free blacks and planter anxiety about a perceived growth in abolitionist sentiment. Under Garrison's management, however, the *Genius* became "absolutely intolerable to the people of Baltimore and the surrounding region." Johnson also quoted Garrison proudly proclaiming "My doctrine of immediate emancipation so alarmed and excited the people everywhere, that where friend Lundy would get one new subscriber I would knock a dozen off."[50] This may have been something of an overstatement by Garrison, but clearly the re-birth of an anti-slavery newspaper in Maryland, especially one published with a bellicose, belligerent and contentious co-editor, coalesced with a growing and powerful black community in Baltimore to encourage an assertive and aggressive response among the white community. Lundy's willingness to support colonization allowed many white Baltimoreans to endure the *Genius* before Garrison joined him in September 1829. Afterward, Garrison's aggressive rhetoric and his increasing antagonism toward colonization made the paper a target.

Another important development that motivated action against Garrison in 1830 was, like the *Genius*, print related: the publication of *An Appeal to the Colored Citizens of the World* by David Walker. The pamphlet was published at the same time Garrison began his association with Lundy, September 1829. Walker condemned white America, urged blacks in America to end their continued submissive behavior and to join together in independent and aggressive resistance, including violence and rebellion if necessary. It was clearly a call to militant action and sent shock waves across the nation.[51] Rather deftly, Walker circulated the pamphlet by using, among other tactics, black sailors to carry it to southern ports along the east coast. In early December 1829, sixty copies of the incendiary pamphlet were seized by officials in Savannah, Georgia, and by the end of the month the state legislature passed a law to quarantine black sailors entering Georgia ports.[52] The furor created by the pamphlet's distribution contributed to prosecutions for inciting insurrections against anyone, black or white, found with it in their possession. Furthermore, several southern states enacted laws which barred the distribution of this kind of "seditious literature," as well as making it a crime to teach a slave to read and write.[53] For instance, an extract of a letter from South Carolina re-printed in the *Boston Commercial Gazette* reported approvingly that a black sailor who had distributed five copies of *Walker's Appeal*, was tried for violating such a law, and sentenced to a year in prison and fined $2000 for distributing the "most outrageous and incendiary publication, calculated and intended to do great harm in the slave holding states."[54] Such was the power of Walker's pamphlet and the fear it engendered in the South.

Although much about David Walker's life must be pieced together from tenuous historical treads, he apparently came by his passionate appeal and appreciation for the onerous status of blacks in the United States from personal experience. According to Peter P. Hinks, Walker was born a free black in Wilmington, North Carolina, to a slave father but free mother, probably around 1796. Despite his status as a freeman, in Wilmington, he undoubtedly witnessed first-hand the brutality of southern slavery; meanwhile, he also developed a strong attachment to Methodism, to which he remained devoted throughout his life. Around 1810, he moved to Charleston, South Carolina, and in 1817 joined the local African Methodist Episcopal (AME) Church. Significantly, this church was at the heart of local controversy in which whites attempted to harass the church and force it to disband. The controversy eventually led to the Denmark Vesey conspiracy of 1822; if Walker was not directly involved in the rebellion, he was certainly familiar with the dispute and its consequences. Walker left Charleston after Vesey's rebellion and found his way to Boston. From 1825 until his death in 1830, he was listed as a Boston resident in the annual city directories. By 1827, he had opened a used-clothing store, married a local woman, Eliza Butler, and became a leading activist for the black community. He was the local agent for *Freedom's Journal*, the first black newspaper in the United States, and one of the founders of nation's first black political organization, the Massachusetts General Colored Association.[55] Although little can be found to directly connect Walker and Garrison, given the relatively small size of Boston's black community and Garrison's connections with that community, as well as Walker's relationship with *Freedom's Journal* and his obvious appreciation for the value of the press, it is hard to believe that they never met.

The most extended remarks Garrison made about Walker's *Appeal* appeared in a brief article in the second issue of *The Liberator*. He deprecated "the spirit and tendency" of the pamphlet; "vengeance belongs to God" not to man, and, Garrison asserted, God will deliver it in His own time, not Walker's. Nevertheless, he also denied the American people's right to denounce Walker's call for vengeance, although Garrison believed that since "we do not preach rebellion ... but submission and peace" he retained that right. He rejected violence as a solution to even the most egregious problems, but asserted that most Americans embraced violence, celebrated violence every Fourth of July, and encouraged violence to overthrow tyranny around the world. Walker had simply adopted "their own language" and, Garrison concluded, "if any people were ever justified in throwing off the yoke of their tyrants, the slaves are that people."[56] Nevertheless, discussion of the *Appeal* was frequently the subject of articles written for *The Liberator* in the first several months of publication, some which included brief commentary or asides from Garrison.[57] Perhaps because the early financial and practical success of his paper was significantly dependent on the support of Black communities in several cities, but especially Boston, Garrison tempered his deprecation of what he called the "general spirit" of the *Appeal*. On January 1, 1831, he criticized it but also called it "one of the most remarkable productions of the age" and on January 29 he did likewise while acknowledging that it contained "many valuable truths and seasonable warnings."

At the *Genius*, however, although Garrison was undoubtedly aware of Walker's pamphlet, he withheld any comment on the *Appeal* until January 1830, when efforts to suppress the publication were already well underway. In a "Black List" article, Garrison reported on the alarm the pamphlet had caused in the Virginia House of Delegates and the Georgia Legislature. In both states, fear over the *Appeal* provoked immediate confiscation of the pamphlet and widespread panic. "We have had this pamphlet on our table for some time past," Garrison reported, and while he disapproved its circulation, he also stated that he admired "the bravery and intelligence of its author." Furthermore, he granted that there was good reason for the alarm and was not surprised "at it effects upon our sensitive southern brethren." Again in February, Garrison reported on the controversy Walker created by noticing that as a consequence of the publication of the *Appeal,* a law was passed in Virginia to prohibit *"instruction of free negroes, mulattoes, or slaves,* either in religious or secular knowledge, under the most aggravated penalties." Once more, in March, reaction to the *Appeal*'s circulation and its seizure in Kentucky were discussed.[58] Garrison's remarks on the *Appeal* in the *Genius,* while always rejecting the use of violence, did not fail to call attention to the culpability of the system of slavery itself to the rationale behind slave insurrections. Southern governors and legislators, he asserted, had good reason to be alarmed by Walker's *Appeal* since rebellion was the natural consequence of tyranny.

Against this backdrop, Francis Todd's libel case against Garrison and Lundy moved forward. Todd was genuinely offended by the articles in the *Genius* and especially by the inference that carrying slaves was the source of his financial success. However, the decision to prosecute Garrison likely reflected a collection of developments in Maryland at the time: the resurgent *Genius,* the growth of an independence black community in Baltimore, and concern about the repercussions of Walker's *Appeal.* Moreover, it seems reasonable to conclude that these factors influenced the decision to change the indictment against Garrison and Lundy from civil to criminal. Todd's lawyers had initially filed a civil suit asking for $5,000 in damages, but on February 19, a Baltimore grand jury indicted Garrison and Lundy with the criminal charge of "contriving and unlawfully, wickedly, and maliciously intending, to hurt, injure and vilify ... [Todd] ... and against the peace, government and dignity of the State." These charges not only exposed the editors to criminal prosecution but to possible jail sentences as well. The case was scheduled for trial on March 1.[59] Criminal prosecution for an alleged libel of a private citizen was a highly unusual step and further evidence, for Henry Mayer, that Garrison's trial "actually bears the hallmarks of a politically inspired prosecution."[60] Taking all the circumstances into account, it is difficult to dispute this conclusion.

Lundy was out of town when the indictment was returned by the grand jury; as a result, his trial was postponed until June. Eventually, the charges against Lundy were dismissed because there was ample evidence that he was not in Baltimore when the offending article was actually published and therefore he could not be held criminally culpable.[61] However, it took some time for the dismissal to be declared official and during those months, Lundy believed that the *Genius,* which he had restarted as a monthly in April 1830, continued to be intimidated by the threat of legal action and therefore had to be restrained in its editorial commentary. After his case was disposed, Lundy accused the Court itself, in an article in the *Genius* titled "The Farce Ended," of using the threat of prosecution and then purposely delaying the trial as an effort to bully and silence him.[62]

Thus, when the trial did convene in March 1830, Garrison was the only defendant; he appeared before Judge Nicholas Brice and was defended by Charles Mitchell, a Baltimore attorney who agreed to represent Garrison pro bono. Brice was the chief judge of the Criminal Court of Baltimore County and a longtime proponent of state regulations to limit the manumission of slaves. He believed that the process of emancipation was moving too quickly, especially in Baltimore, leading to an increase in crime, and threatening the safety of the city.[63] At trial, Mitchell believed that he only had to show that Todd's ship had indeed carried a cargo of slaves to Georgia to prove the truth of the alleged offending statement. Furthermore, the indictment against Garrison did not reference the section of the "Black List" article which insinuated that Todd's financial success resulted from his willingness to carry slaves as cargo. That insinuation would have been more difficult to defend, but since it was not part of the official indictment, Mitchell believed it could not be used by the prosecution during the trial. Over Mitchell's strenuous objections, however, Judge Brice ruled that the jury could not only convict on the terms in the indictment, but that "they might also derive 'auxiliary aid' from the remainder of the article, in making up their verdict." It took only fifteen minutes to return a guilty verdict. On April 3 the Court imposed a fifty dollar fine plus court costs on Garrison.[64] Since he was unable to pay such a large sum, Garrison had no alternative but imprisonment and on April 17, 1830, he entered the Baltimore Jail.[65]

By the time of the trial, Garrison and Lundy had agreed to dissolve their partnership and the last joint issue of the *Genius* was published March 5, 1830. In his brief final editorial commentary, Garrison faulted "adverse circumstances" for ending the partnership. He had no regrets about his contentious language. "Many have censured me for my severity," he wrote, "but, thank God! none have stigmatized me with luke-warmness." In addition, he promised that "my pen cannot remain idle, nor my voice be suppressed" as long as slavery plagued the nation; he did not intend to remain silent for long. In a much longer commentary, Lundy remarked on two causes for ceasing publication of the *Genius*. First was the same problem that had plagued the *Genius* since it began — a lack of patronage. Despite his best efforts and the added services of "two talented writers" to assist him, Lundy was unable to find enough subscribers to sustain the paper. The second cause was "persecution, in some of its worst forms ... meted out with unsparing hands." Personal assaults, threats, and libel suits were, according to Lundy, carried out with the intent of "breaking down our spirits, and destroying the establishment." With regard to the latter, these efforts had worked.

Lundy absolved Garrison of any responsibility for the paper's demise. He admitted that in his absence, Garrison had printed some articles "that did not entirely meet my approbation" but stressed that no actions had been taken with any malicious intent. Lundy praised Garrison's integrity and virtue, and wished him happiness and prosperity in the future. But to those who might find comfort in the paper's failure, Lundy proclaimed that he was not yet prepared to abandon the cause. The *Genius* would soon return, as a monthly. The paper, he promised, "will exclusively treat upon the subject of emancipation," the present editor of the "Ladies Department" will continue her contributions, and "the character of the editor" will remain the same as it was while the paper was "under his exclusive direction." The passion Garrison aroused was perhaps too much for the gentle Quaker, and without Garrison he hoped to return the *Genius* to its past style as a remonstrative, but less belligerent and more reconciliatory, publication.[66]

For his part, Garrison was fast losing any interest in reconciliation and quickly coming to believe that aggressive verbal confrontation was the only hope for reforming American society and, especially, for abolishing slavery. If Garrison had hoped in September 1829 that the tide in the nation was turning against slavery and that a change of heart in politics and religion seemed imminent, in April 1830 he clearly had reason to be despondent. As he entered the jail which would be home for the next 49 days, however, Garrison "was neither cast down nor dismayed."[67] He saw no reason to apologize for his words or his editorial decisions at the *Genius*, and he knew that his cause was just. Garrison willingly embraced the role of martyr but the sense of victory he celebrated as he entered prison was not only spiritual, it was practical as well. If the printing press at the *Genius of Universal Emancipation* was not to be his engine of change, Garrison had at least shown that fuel to stoke that engine was abundant. And, if politics and religion continued to be unwilling to lead the fight to end slavery, then perhaps it was necessary that the printing press be obliged to carry on the battle alone.

On April 17, 1830, Warden David W. Hudson accepted William Lloyd Garrison as the newest prisoner in the Baltimore City Jail. "No man ever went to prison," his children wrote, "with a lighter heart or cleaner conscience."[68] In heroic fashion, Garrison penciled a defiant poem on his prison wall "the next morning after his incarceration" to demonstrate that his spirit had not been destroyed.

> High walls, and huge, the *body* may confine,
>   And iron grates obstruct the prisoner's gaze
> And massive bolts may baffle his design
>   And vigilant keepers watch his devious ways:
> Yet scorns th' immortal *mind* this base control!
>   No chains can bind it, and no cell enclose.
> Swifter than light, it flies from pole to pole
>   And in a flash from earth to heaven it goes!
> It leaps from mount to mount — from vale to vale
>   It wanders, plucking honeyed fruits and flowers;
> It visits home, to hear the fire-side tale,
>   Or in sweet converse pass the joyous hours.
> 'Tis up before the sun, roaming afar
>   And in its watches wearies every star![69]

Unlike most prisoners in the jail, Garrison had considerable freedom to roam about within the prison walls and often took his meals with the warden's family. He also took the time to acquaint himself with his fellow prisoners, took an interest in their status, and aided some of them in writing petitions for clemency. When slave traders came to buy slaves that had been brought to the jail for attempting to escape, Garrison chided the traders, and was unabashed about admonishing them for participation in the sinful activity. Because of this, as long as Garrison remained at the jail, Austin Woolfolk, Benjamin Lundy's adversary and Baltimore's most notorious slave trader, did not visit the jail, as had previously been an almost daily habit.[70] For Garrison, Woolfolk's absence was a minor victory, and perhaps the first of many. He understood the potential power in the image of innocence jailed and, without doubt, he was convinced that the injustice meted out against him by the city's attorney and Justice Brice could provide powerful stimulus for the anti-slavery movement.

From jail, Garrison wrote to Harriet Farnham Horton, a childhood friend in Newburyport. She was the daughter of Martha Farnham, who owned the house in which Garrison was born in Newburyport and who was both Fanny Garrison's landlady and good friend. He told her that he was tired of life in the southern states, because slavery had corrupted everything. "It rests," he wrote, "on every herb, and every tree, and every field, and on the people and the morals." He yearned to return home to New England, "that paradise of our fallen world." Regarding his imprisonment, he joked that he was "as snug as a robin in his cage; but I sing as often, and quite as well, as I did before my wings were clipped." In all seriousness, he also wrote, "the tyranny of the Court has triumphed over every principle of justice and even over the law" and he promised to forward a "copy of my trial" so she could judge for herself.[71]

Garrison's "song" and the "copy of my trial" was the result of the first task he set for himself while in jail: to write and publish a pamphlet describing his trial — ever ready as he was to use the printing press to teach and enlighten. The result was an eight-page document he titled, "A Brief Sketch of the Trial of William Lloyd Garrison, for an alleged libel on Francis Todd, of Massachusetts" which Friend Lundy printed and began circulating in Baltimore around the beginning of May. Garrison then sent his "sketch" to editors around the nation and encouraged them to publish it as well.[72]

The pamphlet, of course, was not a transcript of the trial but rather Garrison's own assessment of how the trial was conducted. It began by calling attention to what he believed was the most fundamental issue of the affair, press freedom. "It is a trite remark," Garrison wrote,

> that whatever relates to the freedom of the press, is intimately connected with the rights of the people. Every new prosecution for libel, therefore (however insignificant in itself), may be viewed as a test, how far that freedom has been restricted by power on the one hand, or perverted by licentiousness on the other.

The pamphlet then described the details of the trial and Garrison demonstrated how power in the hands of corrupt authorities, like Judge Brice, could be used to deny freedom to any editor who did nothing more than have the temerity to publish the truth. Brice, he charged, had denied a proper defense and instructed a jury to use illegitimate, irrelevant, and emotional testimony in order to ensure a guilty verdict. This was, for Garrison, an "abhorrent and atrocious" violation of the Constitution which threatened not only him, but the security of a free press for all newspaper editors, as well as free speech for all citizens. Embracing his martyrdom, he conceded that "a few white victims must be sacrificed to open the eyes of the nation" and that he was "willing to be persecuted, imprisoned, and bound for advocating African rights." Finally, Garrison pledged that he had only just begun to expose the guilt of slaveholders, slave traders, and those who support or protect them, wherever they might live. The trial, conviction, and imprisonment would not intimidate him, nor muffle his voice. There was much more to be done and he promised, "I am only in the *alphabet* of my task; time shall perfect a useful work."[73]

The pamphlet was intended to draw attention in particular to the dangerous consequence posed by libel suits against the liberty of the press, especially in the hands of slave-power sympathizers. In fact, it was not necessary to look any further than Lundy's renewed *Genius* to see the reality of the threat. In the second issue of the new series Lundy reported the results of the libel suit and Garrison's imprisonment. The chilling effect of the prosecution meant that "strange at it may seem to our friends, elsewhere, the *truth* cannot be told, here, relative to the accursed traffic in human flesh, without danger of insult, abuse, and bonds!!!" Furthermore, he declared that his *"press is now muzzled."* Because the physical printing of the *Genius* was not done by Lundy himself and he did not want to expose his printers to potential legal entanglements, he felt compelled to postpone his desire "to expose the conduct of certain persons in this case" until some future issue.[74] Furthermore, Lundy may have been reluctant to be too outspoken since his own trial for libel in the Todd incident was still pending, and would not be dismissed for another month. With publication of the next month's issue, however, the situation had changed. Lundy had now outfitted a printing office, so the paper was now "entirely under his own control" and he was less circumspect in his criticism. He chastised local "despots and oligarches" who claim to love liberty, but who nevertheless have, in both public and private communications, "resorted to personal abuse and legal persecution" in an attempt to intimidate him and destroy the *Genius*. Regardless of their efforts, he pledged that *"my humble labors shall not cease."*[75] But even with his own press and with the freedom to speak his mind, the temperate Quaker could not duplicate the aggressive and antagonistic qualities which Garrison's voice had represented.

Meanwhile, Garrison was carefully planning to use his imprisonment as part of the battle against slavery. Through his pamphlet, Lundy's efforts at the *Genius*, and Garrison's personal correspondence, news of his story and incarceration spread. In June, Lundy reported that "more than an hundred voices have been raised — more than an hundred periodical works have denounced this attack upon ... our proper editorial privileges."[76] The numbers were likely an exaggeration, but there certainly was widespread coverage of the incident and trial. The *Philadelphia Inquirer* reported Garrison's imprisonment and asserted that "the times are out of joint when a philanthropist, in a laudable endeavor to abolish from our national escutcheon the stain of slavery, is sent to prison for his pains."[77] After learning about Garrison's fate, the *Nantucket Inquirer* published a long editorial denouncing slavery as a "great evil, and ought not to exist among a race of intelligent beings." Slaveholders' power and influence in the United States — a republic, which proclaimed "to be the asylum of the oppressed and the sanctuary of Liberty" — had become so sturdy, the editor asserted, that not only were millions "groaning in bondage" but those who spoke for their release had become "an object of persecution." Finally, the editorial reported the actions in Baltimore and asked rhetorically, "Is this our boasted liberty? Is this the freedom on an American press?"[78] Garrison himself would be hard-pressed to compose a more aggressive or scathing commentary.

Exactly how many editorials were as strongly supportive of Garrison as these two is difficult to determine because many newspapers of the era are not extant for examination. Some may have been as brief as the *Mechanics Free Press* of Philadelphia, which limited its response to two sentences. It noted Garrison's imprisonment for denunciation of the "inhuman traffic" in slaves, labeled the punishment a flagrant attack against "the palladium of our dearest rights — the liberty of the press" and regretted that it could not devote more space to the issue.[79] The *Commercial Advertiser* in New York City, the *Portsmouth Journal*, and the *Schenectady Cabinet* were among the many which either re-published a report of Garrison's trial and prison sentence or provided a brief commentary expressing shock at Garrison's plight as well as support for both an end to slavery and for freedom of the press.[80]

Others may have been only marginally supportive. For instance, Garrison wrote directly to Joseph Buckingham of the *Boston Courier,* who was well acquainted with Garrison and who had published his letters in the past. Buckingham himself had been tried for libel in his press at least four times in the 1820s; he claimed that his trials, between 1822 and 1824, were financially and emotionally costly, but were productive nonetheless. The trials helped to change Massachusetts law to allow the truth to be used as defense against charges of an allegedly libelous statement and thus helped to sustain "the freedom and independence of the press."[81] Garrison may have expected him to be especially sympathetic. "I salute you from the walls of my prison" Garrison began, and he again joked about his situation, noting that among the benefits of his current status was that he paid no rent. Buckingham gave Garrison more than a few sentences, but hardly a fulsome level of support. He wrote that some may describe Garrison's actions and words as imprudent, but all must still "give him credit for high and honorable motives, and feel a touch of sympathy for his fate." No word was offered, however, about the threat Garrison's imprisonment posed to a free press. Nevertheless, at Garrison's request, Buckingham printed "A Card" to Francis Todd in which Garrison attacked his fellow-townsman once again for using his ship to transport "the wretched victims of slavery." Garrison asked Todd to put himself, his wife and his children in the place of the slave to be sold at public auction and forcibly separated for life. In closing Garrison once again accused Todd of benefiting from "the fruits of your crime."[82] This was the most libelous element of Garrison's attack on Todd, but Buckingham must have felt secure that the laws of Massachusetts now protected freedom of the press more adequately than the laws of Maryland.

Besides Buckingham, other Bostonians were also aware of Garrison's imprisonment. Oliver Johnson, a fellow printer and future partner, who happened to be in Boston around this time, reported on the reaction of some of the city's clergy. Johnson was only four years younger than Garrison, but was "full of a boy's enthusiasm for my hero," although the two had yet to meet. He was in Boston pursuing his own printing career and frequently visited the Cornhill book store where newspapers from around the nation were available. Among the regular visitors to the store were many of Boston's clergy, including Lyman Beecher. Johnson recalled listening carefully to conversations about Garrison's trial. Few of them expressed more than "a qualified sympathy" for Garrison; in fact, most viewed "the new champion of the slave" as a "fanatic." None, Johnson reported, seemed to appreciate the "injustice and shame" of imprisoning someone for devotion to the anti-slavery cause.[83] Johnson's recollections at least confirmed that the news of Garrison's trial and imprisonment was encouraging discussion about slavery and emancipation; while a full appreciation of the crisis was lacking, public attention and public sentiment was being stimulated, which is, of course, exactly what Garrison wanted.

At the *Newburyport Herald*, Ephraim Allen's response differed little from the general reaction in the *Boston Courier*. Allen commended Garrison's "pure purposes and unshaken courage" and agreed that a free press must be allowed to speak out against the slave trade. However, Allen argued that Garrison's statements about Todd had gone too far, and he concluded that, "we cannot, in our real friendship to him, praise him" for his statements, nor protest the injustice of the court's decision.[84] In truth, Allen's "real friendship" for Garrison have not have been as strong as his friendship with Todd, who was a prominent citizen of Newburyport and as ship-owner may have had commercial connections with Allen. In 1827, Allen and several Newburyport citizens had organized a business in seal fur and sent "vessels round Cape Horn, to cruise among the seal island in the Pacific Ocean."[85] It is also interesting to note that Todd had been a member of the Newburyport Debating Club and therefore likely friends with Caleb Cushing.[86] The old boys' network which had excluded Garrison at the end of his apprenticeship in 1825 was still alive and well in 1830.

Garrison responded to his ex-master's comments in a very long letter which Allen, without comment, published in full. After thanking Allen for his words of praise and for all the kindnesses Garrison had received from Allen over the years, he dissected Allen's comments almost line by line to demonstrate its inaccuracies and inconsistencies. For instance, Garrison argued that if the slave trade was deplorable, as Allen acknowledged it certainly was, then undoubtedly Todd's "occasional transportation of slaves" was just as abhorrent as Austin Woolfolk's regular participation in the trade. Slave trading did not suddenly become acceptable because someone only participated "irregularly," Garrison declared. What was more, Allen had also failed to inform his readers that at the trial Garrison's attorney had proved the truth of the supposed libel. Consequently, Allen had left his readers with the impression that Garrison had indeed slandered an innocent man.

Perhaps most importantly, Allen had misunderstood the reason for Garrison's plea to editors to publicize his trial and imprisonment. He was not seeking the kind of praise which Allen had extended, but truly believed that the trial was a "flagrant infringement upon the liberty of the press ... and dangerous to the freedom of public discussion." He was calling upon newspaper editors to examine the case and "vindicate their prerogative" before similar actions were taken against them. For his own part, Garrison proclaimed his intention to remain stubborn and dogmatic about slavery, intemperance, and war — three issues that were a curse on the nation and contrary to Christian teaching. He would not remain silent, because now was the time "to elicit the sneers of the malevolent, to excite the suspicion of the cold-hearted, to offend the timidity of the wavering, to disturb the repose of the lethargic." He must, and will, continue to be vehement and uncompromising because the times have created hard-hearted individuals who can no longer be "melted by the rays of humanity" but which "require a ponderous sledge and a powerful arm to break them to pieces."[87] Clearly, if anything had been accomplished while he was on trial in Baltimore, it was to reinvigorate Garrison's zeal and set him on the final course toward demonstrating the power of the press to alter society, regardless of political or religious intransigence.

During the months of co-editorship at the *Genius of Universal Emancipation*, much more was on trial in Baltimore than a case of personal libel against Garrison. Before the proceedings in the courtroom, he had prosecuted the political and religious institutions of the nation and his own verdict found them generally deficient in performing their duties to the citizens of a democratic republic. Garrison also searched for evidence of moral content and behavior, which he believed was a fundamental responsibility of the printer's trade, from the editors of the public presses and newspapers — most often with limited success. After his own conviction and sentencing, from the Baltimore jail, Garrison placed the United States system of justice, the Constitution's guarantee of free expression, the nation's political and religious institutions, and even the concept of truth on trial before the American public.

Seven

"And I will be heard"

WRITING FROM JAIL IN BALTIMORE on June 1 Garrison concluded his letter to Ephraim Allen by promising "whether liberated or not, my pen shall not remain idle."[1] In fact, his liberation was being arranged as he wrote; on June 5, 1830, before his letter even reached Newburyport, he was released from jail. One of the most important results of Garrison's pamphlet about his trial was that it came to the attention of the successful New York businessman, Arthur Tappan. Along with his brother Lewis, Tappan had provided financial assistance for many benevolent organizations, although Arthur had turned down Benjamin Lundy's appeal for financial assistance in 1828. In addition to their considerable commercial success, the brothers were driven by their Calvinist faith to promote and provide financial support for moral reform in American society. After reading Garrison's *Brief Sketch* in Lundy's renewed but monthly *Genius*, he wrote to Lundy that he had read the pamphlet "with that deep feeling of abhorrence of slavery and its abettors which every one must feel who is capable of appreciating the blessings of liberty." Consequently, he authorized Lundy to draw on his account for $100 to pay Garrison's fine and court costs, as well as another $100 to assist Lundy and Garrison in re-establishing the *Genius* because "such a paper is much needed to hold up to the American freemen, in all its naked deformity, the subject of slavery as it now exists in our country."[2]

Arthur Tappan's generosity did set Garrison free, but it was unlikely that he would have remained jailed much longer, since at least two other sources were prepared to come to his aid. Oliver Johnson reported that Garrison's political favorite, Henry Clay, at the behest of John Greenleaf Whittier, was "probably getting ready" to effect Garrison's release.[3] Whittier confirmed his effort to elicit Clay's assistance in correspondence published in *The Liberator* in 1864. He had written to Clay to apprise him of Garrison's incarceration, to remind him that in 1829 Garrison was the first editor in New England to nominate Clay for the presidency, and to plead for Clay's assistance in freeing Garrison from jail. Whittier received a letter in reply from Clay informing him that he had written to a friend in Baltimore, Hezekiah Niles, publisher of *Niles' Register*, and instructed him to arrange Garrison's release. Clay learned, however, that Tappan had already paid Garrison's fine and that his "liberation had been effected without the aid he would have otherwise given." Whittier, like Garrison, was ambivalent about Clay and expressed regret that both he, and by implication Garrison, later had to chastise Clay for his sentiments about slavery. It was "always done more in sorrow than in anger," he wrote in 1864, and "with a profound regret that one ... endowed with such wonderful gifts, should allow his great influence to be felt in support of a system which his reason and conscience condemned."[4] In addition to Tappan and Clay, when Garrison arrived back in Boston after his release, he found a check for $100 at the post office from Ebenezer Dole of Hallowell, Maine. The check had been sent to Baltimore and then forwarded to Boston by Lundy. Dole was Garrison's distant cousin who had acquired some wealth in Maine; after he heard about his cousin's plight, he decided to offer financial assistance. This was the first of several generous gifts Dole made to Garrison and the antislavery cause.[5]

After his release, Garrison set out immediately for Newburyport, stopping along the way in New York and Boston. The purpose of his trip was twofold, first, to collect additional information for the civil suit still pending with Todd and second, to attempt to secure financial support for reestablishing the *Genius* on a weekly basis. Lundy prepared a prospectus, dated June 7, 1830, titled "To The Friends of the Anti-Slavery Cause," for Garrison to give to potential supporters. The prospectus proposed that Lundy and Garrison "make another effort" to continue the *Genius,* because "we believe that our cause is fast gaining ground; and that *one* such periodical, at least, faithfully and fearlessly devoted thereto, is absolutely necessary, to expose the enormities of the slave system." Furthermore, they promised that the renewed paper would be dignified in tone, more tolerant of its opponents, and present "more of a *literary* character than formerly."[6] In New York, Garrison paid a visit to Arthur Tappan. Tappan's brother, Lewis, was also present at the meeting and later recalled that Garrison presented himself with "buoyant spirit, and countenance beaming with conscious rectitude, [that] attracted the attention of all."[7] Arthur Tappan was impressed by Garrison's reform ideals and his personal charm and, although he made no additional donation at that time, in

Seven: "And I will be heard"

August he would give Garrison $100, which was eventually used to help launch *The Liberator*.[8] Joseph Buckingham reported Garrison's brief visit to Boston as he passed through on his way to Newburyport. He also wrote that the American Colonization Society should be ashamed of itself for not paying Garrison's fines, and for allowing him "to go to jail for fighting their battles ... if this be a specimen of the philanthropy of these honorable societies, they are little better than societies of honorable hypocrites."[9]

Garrison was back in Baltimore at the beginning of July with little to show for his efforts. It is unclear what evidence he expected to find in Newburyport regarding the pending civil litigation by Todd, but it is clear that he failed to elicit immediate financial support for renewing the *Genius*. In mid–July he finally wrote to Ebenezer Dole to thank him for his "donation only *as a loan on interest*" and to explain how his generosity had been used, since it was not used as originally intended by Dole. Garrison had used part of the funds to pay his travel expenses from Baltimore to Newburyport and back again; the remainder paid outstanding debts of the *Genius*. He also told Dole about the futility of his trip to New England: "I found the minds of the people [in New England] strangely indifferent to the subject of slavery. Their prejudices were invincible — stronger, if possible, than those of the slaveholder." While in New England, Garrison's friends had counseled him to give up the struggle against slavery and return home to Boston. They argued, he wrote, that "it was not my duty ... to spend my time, and talents, and services where persecution, reproach and poverty were the only certain reward ... [while] ... I make myself an exile from home and all that I held dear on earth, and sojourn in a strange land." Their opposition, however, only served "to increase my ardor, and confirm my purpose." Reflecting on those who came to his aid in his legal struggle and on the relative ease of his brief incarceration compared to the degradations of permanent enslavement, Garrison closed the letter with an impassioned plea for someone to vindicate the rights of two million slaves. In the United States today, Garrison angrily declared, only "Death, the great Liberator" can break the slaves' fetters.[10] Garrison did not yet see himself as that someone who was prepared to lead the battle to vindicate the rights of the slave, to take the lead in the anti-slavery effort, or to be slavery's "Liberator." However, considering the reception he experienced during his journey to New England, it is likely Garrison was beginning to consider that there was as much to be accomplished in his "home" as in the "strange land" of Baltimore.

The lack of support for restarting the *Genius* as a weekly doomed the editors' new prospectus, and convinced them to permanently end their partnership. Years later, Garrison attributed the demise of their partnership to insufficient patronage for the *Genius*, principally as a result of his own actions. "The subscription list," he wrote, "I had badly damaged by my demand for immediate and unconditional Emancipation."[11] Furthermore, while reviving the *Genius* was an enticing possibility, it was also apparent there is good reason to believe that both Garrison and Lundy had reservations about resuming their partnership. Lundy was loathe to directly criticize Garrison, but in several ways he signaled his discomfort with Garrison's editorial decisions, as well as his rhetoric. For instance, in March, when the final joint issue had been published, Lundy had indicated that when the paper returned, it would be under his own editorial direction. Also, in the prospectus for a renewed joint effort, which Lundy wrote himself, he promised a dignified paper that would treat its opponents with "a becoming liberality," which may be a not too subtle reference to Garrison's caustic language. Finally, in the *Genius* for May 1830, Lundy reported that an anonymous donor promised to pay for one hundred new subscriptions if Lundy and Garrison resumed the *Genius* as a weekly publication. Lundy expressed his appreciation for the proposal, but said it was still not sufficient to provide financial support for a weekly paper. If, however, the friends of abolition were prepared "to aid its circulation *so as to enable us both to remain at home to superintend it*" then the paper could return as a weekly.[12] Lundy had specific parameters in mind if the co-editorship of the *Genius* was to continue, and they seemed to include maintaining a tighter control over his junior editor.

For his part, Garrison was not about to abandon his combative and bellicose language, nor his aggressive style of journalism. As he told Harriet Horton, he did not regret his actions against Todd and, as he told Ephraim Allen, his vehemence and severity was "not only pardonable, but absolutely necessary."[13] In addition to the "Card" for Francis Todd, published in the *Boston Courier*, Garrison also wrote scathing rebukes to Judge Brice and Richard Gill, the deputy attorney who prosecuted Garrison. Besides showing his contempt for both men, he warned them "beware of my pen"; his passion would not be mitigated simply because they had the power to imprison him.[14] Furthermore, since Garrison interpreted his trial and imprisonment as an attack on the freedom of the press, a retreat to gentler language and a less contentious style of journalism would tacitly acknowledge the efficacy of that attack. Undoubtedly, Garrison found that unacceptable. Finally, his editorial experiences before coming to Baltimore had all been frustrated in one way or another because he lacked the kind of editorial control that gave him complete independence. Resurrecting the *Genius* may have offered the potential for thumbing his nose at Brice, Gill, and the pro-slavery leadership in Baltimore, but even if the financial support had emerged, Garrison was not inclined to mitigate his militancy or augment his dependence. It was time for him to test the limits of his independence — as well as the boundaries of aggressive rhetoric.

Although the partnership had ended, Garrison remained in Baltimore for several weeks and began planning his next endeavor. Todd's civil suit against him was still pending, but once Garrison found out that the trial would not take place until the fall, he decided that he would not stay in Baltimore for another pointless court appearance. Rather, he chose to forego appearing at trial and accept loss by default. When the case was heard in October, the jury heard only the testimony of Todd and his ship's captain, Nicholas Brown; they awarded Todd damages in the amount of $1,000, but the award would never be paid.[15] Garrison commented on the prosecution's testimony and the trial in the first issue of *The Liberator*. He disclaimed any intent to injure Todd or Brown in any way. Rather, he argued that he was motivated by a sense of duty "as an advocate of freedom," and by the desire to show Southerners that Northerners who abetted slavery were "as liable to reprehension as a Maryland slaveholder." Furthermore, he was convinced that the publicity generated by the incident would deter Todd, and perhaps others, from continuing participation in the slave trade. He accepted Todd's statement, which he had made at the October trial, that the incident was the first time any of Todd's ships had carried slaves; Garrison also believed that as a result of his "Black List" commentary and the publicity generated by the trial, it was most certainly Todd's last shipment of slaves as well — not a small accomplishment from his perspective.[16]

If Garrison retained no personal animus against Todd or Brown, he understandably remained quite hostile toward Maryland's courts and its laws. He did not regret his default because his presence at the trial would have been futile. The judge, he argued, was "morally incapable of giving an impartial verdict" and the trial would have had "all the formality, but none of the substance of justice." Worse still, in his estimation, the laws of the state were a paradox. If, as was the case in Maryland, slavery was a legal and respectable business activity, how could a libel be charged against him for defaming Todd's character by his participation in the slave trade? Regardless, Garrison now left the issue in the hands of the public to decide whether he had "exceeded the freedom of the press, or the legitimate province of an independent editor."[17] The repercussions of his "Black List" commentary of November 1829 could not have been anticipated at the time of publication, but it became an important example of Garrison's belief in the responsibility and power of the press to influence public opinion in the fight against slavery. The tumult created by the Todd controversy was but a shadow of the turbulence Garrison now intended to create. In August 1830, however, Garrison was still in Baltimore and without the independent press he so earnestly sought.

In an attempt to resolve that deficiency, Garrison prepared a proposal for a newspaper of his own which he planned to publish in Washington, D.C. The handwritten original of this proposal, which his sons quoted in full in his biography, reported the name of the paper as *The Public Liberator and Journal of the Times*, but in the printed version of the prospectus the name was changed to *The Liberator and the Journal of the Times*. Except for this revision and a few minor changes in wording, the two documents are essentially identical. In both, Garrison argued that the District of Columbia was the most appropriate place to publish an anti-slavery newspaper, not only because it was the nation's capital, but because he expected the struggle to achieve its first victory there — when the slave trade in Washington was ended. The objective of the paper was the abolition of slavery and the "moral and intellectual elevation of our colored population," but it also espoused "the cause of Peace and the promotion of Temperance." In achieving his goals, Garrison intended to use the newspaper to review the proceedings in Congress and the conduct of its members, as well as to maintain a focus on politics, including giving "dignified support to Henry Clay and the American System." In closing, he appealed for support, promised that the first issue would appear as soon as enough subscriptions were received, and requested editors around the country to insert the prospectus in their papers.[18]

According to Oliver Johnson's recollections several decades later, the prospectus was probably published by only two or three newspapers.[19] The *Essex Gazette* in Haverhill, Massachusetts, which was published by Abijah W. Thayer, who knew Garrison from his days in Newburyport and his editorship at *The Free Press*, published the entire prospectus with an accompanying statement encouraging his readers to become subscribers.[20] Also, without any comment, the *National Intelligencer* in Washington, D.C. published the prospectus on August 21. The Whig leaning editors, William Seaton and Joseph Gales, may have appreciated Garrison's support for Henry Clay. There may have been others that did the same, but most newspapers simply reported that a prospectus for the newspaper had been issued and briefly commented about Garrison's plans. The *Boston Recorder* printed a one-sentence report about the proposed *Liberator and Journal of the Times*. In New Hampshire, the *Gazette* printed a longer statement accompanied by a headline which read "NEW CLAY PAPER AT WASHINGTON." The article reported that the prospectus promised support for "the cause of Peace, and the promotion of Temperance" and "dignified support to Henry Clay and the American System," but curiously made no mention of slavery or abolition. At least two other newspapers in New England made similar, although shorter, statements.[21]

As might be expected, a long and vituperative commentary about the proposal came from the south, *The Augusta Chronicle* in Georgia. The article began rather straightforwardly, "A wild-brained fanatic named Wm. Lloyd Garrison ... has issued proposals ... for publishing, in Washington City, a paper to be called the '*Liberator*.'" The new paper was to be devoted to "the abolition of slavery" and, in the opinion of the *Chronicle*'s editor, should be quickly shut down "by the neglect, or scorn and contempt, of an enlightened and liberal people." Furthermore, Garrison was characterized as a "miserable abortion of a mad enthusiast" who was bent on exciting "the prejudices of one part of our people against another — of the South against the North."[22] This commentary represented a kind of preview of the widespread abusive and virulent reaction that later publication of *The Liberator* would routinely generate.

Tepid support in the northern states and absolute contempt in the southern did not bode well for the new paper. Nevertheless, for the first time, Garrison intended to publish a newspaper completely on his own terms, embracing fundamental truths which he believed were critical to a well-ordered society. Furthermore, he would be bound to no benefactor, owner, political party, organization, or co-editor. Near the end of the proposal for his Washington paper, Garrison quoted the 17th century English political theorist, Algernon Sydney, "Implicit faith belongs to fools; and truth is comprehended by examining principles." Sydney was expressing little patience for anyone with reason and common sense who did not "make use of it in those things which concern themselves and their posterity."[23] Garrison certainly agreed. His faith in the political and religious institutions of the United States, which he had found so compelling for most of his yet young life, was being sorely tested by a nation of people, politicians, and religious who were increasingly unwilling to challenge the prevailing and accepted ideology, especially about slavery. He also wrote, "I am opposed to bondage, under its every aspect — whether spiritual, civil, political, mental, or physical." By deciding eventually to shorten the name of his paper to simply *The Liberator*, Garrison may have as clearly indicated its role in his own life, as much as he intended the name to indicate the role he hoped the paper would fulfill for all America's citizens, as well as all America's slaves. "My country is the world; my countrymen are mankind" was the proposal's closing statement (and *The Liberator*'s motto); Garrison was coming to the realization that many more that those physically bond in slavery's chains needed liberation.

Rather quickly, however, Garrison found out how difficult it was to raise the funds he needed for his new paper. One clear indication of that difficulty was the response he received from Arthur Tappan, who had only recently arranged for Garrison's release from prison. As indicated earlier, Tappan sent Garrison $100. The money, however, came with a letter in which Tappan expressed some reservations. He said that he "was not sufficiently acquainted" with Garrison's qualifications "in the editorial and publishing departments to insure success to a paper." Nevertheless, because others had highly recommended him, Tappan "cheerfully" enclosed the check.[24] At their first meeting, Tappan had been impressed by Garrison; both men shared similar perspectives on moral sins, such as gambling and drinking in American society. Before contributing to *The Liberator*, however, Tappan had Garrison investigated. He found that "Garrison's business qualities were doubtful" although none doubted his skills as either a writer or an editor, nor his devotion to the cause.[25] Later Tappan would become more convinced of Garrison's editorial ability and pay for a large number of subscriptions, but for the moment he withheld his unqualified support.[26] Garrison certainly welcomed Tappan's support, lukewarm though it was, but he also realized that he needed to cast a much wider net in order to find the money to finance his new publication. Consequently, Garrison decided to deliver a series of lectures on slavery, colonization, and immediate emancipation as a way to raise the funds he needed.

During his imprisonment in Baltimore, in addition to the *Brief Sketch* of his trial, Garrison had prepared three speeches on slavery and colonization, which he decided to use to bring attention to the plight of the slave, build support for abolition without forced emigration, and generate funding for his proposed newspaper. He attempted to find a meeting room or hall in Baltimore that would allow him to deliver the addresses but, "being regarded as out of my wits," he was unsuccessful.[27] Consequently, at the end of August, Garrison left Baltimore "on an eastern tour for the purpose of delivering public addresses on the subject of slavery, [and] of obtaining subscriptions to my proposed new paper at Washington City."[28] The tour took Garrison to Philadelphia, New York, New Haven, Hartford, Newburyport, and finally Boston. Garrison did not return to Baltimore until June 1864 when he attended the Republican Convention to watch as Abraham Lincoln was nominated for a second term; he also witnessed the convention's unanimous call for a constitutional amendment to abolish slavery.[29] This achievement was far from discernible in August 1830, and the immediate reaction to his lecture tour hardly augured well for Garrison's undertaking.

After leaving Baltimore, the first stop on Garrison's lecture tour was Philadelphia where, after about a week's effort, the Hall of the Franklin Institute allowed him to "deliver an address on the subject of slavery." In fact, he delivered all three addresses on three successive nights from August 31 to September 2, 1830.[30] The *Inquirer* commented: "The declamation of Mr. Garrison is, in some respects, uninviting and defective; but it is impossible for an intelligent auditor to be unimpressed with the strength and beauty of his composition." The audience for the lectures was "almost exclusively members of the Society of Friends and of colored people" who listened attentively to his lectures. Although some of the Quakers may have been troubled by Garrison's harsh tone, they were hardly as critical as the *Inquirer*, since Garrison was preaching to the converted about abolition. Many of the Quakers in Philadelphia were friends of Lundy, subscribers to the *Genius*, and therefore already familiar with Garrison.[31] Included among them were James and Lucretia Mott, who provided hospitality for Garrison on this visit and many other visits to Philadelphia over the next four decades. Their meeting marked the beginning of a long relationship and frequent cooperative efforts in many reform issues including, famously, women's rights. In 1840 when the World's Anti-Slavery Convention in London refused to recognize Lucretia Mott and other American women and seat them as representatives to the convention, Garrison refused to take his own seat and in protest, he chose to remain in the gallery with the women.[32] Several years after their initial meeting, Garrison credited the Motts' "tolerant, catholic spirit" with teaching him, by example, the absurdity of "theological dogmas, which I once regarded as essential to Christianity."[33]

Furthermore, the black community in Philadelphia, like those in Boston and Baltimore, had adamantly opposed the American Colonization Society almost from the moment of its inception. In August 1817, James Forten, Paul Cuffee, and other leaders of the Philadelphia black community held a mass meeting with black citizens of the city during which the American Colonization Society was denounced. They accused the society's policies of contributing to the perpetuation of slavery and called upon all the citizens of the city to reject any connection with the organization. When Garrison lectured in 1830, black Philadelphians still prided themselves on "the spirit of 1817" and were receptive to Garrison's message.[34] His addresses laid the foundation for decades-long support for him from both the Quakers and the black community of Philadelphia, but outside of those two groups he was unable to make a "wide or deep impression upon the citizens generally"—demonstrating a fundamental problem with American society.[35]

He moved on to New York City where he delivered his lectures on September 8 and 9 at the Broadway Hall to "small but respectable audiences" which included Lewis and Arthur Tappan, who heard Garrison's objections to the colonization society for the first time.[36] Aside from a brief notice about the speeches in the *Commercial Advertiser* and in the *Evening Post*, there was no follow-up report in the newspaper about Garrison's reception, the makeup of his audiences, or his demeanor.[37] From New York, he traveled to New Haven and Hartford where he delivered his lectures from the pulpit of black churches to mixed audiences of blacks and whites.

While in Hartford, Garrison wrote to George Shepard, who was minister of the First Congregational Church of Hallowell, Maine. Shepard had written to Garrison and informed him that an anonymous donor was willing to contribute $50 "for the best tract on the subject of slavery." The cause of emancipation had few advocates, Garrison wrote, and he believed a well-written and widely distributed tract could be an excellent aid in publicizing the cause. The proposed subject was so broad, however, that Garrison suggested that the tract ought to be focused on one of two issues, one religious and another political. The first issue was the duty of the Christian ministers and churches to condemn slavery, and the second issue was the duty of society "to restore the slaves to their inalienable rights." Of these two, Garrison voiced a clear preference for the former because he believed that any political or social efforts were doomed "as long the church refuses to act on the subject." For several paragraphs Garrison delivered a strident harangue against those Christian churches which refused to declare slavery to be against the teachings of Christ and, in particular, he rebuked the ministers who themselves owned slaves. The Christian churches "must be purified, as by fire," he wrote.[38] While there is no record that the tract that Shepard proposed, if written, was ever published, Garrison's response clearly demonstrated his continuing concern about the political and, especially, religious acquiescence to slavery, as well as his faith in the power of the printed word to promote change.

In closing the letter, Garrison told Shepard that he would continue his "eastern tour" and was leaving the next day, September 14th, for Boston. If so, his stay there was brief for we next find Garrison in Newburyport where he hoped that "his native town should be the first place in Massachusetts to hear his lectures on slavery." Unfortunately, his reception was disappointing — to say the least. The pastor of the Second Presbyterian Church, Daniel Dana, quickly agreed to give Garrison the use of the church meeting hall, but when Garrison and his audience arrived, the doors to the hall were locked. The Trustees of the church had evidently overruled Dana. In disgust, Garrison left Newburyport for Amesbury, Massachusetts, just across the Merrimack River from Newburyport, where he was permitted to deliver his lectures at the local lyceums. Meanwhile, when the minister of the Second Congregationalist Church of Newburyport, Luther Dimmick, found out that Garrison had been locked out of the Presbyterian Church, he offered his church "for as many lectures as [Garrison] wanted." After delivering his lectures on September 24,

25, and 26 in Amesbury, Garrison returned to Newburyport and finally delivered one lecture on September 28. However, when he returned on the next night, he was barred from the church — once again the Trustees of a church had overruled their pastor.[39] Garrison had struggled to find venues for his anti-slavery lectures wherever he went on his tour from Baltimore, but the reaction of his hometown was a particularly bitter blow.

While his presentations were closed out in Newburyport, Ephraim Allen did print a long, and generally very complimentary, letter about Garrison's lectures in Amesbury in the *Newburyport Herald*. This letter is, in fact, the only record we have regarding the content of his lectures. The correspondence was signed "N" and the tone indicated some familiarity with Allen. "N" reported that the first lecture was so well attended that a larger hall had to be found for the following two lectures; in the new venue, both lectures were delivered to "full and respectable" audiences. In Garrison's first lecture, he refuted "the strongest and most popular objections to the immediate abolition of slavery" and demonstrated not only that immediate emancipation was necessary but that justice required it. The second lecture described slavery as it currently existed "in *law* and in *fact* in the United States and gave examples of the cruelty imposed on the slaves by Southerners," including stories of slavery's brutality which Garrison himself had witnessed. "N" claimed that Garrison's vivid presentation moved many in the audience who, like he, felt for the first time affected by a new understanding of the reality of the slaves' condition. In the final lecture, Garrison admonished the audience that "the crime, the infamy, and the curse of Slavery are national, and that we (yes, Mr. Allen) *we New-Englanders* are equally culpable with the slave dealers and slaveowners." Someone who accepts stolen goods, Garrison argued, is as guilty as the thief who stole the goods, but in the case of slavery, the "stolen merchandise" is a human being "like ourselves, differing only in the color of their skins." Garrison also cautioned his listeners about the American Colonization Society, who were "lulling the American people to sleep." While granting that the society was supported by many good men, he warned that many more in the society had selfish motives. Their purpose was not to remove slaves, but rather to remove free blacks "who they well know are constantly instilling the principles of liberty into the minds of their enslaved brethren." The correspondent acknowledged that some may accuse Garrison of extreme "enthusiasm" in his agitation about slavery, but none can doubt his determination and sincerity "in a good cause." Finally, he concluded dramatically with the hope that "the fair tree of Liberty" may provide shade and protection for all children in future generations, "without distinction of color."[40]

Allen's willingness to publish this letter was small recompense for Garrison. He left Newburyport on the morning of September 30, but not before sending a letter expressing anger over the treatment he received from his hometown to Allen. "Twice have the inhabitants of this town been deceived," he wrote, with regard to his lectures. He had pledged to deliver them in his hometown, but circumstances "beyond my control" prevented him from fulfilling that pledge. Those who had used their power to exclude him were, he charged, "discreditable to themselves and [this] place." Furthermore, Garrison argued, every meeting house in the town would have been opened to him if he came to plead for twenty white men in chains, but the reality of two million black men, women, and children in chains "in this land of liberty" excited no similar response. For Garrison, this was, needless to say, an unacceptable situation. He announced that he was now on his way to Boston, but he remained undeterred by Newburyport's disappointing reception and reaction; he declared his intention to continue his devotion to "the cause of universal liberty."[41]

Garrison finally reached Boston with little to show for his efforts to raise funds for publishing his newspaper in Washington. In Boston, he initially found a somewhat sympathetic welcome from the editor of the *Boston Evening Transcript*, Lynde Walter. In an editorial commentary, Walter summarized Garrison's trial and incarceration in Baltimore; reported on his disappointing reception in Newburyport, where town leaders "uncharitably closed the doors of Churches and Public Halls" to his lectures; and welcomed his arrival in Boston. He also described Garrison as a "visionary enthusiast" who was selflessly devoted to a project "which he can never hope to see perfected," but for which he will be remembered as "an early and laborious pioneer."[42]

Walter's kind reception for Garrison and Garrison's zeal to free the southern slaves, however, did not translate to sympathy or compassion for the free black population of Boston. Just a few days earlier Walter had published an editorial on "Our Colored Population" which argued that blacks in Boston were already "free enough" and did not need or deserve more freedom. If they had not been granted political rights, he argued, then neither are they required "to perform military service," and meanwhile, they are protected by the same laws as white citizens, and are sheltered from the hardships imposed "upon their less favorable brethren of the South." The problem, he asserted, was "not that we do not treat the colored man well, but that he has been treated too well." Furthermore, the onus for the demands of free blacks in Boston for greater rights fell to "certain very good people" who nevertheless did not understand "the terrible consequences [of] their injudicious interference."[43] Garrison certainly appreciated Walter's "kindly reception," but it is unlikely that Walter's prejudice against granting full civil rights to the free blacks of Boston escaped his attention.[44] It was one more sign of the cold-hearted obstinacy in New

England that inhibited their support for the immediate abolition of slavery and extension of political and civil rights to all.

Regardless of Walter's attitude toward free blacks, he welcomed correspondence from Garrison, who wrote two articles "For the Transcript" in the next several weeks. Walter's support may have been less than desirable, but Garrison embraced the opportunity to use the *Transcript* to get his message into print and into the hands of the public. The first article was headlined "OUGHT WE NOT BLUSH" and reported on the hypocrisy of Americans, especially "our southern slaveholders," who celebrated the triumph of republicanism in Europe while millions in the United States were "held in a state of servitude which, for cruelty and debasement finds no parallel in European despotism."[45] Several days later, Garrison reported on two runaway slaves, a man and his wife, who had recently arrived in Boston as stowaways on a ship from New Orleans. They were discovered when hunger forced them to reveal themselves a few days after the ship had left New Orleans; they were immediately arrested by local authorities when the ship arrived in Boston. In accordance with Federal fugitive slave laws, Boston courts returned them in chains to the "galling yoke of bondage" of a New Orleans' planter who claimed them and offered a reward for the return of his "property." Garrison's outrage that slavery was so casually supported and protected in New England was palpable.[46] Five months earlier, from his Baltimore prison, he had written of his desire to return to New England — "that paradise of our fallen world" — but now the luster of that paradise was clearly becoming diminished.[47]

Meanwhile, during his first two weeks in Boston, Garrison searched for a place where he could deliver his lectures free of charge. Eventually, he prevailed upon Joseph Buckingham at the *Courier* to print an advertisement which requested the free use of a hall or meeting place for three nights of lectures "to vindicate the rights of TWO MILLIONS of American citizens." Because there was no charge to attend the addresses and they were open to all as a "public benefit," Garrison could not afford any fee for use of the hall. If his appeal was unsuccessful, Garrison promised to "address the citizens of Boston in the open air, on the Common."[48] Almost immediately, a response was received; however, it was not from "any of the Christian ministers or churches."[49] Rather, Julien Hall was offered by a decidedly non–Christian organization called, The First Society of the Free Thinkers, which was at the time under the leadership of Abner Kneeland. During his ministerial career, Kneeland had moved from orthodox Protestantism, to liberal Universalist, and finally, in 1829, announced that he was ending his attachment to Christianity altogether.[50] Both the Society of Free Thinkers and Kneeland had only recently established themselves in Boston, and unlike the regular ministers in the city, they were willing to welcome a radical voice to their hall. After offering Julien Hall, however, they did little to support the abolitionist cause. These "infidels," as Garrison later described them, "certainly took no interest in our proceedings ... and contributed nothing to our funds," but they did stand as a "rebuke to the pro-slavery Christian church" by coming forward to offer Julien Hall for his lectures, while Boston's churches remained closed to both Garrison and the cause of emancipation.[51]

On Friday morning, October 15, the *Boston Evening Transcript* announced Garrison's first lecture at Julien Hall, and, on Saturday and the following Monday, similar notices announced his second and third addresses.[52] The hall that night was nearly full, including the Reverends Lyman Beecher and Ezra Gannett, John Tappan, brother of Arthur and Lewis, as well a young Unitarian minister named Samuel J. May who persuaded his cousin, Samuel E. Sewall, and brother-in-law, A. Bronson Alcott, to accompany him. May had never met Garrison but was familiar with his career and had been impressed by his writings in the *Genius*. May later wrote that "Providence" had brought him from his church in Brooklyn, Connecticut, to visit Boston at the time of Garrison's address. "Never before," he proclaimed, "was I so affected by the speech of man." He described Garrison's calm determination as he rose to speak and

> delivered such a lecture as he only, I believe, at that time, could have written; for he only had his eyes so anointed that he could see that outrages perpetrated upon Africans were wrongs done to our common humanity; he only, I believe, had had his ears so completely unstopped of "prejudice against color" that the cries of enslaved black men and black women sounded to him as if they came from brothers and sisters.

When the address was over, May convinced Sewell and Alcott to come with him and introduce themselves to Garrison. At that meeting, May told Garrison that he was not yet prepared to endorse everything Garrison had proposed, but he committed himself to help him in his "great work." Sewall made a similar promise and Alcott invited them all to return to his home, where until midnight they listened to Garrison passionately discourse on immediate, unconditional emancipation.[53]

The next morning, May called on Garrison at Collier's boarding house, staying until mid-afternoon. Garrison told May that he needed to return to the printing trade for "his own support" but believed that he first had to "communicate to persons of prominent influence" the true conditions of slavery. Once they became fully apprised of the need for action, he expected these men to fulfill their obligation to diligently lead the movement for abolition. In mid-October of 1830, Garrison still viewed printing as a livelihood, albeit in service to a greater cause, but it was not yet the cause itself. Garrison showed

May letters he had written to William Ellery Channing, Lyman Beecher, Daniel Webster, and other prominent political and religious leaders in New England "begging them ... to interpose their great power in the Church and State to save our country from the terrible calamity" that slavery threatened for the whole nation.[54] However, none had yet chosen to step forward and embrace the cause.

One of those New England ministerial leaders, the Reverend Lyman Beecher, had attended Garrison's first lecture, but, unlike May, Beecher was not inspired by Garrison's rhetoric. He told Garrison that he could not offer his support for abolition because he already "had too many irons in the fire." Reportedly, Garrison warned Beecher that he "had better let all your irons burn than neglect your duty to the slave." But Beecher was not moved. "Your zeal is commendable," he advised Garrison, "but you are misguided. If you will give up your fanatical notions and be guided by us (the clergy), we will make you the Wilberforce of America."[55] Clearly, however, Garrison was uninterested in accepting the guidance of clergy who, he believed, were already culpable for the national evil of slavery and who summarily dismissed the need for their immediate participation in combating this sin. May later confirmed Garrison's appraisal. "The churches and ministers" of nearly every denomination, he wrote, "gathered about the 'Peculiar Institution' for its *protection*; and vehemently denounced ... all those who insisted upon its abolition"; and, he asserted, eventually "[Garrison] soon discovered to his astonishment, that the American Church was the bulwark of American slaveholders."[56] Garrison had told May that he wished to find someone of political or religious prominence to lead the anti-slavery struggle, but the difficulty of this wish was twofold. On the one hand, leaders like Beecher were unwilling to take up the cause, and, on the other hand, Garrison was as yet unwilling to lead the struggle himself.

Meanwhile, May immediately took his new commitment to anti-slavery to the pulpit. He had been invited to preach at Alexander Young's New South Street Church in Boston on the Sunday following Garrison's lecture. The sermon he had planned to deliver that Sunday discussed prejudice, but he revised it and turned it into an attack on racism, which, he argued, provided a foundation and support for American slavery. He warned the congregation that prejudice against "the color of these poor people" contributed to New England's blindness to the slaves' suffering. Finally, he shocked his listeners by demanding an end to slavery, even if it threatened the existence of the American Republic, and advised them to attend Garrison's lecture the next evening. Reaction to his sermon was immediate, powerful, and negative. Young informed May that he would never again be invited to speak in his church. All of Boston's

Unitarian churches, except for those of William Ellery Channing and Ralph Waldo Emerson, closed their doors to May's preaching. Despite this reaction, and inspired by Garrison, May audaciously continued to advocate on behalf of slaves and free blacks. In 1835, when his Brooklyn congregation demanded that he either give up abolition or leave the church, he chose to leave.[57] Before May heard Garrison in October 1830, his lecture tour had failed to arouse the response Garrison sought, much less raise the funds he needed for his paper in Washington, but finally, at least, he had ignited a new and impassioned disciple.

Around this time, Garrison also learned that Lundy had decided to move the *Genius* to Washington. Since the Todd incident in November 1829, and the subsequent threats of legal actions against him, Lundy had been unsuccessful in his attempts to revitalize the paper. In the first edition of the *Genius* published in Washington, Lundy claimed that he had begun to make plans to move a year ago, but that "violent persecution" forced a postponement until now. He also noted that the move to Washington offered an opportunity to revive the paper. At the nation's capital he had access to "intelligent and influential men, from every part of the Union, and thus an opportunity to increase the facilities of collecting and disseminating information" with regard to the abolition of slavery.[58] Lundy was aware that Garrison had issued his prospectus for *The Liberator* in Washington, and although he had his reservations about Garrison's language, immediatism, and rejection of colonization, there is nothing to support the notion that Lundy moved to Washington in order to frustrate Garrison's plans.[59]

Nonetheless, Lundy's move certainly contributed to Garrison's need to decide on a new location for *The Liberator*. By October 1830, circumstances beyond Lundy's move to Washington may have already begun to prod him toward the decision to publish in Boston. First of all, the American Colonization Society had taken measures to frustrate Garrison's attempt to publish in Washington. There had been some speculation that Garrison considered using the donation he had received from Tappan in August to purchase the printing office of the *Washington Spectator*. The paper was edited by Walter Colton, who had supported colonization but who was also experiencing financial problems. One of the society's agents, Elliot Cresson, wrote to warn the society about Garrison, who he called "a second Walker." Cresson suggested that "the board had much better buy C[olton] out and break up the establishment" rather than allow Garrison into Washington.[60] Garrison's animus toward the American Colonization Society was becoming stronger by this time, but it was undoubtedly augmented by Cresson's action and would only grow in the future. In 1833, during Garrison's first trip to England, he would have a chance to seek some revenge because, at the same time, Cresson was also touring England as agent and advocate for the society. Garrison pursued Cresson throughout the country, in person and in print. He seriously limited Cresson's effectiveness in winning support for the colonization society by challenging him to public debates about colonization and by repeatedly attacking him in the London press. Garrison proposed a public debate with Cresson in a letter published by the *London Times* and promised to pay the mayor of New York "20 guineas ... for the education of the coloured children of that city" should he lose the debate.[61] Although they were present at each other's lectures several times, Cresson and Garrison never debated directly; however, they did exchange a series of letters in a London newspaper, *The Patriot*, between July and September 1833.

More instrumental, perhaps, in deciding where to publish his paper was the fact that neither of the two goals for Garrison's lecture tour, raising awareness of slavery and raising funds for *The Liberator* in Washington, materialized. However, what did become increasingly clear to Garrison as he lectured in the North was the intransigence of northerners in general and his own New England brethren in particular with regard to abolition. In a letter explaining his choice of Boston, Garrison claimed that he had no intention of publishing there until after he returned to the city in October 1830.[62] On his way to Boston, Garrison had spoken in Philadelphia and New York to large, active, and receptive black communities who had long been opponents of both slavery and colonization and who were prepared to join a new battle against them. Aside from Quakers, however, few white communities in the northern states had either attended or listened politely; they were unmoved or ignored him or, as with his reception in Newburyport, were adamantly opposed to his presence. In Boston, when he was finally allowed to speak, it was at a venue provided by a group of radical religious "freethinkers" not by the traditional Christian churches of the city. Furthermore, the orthodox religious leaders rejected Garrison as too harsh and extremist, while they also dismissed immediate emancipation as too fanatical as a response to slavery.

Resistance to anti-slavery activity from northerners was, of course, not new for Garrison. A year earlier, before the Todd incident, in response to a letter chastising him for his overzealousness, he wrote, "One thing has struck me with surprise—that the burden of complaint against the freedom of my strictures has originated in the *non-slaveholding states*, and among *ministers of the gospel* and *church members!*"[63] With regard to the churches in particular, Garrison remained embittered by their early, strong, and vocal hostility to abolition. After the Civil War and emancipation he indignantly criticized the suggestion that, at its beginning, the churches had simply failed to offer their "hearty cooperation and ready acquiescence" in the struggle. "On the contrary," he argued, the churches offered "the most determined hostility and relentless persecution" toward himself and the cause of abolition.[64]

In his biography of Garrison, Oliver Johnson reported that in the last few months of 1830 Garrison realized that it would be fruitless to appeal to "Richmond, Charleston, and New Orleans, while Boston, New York, and Philadelphia were apologizing for [slavery]." In addition, Johnson quoted a letter from Garrison about New England in which Garrison wrote, "I found contempt more bitter, opposition more active, detraction more relentless, prejudice more stubborn and apathy more frozen than among slave owners themselves."[65] Indeed, in his letter from jail to Ephraim Allen, he wrote that Todd was only one of many northern shippers who transported slaves and he had come to the realization that "the transportation of slaves is almost entirely effected in New-England bottoms!" Northern merchants wished his silence "because they are guilty, and dread exposure."[66] Therefore, in combination with Lundy's decision to move to Washington, the realization that slavery was as strongly supported in the North as in the South helped to convince Garrison that Boston was the best location for *The Liberator*.

Additional support for publishing *The Liberator* in Boston also came from the one significant success Garrison had on his lecture tour, the conversion of Samuel May to abolitionism.[67] May's own experience with the reaction to his sermon on the Sunday after he heard Garrison's lecture convinced him that the churches and people of New England were especially blind to the moral evil of slavery. After delivering his anti-slavery sermon, "gentlemen of property and standing" persuaded May's father to plead with his son to abandon his support for Garrison. Several days later, May submitted the sermon for publication by the tract society of the American Unitarian Association. However, the manager of those tracts, the Reverend Henry Ware, Jr., advised May that, in order to publish the sermon, all the revisions that he had made to give the sermon its anti-slavery sentiment had to be removed. This only helped to convince May that the entire country was responsible for the outrages perpetrated on the nation's slave population — "Northern people, scarcely less than that of the Southern." In light of the contributions of New England to the ideals of the American Revolution and the support they gave to the "cause of human freedom" in other areas of the world, "a more glaring inconsistency does not appear in the whole history of mankind."[68] May's conversion and personal commitment to abolition combined with the hardhearted reaction of his fellow clergy, including those of May's own liberal Unitarian Association, was further evidence to Garrison that *The Liberator* would be as effective in Boston as it would be in Washington.

Seven: "And I will be heard"

Finally, a skirmish between Garrison and Lynde Walter of the *Transcript* offered Garrison final confirmation that Boston was as much (or more) in need of an anti-slavery newspaper as was the rest of the nation. What was more, the controversy may have helped Garrison to see firsthand the potential impact a northern anti-slavery newspaper might exert beyond its own region and, in particular, on southern interests and concerns. As indicated earlier, Walter's *Transcript* had given Garrison a relatively sympathetic welcome when he returned to Boston; twice articles written by Garrison about slavery were published. Walter, of course exchanged his paper with other editors around the country, and on November 1, in response to Garrison's October 12 article which accused southern slaveholders of being hypocrites, the paper printed what it called "a fair offset" taken from the *City Gazette* of Charleston, South Carolina. The brief notice was headed "IMPERTINENCE" and accused Garrison of engaging in the kind of libel for which he had been punished in Baltimore. In addition it asked, "Could not this man be provided with some decent honest employment ... which will keep him out of mischief, and prevent him from meddling with the concerns of those about whom he knows nothing?"[69] The notice provoked a blistering response from Garrison which in turn elicited a stern rebuke from Walter.

In its next issue, the *Transcript* published Garrison's letter. First, he defended the original charge of hypocrisy he had made against southerners who toasted freedom in France while two million slaves were bound in the United States. Then Garrison told the Charleston *Gazette* editor that he was "a *New England mechanic who is not ashamed of his trade*" and suggested that the editor ought to urge "purse proud, indolent and profligate slaveholders to alter their vile pursuits." Was it "decent honest employment," Garrison asked, to treat human beings like brutes, to whip them savagely, to withhold religious training, to rip families apart, and to steal their labor while giving them little in return? Indeed, Garrison argued, if in his trade he became "so mean and dastardly" that he enslaved his fellow countrymen, then, "if capital punishment be lawful," he deserved the gallows. However, it was not he, a printer by trade, who acted in this manner, but rather the southern slaveholders, who were neither Christians nor patriots and whose "professions of patriotism and piety" only confirmed their hypocrisy. In his closing paragraphs, Garrison predicted that the end of slavery would be "recorded in blood" if the country did not act immediately and use "the energy of enlightened public opinion" to bring about emancipation. Left unsaid was the means of creating that "enlightened public opinion" but it could not have been far from Garrison's mind.

Walter wrote a long introduction to Garrison's letter, in which he said that he published the correspondence with reluctance. By publishing the letter, however, Walter clearly intended to prove Garrison's fanaticism and consequently discredit him. Until recently, Walter wrote, he had considered Garrison to be "an ardent enthusiast in a good cause," but Garrison's letter as well as his recent series of lectures displayed too much "intemperance of feeling and expression." Slavery was a curse, Walter contended, that had pre-existed the nation and that could be removed only "gradually ... and by cool and deliberate argument." Garrison's overzealous remarks and overheated rhetoric did not help to advance the anti-slavery cause and, in fact, it destroyed his influence with "the very persons whose influence and assistance he most requires." In closing, Walter reiterated an old and familiar argument. He declared, "We have no slaves here, and New Englanders do not need the benefit of his lectures. They can do us no good, and they may do our society harm."[70] Walter confirmed for Garrison something he already knew: the very persons whose "influence and assistance" he desired were definitely not listening. Those "persons" were, of course, leading citizens, politicians, ministers, and editors in the community.

The accusations from Charleston against Garrison's trade may have been particularly instructive. It was not his occupation, as a printer, newspaper publisher and editor, which neglected the slave and condemned them to unspeakable horrors. No, it was other occupations, including not only the slave-owners, but the politicians and ministers who were supposed to provide moral leadership for the nation — not to mention the "influence and assistance" Walter though was most important. Furthermore, it was also the unprincipled and unscrupulous newspaper editors, in both the North and the South, who provided support and apology for the system of slavery. Garrison was neither politician nor minister, but a printer by trade. It was his trade that could challenge the hypocrisy of the nation's Christians and patriots, and Garrison was not about to abandon the kind of "meddling" which was not only the prerogative of the printer, but was, as he had so often declared, the printer's obligation as well.

Walter's *Transcript* had been the only one of Boston's regular newspapers to publish Garrison's views, but now even it severely criticized him and no longer published his commentary. New England, Walter told Garrison, not only did not need immediate emancipation, but it did not need to listen to Garrison's lectures. What more evidence did Garrison need to convince him that a strong voice against slavery was as absent in the North as it was in the South? What more was needed to demonstrate that New England and Boston required his voice, and *The Liberator*, in order to wage the abolition battle? We do not know the exact date Garrison decided to publish in Boston, but about the time of this exchange in the *Transcript*, the die was cast. He became determined, as he wrote in his inaugural editorial, "to lift up the standard of emancipation in the eyes of the nation, *within sight of Bunker Hill, and in the birth-place of Liberty*."[71] His boyhood friend and fellow printer, Isaac Knapp, agreed to a partnership, and a few weeks later, on January 1, 1831, without subscribers and without money, with paper procured on credit and with a borrowed press, the first issue of *The Liberator* appeared in Boston — and reappeared every Saturday for the next 35 years.[72]

Eight

"The press is able to cope"

PUBLICATION OF *The Liberator* was the culmination of a journey Garrison had begun with his apprenticeship at the *Herald* in 1818. From that time until this point in his career Garrison had certainly not shied away from espousing unpopular opinions in his press. In his first editorial effort at *The Free Press,* he championed the Massachusetts claim for compensation from the War of 1812, political corruption, and the undue influence of special interests and power brokers in local politics. Furthermore, Garrison directly challenged his former master and benefactor, Ephraim Allen, over what Garrison believed was Allen's misplaced praise for the recently deceased Thomas Jefferson. In consequence, Garrison was forced to sell his paper. As editor of the *Philanthropist* in Boston, Garrison entered the emerging antebellum reform movements. He used the paper's principal issue, temperance, as a foundation on which to build support for other controversial reforms, such as abolishing imprisonment for debt, peace and non-resistance, sabbatarianism, women's role in society, justice for the nation's Indians, and slavery. The end of his editorship at the *Philanthropist* came, Garrison claimed, because he wanted to pursue new opportunities, perhaps related to his recent meeting with Benjamin Lundy and anti-slavery. But there is also some evidence that the breadth of his reform sentiments and his unwillingness to completely abandon political issues contributed as well to bringing his tenure at the *Philanthropist* to a quick end.

The appeal for Garrison in his next newspaper, the *Journal of the Times*, in Bennington, Vermont, was the complete editorial freedom he exercised, as long as he supported John Quincy Adams' presidential campaign. In the newspaper Garrison advocated anti-slavery, temperance, peace, moral reform, and, lastly, Adams' election. He supported Adams strongly enough to satisfy his commitment to the paper's proprietor, but Garrison's robust advocacy of reform issues, and especially his appeals for moral reform, rankled many. Once again, after six months, Garrison suddenly announced he was leaving to respond to a "higher enterprise." That enterprise was, of course, his partnership with Benjamin Lundy at the *Genius of Universal Emancipation* in Baltimore. In the *Genius*, Garrison took the most controversial position of his young career — support for immediate emancipation accompanied by increasingly sharp questioning of the colonization movement. While Lundy defended Garrison's right to express this view, even he found his co-editor's ideas and language troublesome. Immediate emancipation and a penchant for acerbic rhetoric eventually put Garrison in jail for libel and brought an end to the partnership. While Lundy certainly regretted the loss of a powerful voice, he also understood the potential danger that Garrison's aggressive and contentious inclinations presented to the continued existence of the *Genius*. As editor of four different newspapers, Garrison had not learned to eschew controversy, but rather increasingly found it to be a necessary and vital element in the role that a newspaper and a newspaper's editor were required to perform for society.

What was more, while mixing ink and setting type as an apprentice, Garrison had learned the important contribution that the press and newspapers rendered in promoting and spreading education and in informing a democratic society about critical political and moral issues. As his career progressed, he repeatedly championed the duties of the editor to inform, educate, and stand at the forefront of social and political improvement. In one of his first published letters, while still an apprentice, Garrison admonished "the public newspapers" which used rumors rather than facts to stir public opinion and interest.[1] When forced to relinquish *The Free Press*, Garrison strongly editorialized about the proper duty of a newspaper editor to challenge "public follies and vices" in spite of the cost, which in this case was the silencing of Garrison's voice.[2] During his editorship of the *Philanthropist*, Garrison regularly spoke about the power of the press to contribute to the reformation of society, and about the responsibilities of the newspaper editor to conduct his paper accordingly. Responding to an attack by his longtime nemesis, John Neal, who called all newspapers "utterly worthless," Garrison defended newspapers of moral character as "a valuable acquisition to the country."[3] At the *Philanthropist*, Garrison began his practice of regularly passing judgment on other newspapers and their editors. Those which advocated correct political and moral convictions were praised; those which did not were rebuked. He continued and expanded on this practice in the *Journal of the Times* and the *Genius*, as well as, of course, *The Liberator*.

At the *Journal of the Times*, Garrison published a list of qualifications for newspaper editors. They required five traits: principle, and the "integrity of conscience"; courage, to "attack the follies of the times"; independence, "such as power cannot awe, nor wealth bribe"; genius, which "adds to the opulence of the intellectual world"; and industry, without which "it is impossible to thrive." Without these qualifications, the unprincipled, timid, dependent, or lazy editor would "do more mischief that a band of robbers" to undermine and destroy the American republic.[4] By the time he ended his tenure at the *Journal of the Times*, Garrison classified himself as part of a "new race of editors" for whom the newspaper had a greater purpose than financial success; the newspaper was a venue for reforming and reshaping the nation — and the world.[5] He carried this attitude to Baltimore and the *Genius of Universal Emancipation*, where he continued to emphasize the social and moral obligations of the newspaper editor. He praised the good newspapers and censured the bad, especially those newspaper editors who, by accepting advertisements for slave auctions, were willing to participate in and provide support for the slave trade. After he was jailed for an alleged libel, he used the Todd incident to remind his fellow editors about the threat to the liberty of the press that his prosecution represented. In a letter that took Ephraim Allen to task for his lackluster response to Garrison's trial and conviction, Garrison also reminded Allen that the threat was something ignored by editors at their own peril. The liberty of the press as it should be practiced by newspaper editors in the United States was the safeguard of "all your civil, political and religious rights."[6]

By early November 1830, Garrison had reached a new understanding about slavery and its protected status in American society in both the North and South. This understanding required him to take the newspaper's role in society further than he had formerly anticipated. The usual supporters and conductors of social change, politics and the church, had willfully and unalterably abandoned their responsibility. As a result, Garrison decided that the newspaper press must do more than simply provide support for correct moral action in society. The press had to go beyond its function as a source of information for those leading change in American society, or as an auxiliary to those who should provide moral leadership in society; the press itself must take the lead. As Edmund Quincy explained, Garrison began *The Liberator* at a time when

> slavery had intermarried itself so indissolubly with the political and ecclesiastical institutions of the country, as well as with its commercial and social arrangements, that it seemed as if it might defy Almighty power itself to put them asunder.[7]

Furthermore, Garrison had not planned to lead the abolitionist movement.

As committed as he became to anti-slavery activity at the *National Philanthropist* and at the *Journal of the Times*, he believed that his role was primarily supportive and instructive, as was the role of the newspaper in the political processes of a democratic society. When he delivered his Park Street Address in July 1829 and warned his listeners about the impending threat caused by the evil of slavery, he also told his audience, "I regret that a better advocate has not been found, to enchain your attention, and to warm your blood."[8] He presented his warning because no one else was prepared to do so, and in the hope that his warning would be heeded and better advocates would emerge. While he certainly believed that it was his obligation to speak and publish the truth, he expected only to be an auxiliary and to provide support for the traditional political and religious leaders of society.

Even as late as August 1830, when he initially decided to publish *The Liberator* in Washington, he told Oliver Johnson that he had no desire to "take the place of the *Genius*, or to diminish the circulation of the latter."[9] At that time, he envisioned *The Liberator* as a supplement to the *Genius*, albeit a radical one, in the anti-slavery struggle. Samuel May also attested to Garrison's reluctance to take on the leadership of the abolitionist movement. When May visited Garrison after he had been converted to abolitionism in October 1830, he learned about Garrison's efforts to appeal to political and religious leaders to come forward and guide the anti-slavery cause. None responded. "Mr. Garrison," May wrote, "found himself ... impelled to become the leader of the great antislavery reform."[10] Garrison testified to this himself at the gathering to celebrate the anniversary of his apprenticeship a year before his death. Speaking about his lecture series of August 1830, Garrison told his audience,

> I never dreamed of being foremost in [the antislavery movement], but always, at that time certainly, and for a considerable period looked to our eminent men, to our distinguished statesmen and our prominent divines who, I then thought, if they could have their attention turned to the subject, would surely take the lead in so great a work.[11]

But the "eminent men" of the nation were unwilling. *The Liberator* and its editor then emerged not just to support the abolitionist movement, but to lead and direct it.

Garrison did not issue a new prospectus before the first issue of *The Liberator* appeared on January 1, 1831. He reasoned that it was unnecessary because the August prospectus for *The Liberator* in Washington had already received sufficient attention. However, a new prospectus for the paper was issued and published at the end of May 1831. Some significant differences between it and the earlier prospectus demonstrate the alterations which Garrison felt were necessary to redefine his role in the anti-slavery movement. There was no appeal to Christianity or religious principles. During his lecture tour in August 1830, mainstream church halls routinely remained closed to his message — including being locked out twice at churches in his hometown of Newburyport. Meanwhile he was welcome in black churches, Quaker meeting halls, and in Boston at Abner Kneeland's non-Christian "Society of Free Thinkers." When prominent white ministers, such as the Reverend Lyman Beecher, did attend, they dismissed Garrison's call for emancipation as fanatical and misguided. "God" and "the Creator" were the source of all human rights and the "light of the gospel" was meant to shine for all, black and white, but it was not to be found inside most churches, south or north; it would, however, be found on the pages of *The Liberator*.

Missing completely from the new prospectus was any reference to Garrison's political affiliation or support for any politician, political party, or political ideology. In August 1830, Garrison defined himself politically as a republican and promised "dignified support [for] Henry Clay and the American System." He had repeatedly endorsed Clay and as recently as February 1830 praised Clay's talent, honesty, patriotism, and proclaimed him "the champion who is destined to save this country from anarchy, corruption, and ruin."[12] It is difficult to rationalize this kind of praise from Garrison for a man who was a slaveholder. The reality could be that Garrison may have been willfully deceiving himself about Clay or naively believed that Clay did not own slaves. As difficult to believe as this might be, there is some evidence. Twice in April 1831 in *The Liberator*, he suggested as much. In a brief article about a new biography of Clay, Garrison asks: "We should like to know whether Mr. Clay is a slaveholder, and if so, to what extent? Some have assured us that he is not; others, that he owns a FEW slaves."[13] More directly, a week later he requested a fellow editor to inform his readers "that we formerly supported Mr. Clay on the supposition that he was not a slave owner."[14] Exactly when Garrison recognized this reality is not known, but it is not difficult to image the level of cynicism and anger the realization would have generated in Garrison.

Years later, Garrison wrote Clay and the venom of his disillusionment had remained powerful. He acknowledged Clay's "shining abilities" but also called him a "pitiable object" incapable of "a clear perception of human rights and obligations." John C. Calhoun was, Garrison asserted, a "more honest, trust-worthy and harmless man" than Clay. Calhoun was not a hypocrite about slavery while Clay's "oily tongue and wily compromises" deceived people about his "pretended desire to see [slavery] come to an end, not now, but at a future period long protracted."¹⁵ In 1830, the reception and support Garrison received from black communities in Baltimore, Philadelphia, Boston, and other cities during his tour, as well as his growing disenchantment with colonization, together with the realization that his political "champion" did in fact own slaves finally helped him recognize that the political institutions of the nation were as faithless and dishonest as the religious institutions — and that neither were capable of saving the nation "from anarchy, corruption, and ruin."

Also missing was Garrison's initial promise to use the paper to advocate peace and temperance. Earlier, he had called these two issues "equally dear to my heart" and promised "my zealous and unequivocal support." In the new prospectus, however, Garrison advocated only "LIBERTY AND EQUALITY," which he defined as emancipation for the nation's two million slaves and "complete enfranchisement" which required "social, political, intellectual and religious advancement" for the nation's three hundred thousand "free people of color."

More important than what was missing in the May 1831 prospectus was what was new. Since publication of *The Liberator* began in January, the new prospectus argued, "emancipation" and the "rights of man" were beginning to be universally asserted, while the "towers of civil and ecclesiastical domination" were being undermined. We can definitely acknowledge a certain amount of hyperbole in this statement, but from Garrison's perspective, these "towers of ... domination" had steadfastly refused to listen to his warnings and to accept their duty to defend the humanity and natural rights of the enslaved. The twin appeals Garrison had made, beginning with his Park Street Address of July 1829, to politics and church, and which, by October 1830, both had rejected, were now succumbing to the rhetoric of *The Liberator*. What was more, the overthrow of slavery would not come by the power of religious or political authority or leadership, but, Garrison argued "we expect to conquer through the majesty of public opinion ... and the moral power of the nation." Finally, he asserted, that despite the horrific nature of slavery, "the press is able to cope with it; and without the agency of the press, no impression can be made, no plan perfected, no victory achieved."¹⁶ Civil and ecclesiastical obduracy and their perceived authority would not deter the power of the press to reform the nation.

The public institutions of politics and church had rejected Garrison's appeal to lead and had spurned, he believed, their duty to the nation and to humanity. As a result of this capitulation, Garrison turned to the printing press to lead the struggle for abolition. When Garrison wrote his now famous introductory statement on January 1, 1831, and declared in bold letters "**and**

I will be heard," it was more than a promise to speak forcefully, powerfully, and vociferously. It was an indictment against those who refused to be faithful to their religious or political ideology and against those who had rejected Garrison's admonitions. The printing press became his instrument of reform. Success was far from assured, but meanwhile, the "printer's stand" became the bulwark of emancipation.

Chapter Notes

Chapter One

1. *The Liberator*, December 29, 1865.
2. William Lloyd Garrison, Boston, to George W. Stacy, October 23, 1878, Special Collections, Boston Public Library (Ms # A.1.1 v. 9, p. 55).
3. Samuel J. May, *Some Recollections of Our Antislavery Conflict* (Boston: Fields, Osgood, & Co., 1869; reprint, New York: Arno Press, 1968), 4–5.
4. Oliver Johnson, *William Lloyd Garrison and His Times; or Sketches of the Anti-Slavery Movement in America, and of the Man Who Was Its Founder and Moral Leader* (Boston: B.B. Russell & Co.,1880), 379.
5. Oliver Johnson, "The Abolitionists Vindicated" (1887), American Antiquarian Society (Miscellaneous MSS. "J," Box 3, Folder 3).
6. John L. Meyers, *Henry Wilson and the Era of Reconstruction* (Lanham, MD: University Press of America, 2009), xii.
7. Henry Wilson, *The History of the Rise and Fall of the Slave Power in America* (Boston: James R. Osgood and Company, 1872), 176.
8. William Lloyd Garrison, Roxbury, to Henry Wilson, May 2, 1872, Special Collections, Boston Public Library (Ms # A.1.1 v. 8, p. 14a).
9. Walter M. Merrill, ed., *The Letters of William Lloyd Garrison, Volume VI* (Cambridge, MA: Belknap Press, 1981), Letter to Henry Adams, July 27, 1874, 333–4.
10. Francis Jackson Garrison and Wendell Phillips Garrison, *William Lloyd Garrison, 1805–1879: The Story of His Life Told by His Children* (Boston: Houghton, Mifflin, 1894), IV, 257.
11. Merrill, *The Letters of William Lloyd Garrison*, Vol. VI, Garrison to "Esteemed Friends," Boston, March 17, 1873.
12. William Lloyd Garrison, Boston, to Samuel May, Jr., December 19, 1874, Special Collections, Boston Public Library (Ms # A.1.1 v. 8, p. 66).
13. Merrill, *The Letters of William Lloyd Garrison*, Vol. VI, Microform, Garrison to Wendell P. Garrison, Roxbury, March 2, 1873.
14. Garrison and Garrison, *Life*, IV, 258.
15. Johnie D. Smith, "Grimké, Archibald Henry," *American National Biography Online*.
16. James Schouler, *History of the United States of America Under the Constitution* (New York: Dodd, Mead, 1892), IV, 210–21.
17. James Ford Rhodes, *History of the United States from the Compromise of 1850* (New York: Harper & Brothers, 1893), I, 62–3.
18. Ulrich Bonnell Phillips, *American Negro Slavery: A Survey of the Supply, Employment and Control of Negro Labor As Determined by the Plantation Regime* (New York: D. Appleton, 1918; reprint, Baton Rouge: Louisiana State University, 1966), 342–343.
19. John Jay Chapman, *William Lloyd Garrison* (Boston: Atlantic Monthly Press,

1921; reprint, New York: Beekman, 1974), 6–7.

20. Gilbert Hobbs Barnes, *The Antislavery Impulse, 1830–1844* (New York: D. Appleton, 1933), 51, 174–5.

21. Hazel Catherine Wolf, *On Freedom's Alter: The Martyr Complex in the Abolition Movement* (Madison: University of Wisconsin Press, 1952), 19, 146–7.

22. Stanley M. Elkins, *Slavery: A Problem of American Institutional and Intellectual Life*, 3d ed. (Chicago: University of Chicago Press, 1976), 183–4.

23. Russell B. Nye, *William Lloyd Garrison and the Humanitarian Reformers* (Boston: Little, Brown, 1955), 205–6.

24. Walter M. Merrill, *Against Wind and Tide: A Biography of Wm. Lloyd Garrison* (Cambridge: Harvard University Press, 1963), xvi.

25. John L. Thomas, *The Liberator, William Lloyd Garrison: A Biography* (Boston: Little, Brown, 1963), 5.

26. Aileen S. Kraditor, *Means and Ends in American Abolitionism: Garrison and His Critics on Strategy and Tactics, 1834–1850* (New York: Vintage, 1967), ix.

27. Kraditor, *Means and Ends in American Abolitionism*, 260.

28. Merton L. Dillon, *The Abolitionists: The Growth of a Dissenting Minority* (DeKalb: Northern Illinois University Press, 1974), 122–4.

29. James Stewart Brewer, *Holy Warriors: The Abolitionists and American Society* (New York: Hill & Wang, 1976), 187.

30. Lawrence Friedman, *Gregarious Saints: Self and Community in American Abolitionism, 1830–1870* (New York: Cambridge University Press, 1982), 5.

31. Henry Mayer, *All on Fire: William Lloyd Garrison and the Abolition of Slavery* (New York: St. Martin's Press, 1998), 631.

32. Frank Luther Mott, *American Journalism: A History of Newspapers in the United States, 1690–1960* (New York: Macmillan, 1962) and Edwin Emery and Michael Emery, *The Press and America: An Interpretation of the Mass Media*, 8th ed. (Boston: Allyn and Bacon, 1996) are both excellent general studies of American journalism and examples of the focus on these two developments.

33. James L. Crouthamel, "The Newspaper Revolution in New York, 1830–1860," *New York History* 45 (April 1964), 94–95. For more details, see also Frank M. O'Brien, *The Story of the Sun* (New York: George H. Doran, 1918) and James L. Crouthamel, *Bennet's New York Herald and the Rise of the Popular Press* (Syracuse: Syracuse University Press, 1989).

34. William E. Huntzicker, *The Popular Press, 1833–1865*, (Westport: Greenwood Press, 1999), 163. Michael Schudson, *Discovering the News: A Social History of American Newspapers* (New York: BasicBooks, 1978) goes so far as to credit the journalistic revolution brought about by the "penny press" with creating "the world in which modern journalism took root."

35. Gerald J. Baldasty, *The Commercialization of News in the Nineteenth Century* (Madison: University of Wisconsin Press, 1992), 139.

36. Stephen Botein, "'Meer Mechanics' and an Open Press: The Business of Political Strategies of Colonial American Printers," *Perspectives in American History* 9 (1975), 130–211.

37. Arthur M. Schlesinger, *Prelude to Independence: The Newspaper War on Great Britain* (1957; reprint, Boston: Northeastern University Press, 1980), 189.

38. Mott, *American Journalism*, 79–80.

39. Schlesinger, *Prelude to Independence*, 46.

40. Botein, "Meer Mechanics," 215. Schlesinger, *Prelude to Independence*, 82. Bernard Bailyn, *The Ideological Origins of the American Revolution* (Cambridge, MA: Belknap Press, 1967) also acknowledges the important role newspapers exhibited in the years leading to American Independence.

41. John Adams letter to Thomas Jefferson, August 15, 1815, in Lester J. Cappon, ed., *The Adams-Jefferson Letters*, vol. II (Chapel Hill: University of North Carolina Press, 1959), 455.

42. Jeffery Pasley, *"The Tyranny of Printers": Newspaper Politics in the Early American Republic* (Charlottesville: University of Virginia Press, 2001), 41.

43. Jefferson letter to Edward Carrington, January 16, 1787, in Julian Boyd, ed., *The Papers of Thomas Jefferson*, vol. 11 (Princeton: Princeton University Press, 1955), 49.

44. Pasley, "The Tyranny of Printers," 48–50.

45. Botein, "'Meer Mechanics,'" 160.
46. Pasley, "The Tyranny of Printers," 9, 78.
47. John Ferling, *Adams vs. Jefferson: The Tumultuous Election of 1800* (New York: Oxford University Press, 2004), 143.
48. Donald H. Stewart, *The Opposition Press in the Federalist Period* (Albany: State University of New York Press, 1969), 640.
49. David Hacker Fischer, *The Revolution of American Conservatism: The Federalist Party in the Era of Jeffersonian Democracy* (New York: Harper & Row, 1965), 135–7.
50. Alexander Hamilton letter to James A. Bayard, in Henry Cabot Lodge, ed., *The Works of Alexander Hamilton*, vol. X (New York: G.P. Putman's Sons, 1904), 432–437.
51. American Antiquarian Society, *Transactions and Collections of the American Antiquarian Society*, vol. VI (Albany: Joel Munsell, 1874; reprint, New York: Johnson Reprint, 1971), 294–305.
52. Pasley, Tyranny of Printers, 403.
53. Gerald J. Baldasty, "The Press and Politics in the Age of Jackson," *Journalism Monographs*, Volume 89 (1984): 5.
54. Pasley, *Tyranny of Printers*, 12.
55. Sean Wilentz, *The Rise of American Democracy: Jefferson to Lincoln* (New York: W.W. Norton, 2005), xviii.
56. Baldasty, "The Press and Politics in the Age of Jackson," 20.
57. Baldasty, "The Press and Politics in the Age of Jackson," 5. The significance of the press to Jefferson's victory is also discussed in Donald H. Steward, *The Opposition Press in the Federalist Period*.
58. Michael Schudson, *The Good Citizen: A History of American Civic Life* (Cambridge: Harvard University Press, 1999), 121–2.
59. Hazel Dicken-Garcia, *Journalistic Standards in Nineteenth-Century America* (Madison: University of Wisconsin Press, 1989), 109. Carol Sue Humphrey, *The Press of the Young Republic, 1783–1833*, (Westport: Greenwood Press, 1996) argued that this trend was underway by the time the penny press emerged.
60. Dicken-Garcia, *Journalistic Standards*, 109; Schudson, *The Good Citizen*, 123.
61. Robert A. Fanuzi, "'The Organ of An Individual': William Lloyd Garrison and the *Liberator*," *Prospects* 23 (1998): 107–127.
62. David Paul Nord, "Tocqueville, Garrison and the Perfection of Journalism," *Journalism History* 13.2 (Summer 1986): 59.
63. Alexis deToqueville, *Democracy in America*, ed. J.P. Mayer, trans. George Lawrence (New York: HarperPerennial, 1988), 517.
64. *Journal of the Times*, March 27, 1829.
65. David Paul Nord, "Religious Reading and Readers in Antebellum America," *Journal of the Early Republic* 15 (Summer 1995): 241–271.
66. Nord, "Religious Reading," 245. Nord also argued that the American Anti-Slavery Society adopted the printing, distribution, and organizational methods of the bible and tract societies in 1835 in "The Evangelical Origins of Mass Media in America, 1815–1835, "*Journalism Monographs* 84 (May 1984): 2–30.
67. Garrison and Garrison, *Life*, vol. IV, 290.
68. *Daily Evening Traveller* (Boston), October 15, 1878.

Chapter Two

1. *Tributes to William Lloyd Garrison, at the Funeral Services, May 28, 1879* (Boston: Houghton, Osgood and Company, 1879), 39–40.
2. *The Liberator*, January 1, 1831.
3. Francis Jackson Garrison and Wendell Phillips Garrison, *William Lloyd Garrison, 1805–1879: The Story of His Life Told by His Children* (Boston: Houghton, Mifflin, 1894), I, 12–24.
4. Years of economic disruptions, including the embargo, blockade, and war with England, had devastated the once bustling port city of Newburyport. From 1807 through the early 1840s, business, property values, and population were in steep decline. Stephan Thernstrom, *Poverty and Progress: Social Mobility in a Nineteenth Century City* (Cambridge: Harvard University Press, 1964), 10–11.
5. Garrison and Garrison, *Life*, I, 27, 28.
6. Garrison and Garrison, *Life*, I, 32.
7. Garrison and Garrison, *Life*, I, 32–33.
8. Walter M. Merrill, ed., *The Letters of William Lloyd Garrison* (Cambridge: Belknap Press, 1971), I, Garrison to Frances Maria Lloyd Garrison, May 26, 1823, 11.
9. Garrison and Garrison, *Life*, I, 35.

10. Mrs. E. Vale Smith, *History of Newburyport: From the Earliest Settlement of the Country to the Present Time* (Newburyport, 1854), 258–9.
11. *Newburyport Herald*, March 13, 1846.
12. Paul Martin Tonsing, *The Power of the Press: History and Development of Printing Presses from the Fifteenth to the Twenty-First Century* (Fort Worth: P & T, 1998), 16.
13. Tonsing, *The Power of the Press*, 33–44.
14. Rollo G. Silver, *The American Printer, 1787–1825* (Charlottesville: University Press of Virginia, 1967), 40–62. This book provides a helpful overview of the changes in American presses during this period.
15. W.J. Rorabaugh, *The Craft Apprentice: From Franklin to the Machine Age in America* (New York: Oxford University Press, 1986). The transformation of the apprenticeship system is also discussed in Sean Wilentz, *Chants Democratic: New York City and the Rise of the American Working Class, 1788–1850* (New York: Oxford University Press, 1984), 33.
16. Rorabaugh, *The Craft Apprentice*, viii.
17. Rorabaugh, *The Craft Apprentice*, 17–31.
18. Rorabaugh, The Craft Apprentice, 76–77.
19. Robert A. Gross, *The Minutemen and Their World* (New York: Hill & Wang, 1976), 171.
20. Alan Taylor, *William Cooper's Town: Power and Persuasion on the Frontier of the Early American Republic* (New York: Vintage, 1996), 205–213.
21. Joseph F. Kett, *The Pursuit of Knowledge Under Difficulties: From Self-Improvement to Adult Education in America* (Stanford: Stanford University Press, 1994), 76.
22. Ronald Walters, *American Reformers 1815–1860*, rev. ed. (New York: Hill & Wang, 1997), 9.
23. Rorabaugh, *The Craft Apprentice*, 121.
24. Rorabaugh, *The Craft Apprentice*, 121.
25. Rorabaugh, *The Craft Apprentice*, 122
26. Charles E. Clark, *The Public Prints: The Newspaper in Anglo-American Culture, 1665–1740* (New York: Oxford University Press, 1994), 194–5.
27. Clark, *The Public Prints*, 196.
28. David Hackett Fischer, *The Revolution of American Conservation: The Federalist Party in the Era of Jeffersonian Democracy* (New York: Harper & Row, 1965), 180.
29. Garrison and Garrison, *Life*, I, 42.
30. Horace Greeley, *Recollections of a Busy Life* (New York: J.B. Ford & Co., 1868), 64.
31. William Dean Howells, *Years of My Youth and Three Essays* (Bloomington: Indiana University Press, 1975), 77.
32. Howells, *Years of My Youth*, 16.
33. *Daily Evening Traveller* (Boston), October 15, 1878.
34. John L. Thomas, *The Liberator, William Lloyd Garrison: A Biography* (Boston: Little, Brown, 1963), 28.
35. Garrison and Garrison, *Life*, I, 73.
36. Garrison and Garrison, *Life*, I, 55.
37. Garrison and Garrison, *Life*, I, 55–56.
38. John J. Currier, *History of Newburyport, Massachusetts, 1764–1909* (Printed for the author, Newburyport, 1909), II, 172–173.
39. Catalogue of the Merrimack Circulating Library Kept by W & J Gilman, Booksellers (Printed by W & J Gilman, State Street, circa 1821).
40. *Newburyport Herald*, May 10, 1822.
41. Garrison and Garrison, *Life*, I, 42.
42. Claude M. Fuess, *The Life of Caleb Cushing*, vols. I and II (New York: Harcourt, Brace & World, 1923; reprint, Hamden, CT: Archon Books, 1965).
43. *Newburyport Herald*, December 21, 1821.
44. Garrison and Garrison, *Life*, I, 48.
45. Fuess, *The Life of Caleb Cushing*, I, 40–41.
46. *Newburyport Herald*, July 12, 1822.
47. Fuess, *The Life of Caleb Cushing*, I, 51–53.
48. Merrill, *Letters*, I, 11.
49. *Newburyport Herald*, April 22, 1822.
50. Walter M. Merrill, ed., *The Letters of William Lloyd Garrison,* Vol. VI. Microform Supplement (Historical Society of Pennsylvania; Ann Arbor: University Microforms International, 1979), Garrison to Wendell P. Garrison, January 6, 1879.
51. Daniel J. Boorstin, *The Americans: The National Experience* (New York: Random House, 1965), 312–313, and Louis W. Potts, "The Franklin Debate Society: Culture in the Missouri Frontier," *Missouri Historical Review* 86 (1991), 1–3.
52. Alexis de Tocqueville, *Democracy in America*, ed. J.P. Mayer, trans. George Lawrence (New York: HarperPerennial, 1992), vol. I, pt. I, 243.

53. *Newburyport Herald*, March 2, 1821.
54. Caleb Cushing, *The History and Present State of the Town of Newburyport* (Newburyport: Ephraim Allen, 1826), 70–1.
55. *Constitution of the Newburyport Debating Society Adopted January 24th 1823, with a List of Officers and Name of Members of the Society* (Newburyport: W & J Gilman, 1823).
56. *Newburyport Herald*, September 3, 1824.
57. *Newburyport Herald*, March 27, 1821.
58. *Constitution of the Newburyport Debating Society*, 5.
59. Cushing, *History ... of Newburyport*, 70.
60. *Newburyport Herald*, December 17, 1824.
61. *Newburyport Herald*, January 18, 1825.
62. Cushing, *History ... of Newburyport*, 70.
63. Garrison and Garrison, *Life*, I, 56.
64. Currier, *History of Newburyport*, I, 433.
65. *Address Delivered Before the Members of the Franklin Debating Club on the Morning of the 5th of July, 1824, Being the Forty-Ninth Anniversary of American Independence* (Newburyport: Printed at the Herald Office, 1824).
66. Garrison and Garrison, *Life*, I, 56, footnote.
67. *Address Delivered Before the Members of the Franklin Debating Club*, 1–7.
68. *Newburyport Herald*, November 11 and November 24, 1825.
69. *Newburyport Herald*, September 23, October 28, and December 9, 1825.
70. *Tributes to William Lloyd Garrison*, 40.
71. Reprinted in the *Newburyport Herald*, July 16, 1822 (italics added).
72. Garrison's debate club is reminiscent of what Franklin described as "a club for mutual improvement which we called the Junto" in his autobiography. Russel B. Nye, ed., *Autobiography and Other Writings by Benjamin Franklin* (Boston: Houghton Mifflin, 1958), 54.
73. Merrill, *Letters*, I, 20.
74. Garrison and Garrison, *Life*, I, 43.
75. *Newburyport Herald*, May 21, 1822.
76. *Newburyport Herald*, May 24, 1822.
77. The breach-of-marriage-promise suit became common in the post-revolutionary era as protection for virtuous women against victimization and as a means of promoting republican ideals about gender responsibilities. By the end of the nineteenth-century and primarily as the result of changes in social attitudes, these suits, while still available, were rare. Michael Grossberg, *Governing the Hearth: Law and The Family in Nineteenth-Century America* (Chapel Hill: The University of North Carolina Press, 1985), 33–63.
78. *Newburyport Herald*, May 14, 1822, reprinted article from the *New York National Advocate*.
79. Garrison and Garrison, *Life*, I, 48, and Fuess, *The Life of Caleb Cushing*, I, 52.
80. Merrill, *Letters*, I, 5–31.
81. Bernard Bailyn, *The Ideological Origins of the American Revolution* (Cambridge: Belknap Press, 1967), 132.
82. *Newburyport Herald*, July 16, 19, 26, 1822.
83. Merrill, *Letters*, I, 9, footnote.
84. *Newburyport Herald*, August 6, 1822.
85. *Newburyport Herald*, March 14, April 1 and 3, 1823.
86. Lynn Hudson Parsons, *The Birth of Modern Politics: Andrew Jackson, John Quincy Adams, and the Election of 1828* (New York: Oxford University Press, 2009), 43.
87. Stanley Elkins and Eric McKitrick, *The Age of Federalism* (New York: Oxford University Press, 1993), 691–694.
88. *Dictionary of American Biography*, ed. Allen Johnson (New York: Charles Scribner Sons, 1964), "Otis, Harrison Gray," VII, 98–100.
89. *Columbian Centinel*, May 31, 1823.
90. *Newburyport Herald*, April 22, May 2 and 16, 1823.
91. *The Liberator*, January 1, 1831.
92. Merrill, *Letters*, I, 11, Garrison's italics.
93. Garrison and Garrison, *Life*, I, 51.
94. Timothy Pickering (1745–1829) was a lawyer turned soldier who rose to the rank of General during the Revolution. Later he served as secretary of war and then as secretary of state under Washington and Adams. His hatred for the French Revolution and revulsion at Jeffersonian policies led him to argue that the creation of a New England Confederation was not only feasible but also advisable. *Dictionary of American Biography*, "Pickering, Timothy," VII, 565–68.
95. Joanne B. Freeman, *Affairs of Honor: National Politics in the New Republic* (New Haven: Yale University Press, 2001), 148–158.

96. Harry R. Warfel, ed., *Letters of Noah Webster* (New York: Library Publishers, 1953), letter to Alexander Hamilton, New Haven, September, 1800, 222–6; Harlow Giles Unger, *Noah Webster: The Life and Times of an American Patriot* (New York: John Wiley & Sons, 1998), 236.
97. *The Salem Gazette*, June 11, 1824.
98. *The Salem Gazette*, June 29, 1824.
99. *The Salem Gazette*, July 27, 1824.
100. *The Salem Gazette*, August 6, 10, 20, September 7, October 22, and 29, 1824.
101. Philip S. Foner, ed., *The Life and Major Writings of Thomas Paine* (Secaucus: The Citadel Press, 1974), 48–50.
102. *The Salem Gazette*, October 29, 1824.
103. *Newburyport Herald*, July 26, 1822.
104. *Newburyport Herald*, April 1, 1823.
105. *Newburyport Herald*, May 16, 1823.
106. *The Salem Gazette*, June 29, 1824.
107. *The Salem Gazette*, August 10, 1824.
108. *Newburyport Herald*, May 17, 1825.
109. Donald A. Sears, *John Neal* (Boston: Twayne, 1978), 9.
110. Coffin had also been an apprentice in Ephraim Allen's office but was about eight years older than Garrison and there is no record that the two ever met. Smith, *History of Newburyport*, 261.
111. *Dictionary of American Biography*, "Fessenden, Thomas," III, 347.
112. *The Liberator*, November 13, 1835.
113. *The Liberator*, November 3, 1865.
114. The author is identified in Merrill, *Letters*, I, 31. Since the novel was published anonymously, Garrison did not know for certain who the author was. He suggests in a footnote to his article that it was "Miss Evans, of Portsmouth, sister of Estwick Evans, Esq." and he was right.
115. *Newburyport Herald*, October 14, 1825.
116. See Herbert Ross Brown, *The Sentimental Novel in America, 1789–1860* (Durham: Duke University Press, 1940); Linda K. Kerber, *Women of the Republic: Intellect and Ideology in Revolutionary America* (New York: W.W. Norton, 1980); Nina Baym, *Novels, Readers, and Reviewers: Responses to Fiction in Antebellum America* (Ithaca: Cornell University Press, 1984); and Cathy N. Davidson, *Revolution and the Word: The Rise of the Novel in America* (New York: Oxford University Press, 1986).

117. Fuess, *The Life of Caleb Cushing*, I, 78.
118. Fuess, *The Life of Caleb Cushing*, I, 151.
119. *Tributes to William Lloyd Garrison*, 40.

Chapter Three

1. *Daily Evening Traveller* (Boston), October 15, 1878.
2. *The Liberator,* January 1, 1851.
3. *The Patriot* (London), August 21, 1833.
4. Francis Jackson Garrison and Wendell Phillips Garrison, *William Lloyd Garrison, 1805–1879: The Story of His Life Told by His Children* (Boston: Houghton, Mifflin, 1894), I, 55. Wendell and Francis Garrison also suggest that the portrait was accurate in the "dress of the subject," but was in fact not really a good resemblance of the young Garrison, *Life*, I, xv.
5. Sean Wilentz, *Chants Democratic: New York City and the Rise of the American Working Class, 1788–1850* (New York: Oxford University Press, 1984), 102. The changing role and status of the artisan took on new political and social significance as a result of the American Revolution, was felt throughout the country, and are also examined in Howard B. Rock, Paul A. Gilje, and Robert Asher, eds., *American Artisans: Crafting Social Identity, 1750–1850* (Baltimore: Johns Hopkins University Press, 1995).
6. Garrison and Garrison, *Life*, I, 55.
7. Garrison and Garrison, *Life*, I, 59.
8. *The Free Press* March 22, 1826.
9. *Daily Evening Traveller* (Boston), October 15, 1878; Garrison and Garrison, *Life*, I, 60.
10. *Journal of the Times*, March 13, 1829.
11. *Newburyport Herald*, December 15, 1826.
12. David Hackett Fischer, *The Revolution of American Conservatism: The Federalist Party in the Era of Jeffersonian Democracy* (New York: Harper & Row, 1965), 129, 415.
13. Henry Mayer, *All on Fire: William Lloyd Garrison and the Abolition of Slavery* (New York: St. Martin's Press, 1998), 35.
14. Walter M. Merrill, ed., *The Letters of William Lloyd Garrison*, Vol. VI. Microform Supplement (Historical Society of Pennsylvania; Ann Arbor: University Microforms In-

ternational, 1979), Garrison to Wendell P. Garrison, January 6, 1879.

15. *The Free Press*, March 22, 1826.
16. *The Free Press*, March 29, 1826.
17. *The Free Press*, April 5, April 20, April 27, May 11, 1826.
18. *The Free Press*, April 20, 1826.
19. *The Free Press*, April 5, 1826. Interestingly, after Garrison sold *The Free Press* in September 1826, it returned to Saturday publication. *The Free Press*, October 28, 1826.
20. *The Free Press*, March 22, 1826.
21. *The Free Press*, September 21, 1826. In his opening comments in *The Liberator*, January 1, 1831, Garrison famously declared that with regard to the abolition of slavery, "I am in earnest — I will not equivocate — I will not excuse — I will not retreat a single inch — AND I WILL BE HEARD."
22. *The Free Press*, April 5, 1826, and April 13, 1826.
23. Garrison and Garrison, *Life*, II, 273.
24. *The Free Press*, May 25, 1826.
25. *The Free Press*, May 11, 1826.
26. *The Free Press*, June 22, 1826.
27. *The Free Press*, June 29, 1826.
28. *Newburyport Herald*, July 12, August 2, 1822.
29. Newburyport Herald, July 4, 1826.
30. Many of the arrangements for the anniversary were made by the town's "Franklin Debating Society" which Garrison had organized a few years earlier, but there is no mention of his current involvement with the society. *The Free Press*, July 7, 1826.
31. *The Free Press*, July 13, 1826.
32. *Newburyport Herald*, July 11, 1826.
33. *Newburyport Herald*, July 14, 1826.
34. *The Free Press*, July 20, 1826.
35. *Newburyport Herald*, July 21, 1826.
36. *Newburyport Herald*, July 25, 1826.
37. *Newburyport Herald*, September 22, 1826.
38. *The Free Press* August 3, 1826.
39. *The Free Press*, August 10, 1826.
40. *The Free Press*, August 3 and August 17, 1826.
41. *The Free Press*, July 27, August 3, August 10, August 17, and August 31, 1826.
42. Garrison and Garrison, I, 63.
43. *Newburyport Herald*, August 18, 1826.
44. *The Free Press*, August 24, 1826.
45. *The Free Press*, May 4, 1826 and May 25, 1826.
46. *The Free Press*, September 14, 1826.
47. Claude M. Fuess, *The Life of Caleb Cushing*, vols. I and II (New York: Harcourt, Brace & World, 1923; reprint, Hamden, CT: Archon Books, 1965), 72–74.
48. Mayer, *All on Fire*, 40–43.
49. *The Free Press*, September 14, 1826.
50. *The Free Press*, August 10, 1826.
51. Support for Cushing was announced in *The Free Press* of October 5, 1826. However, Harris began a secret campaign for Cushing in *The Free Press* of September 21 with the first in a series of articles signed "C" but which were later revealed to have been written by Cushing himself. Walter M. Merrill, "Prologue to Reform — Garrison's Early Career," *Essex Institute Historical Collection* XCII, no. 2 (1956): 163.
52. *The Free Press*, September 21, 1826.
53. Merrill, ed., *Letters*, vol. VI (Microform), to Wendell Phillips Garrison, January 6, 1879. Only a few brief articles attributed to Garrison have not been found but there were many anti–Cushing articles in the local papers written under various pseudonyms, some of which may have been written by Garrison.
54. *Newburyport Herald*, November 7, 1826.
55. Feuss, *The Life of Caleb Cushing*, 78.
56. Garrison and Garrison, *Life*, I, 73.
57. Garrison and Garrison, *Life*, I, 277–280.
58. Garrison and Garrison, *Life*, I, 73.
59. Garrison and Garrison, *Life*, I, 79.
60. *Boston Courier*, September 23, 1826.
61. Fischer, *Revolution of American Conservatism*, 272–4.
62. *Boston Courier*, December 13, 1826.
63. These words also suggest a deep faith in the "True Whig" or "Commonwealthman" traditions identified by Bailyn as fundamental to American revolutionary ideology. Bernard Bailyn, *The Ideological Origins of the American Revolution* (Cambridge: Belknap Press, 1967).
64. *Boston Courier*, July 14, 1827.
65. *Newburyport Herald*, April 24, 1827.
66. *Newburyport Herald*, May 8, 1827.
67. *Newburyport Herald*, June 12, 1827.
68. Garrison and Garrison, *Life*, I, 73–4.
69. Joseph Tinker Buckingham, *Personal Memoirs and Recollections of Editorial Life* (Boston: Ticknor, Reed, and Fields, 1852), II, 34.

70. *Boston Courier*, July 12, 1827.
71. *Boston Courier*, July 13, 1827.
72. *Boston Courier*, July 15, 1827.
73. *Boston Courier*, July 14, 1827.
74. *Boston Courier*, July 23, 1827.
75. *Newburyport Herald*, July 27, 1827.
76. Merrill, "Prologue to Reform," 164.
77. Garrison and Garrison, *Life*, I, 85.
78. *National Philanthropist*, January 4, 1828.
79. *National Philanthropist*, March 4, 1826.
80. *National Philanthropist*, July 4, 1828.
81. The change in women's role in American society as the result of the Revolution and post–Revolutionary society has been examined in several books, including Nancy Cott, *The Bonds of Womanhood: Woman's Sphere in New England, 1780–1835* (New Haven: Yale University Press, 1977); Cathy Davidson, *Revolution and the Word: The Rise of the Novel in America* (New York: Oxford University Press, 1986); Linda Kerber, *Women of the Republic: Intellect and Ideology in Revolutionary America* (New York: W.W. Norton, 1980); and Mary Beth Norton, *Liberty's Daughters: The Revolutionary Experience of American Women, 1750–1800* (Boston: Little, Brown, 1980).
82. *National Philanthropist*, April 4, 1828.
83. *National Philanthropist*, April 25, 1828.
84. *National Philanthropist*, May 9, 1828.
85. *National Philanthropist*, May 16 and May 23, 1828.
86. In fact, at the time of his offer, three towns in Massachusetts had already formed such societies, Garrison and Garrison, *Life*, I, 86. In an editorial comment, *National Philanthropist*, June 20, 1828, Garrison acknowledged that he was informed of a Female Temperance Society in Mendon. He praised their determination and promised to forward a copy of the paper regularly.
87. *National Philanthropist*, February 15, 1828.
88. *National Philanthropist*, March 14, 1828.
89. *National Philanthropist*, April 25, 1828.
90. *National Philanthropist*, May 5, 1828.
91. *National Philanthropist*, May 23, 1828.
92. "From the Portland Yankee by John Neal," *Eastport Sentinel* (Maine), April 5, 1828.
93. *National Philanthropist*, January 4, 1828.
94. *National Philanthropist*, January 11, January 18, January 25, February 8 and 15, 1828; Fischer, *Revolution of American Conservatism, 134–5.*
95. Daniel Walker Howe, *What Hath God Wrought: The Transformation of America, 1815–1848* (New York: Oxford University Press, 2007), 274–5.
96. *National Philanthropist*, May 30 and June 6, 1828.
97. *National Philanthropist* June 20 and June 27, 1828.
98. *National Philanthropist*, July 4, 1828.
99. Garrison and Garrison, *Life*, I, 93.
100. For the most authoritative biography of Benjamin Lundy, see Merton L. Dillon, *Benjamin Lundy and the Struggle for Negro Freedom* (Urbana: University of Illinois Press, 1966).
101. *The Liberator*, September 20, 1839.
102. *The Yankee*, August 13, 1828.
103. Garrison and Garrison, *Life*, I, 96.
104. *The Yankee*, February 27 and March 12, 1828.
105. *The Yankee*, July 23, 1828.
106. *The Yankee*, August 13, 1828.
107. *The Yankee*, August 20, 1828.
108. Russell Nye, *William Lloyd Garrison and the Humanitarian Reformers* (Boston: Little, Brown, 1955), 21.
109. Abby Maria Hemenway, ed., *The Vermont Gazetteer: A History Embracing the History of Each Town*, vol. 3 (Burlington, 1868), 252.
110. Garrison and Garrison, *Life*, I, 101–2.
111. *Proceedings of the American Anti-Slavery Society at Its Third Decade* (New York: American Anti-Slavery Society, 1864; reprint, New York: Arno Press, 1969), 121.
112. *Journal of the Times*, October 3, 1828.
113. Generally, Garrison's modern biographers agree. John L. Thomas, *The Liberator* (Boston: Little, Brown, 1963), 84, wrote, "What Bennington subscribers saw was a spiritless campaign for Adams"; Walter M. Merrill, *Against Wind and Tide* (Cambridge: Harvard University Press, 1963), 21, said "Garrison's support of Adams ... was unenthusiastic and indirect"; Mayer, *All on Fire*, 58, on the other hand admitted that Adams' supporters in Bennington "received full value"

from editor Garrison although reform issues remained his principal concern.

114. *Journal of the Times*, October 3, 1828.
115. *Journal of the Times*, October 17, 1828.
116. *Journal of the Times*, October 31, 1828.
117. *Journal of the Times*, November 21, 1828.
118. *Journal of the Times*, November 28, December 5 and 19, 1828, and January 9, 1828.
119. Journal of the Times, November 28, 1828.
120. *Journal of the Times*, December 5, 1828.
121. *Journal of the Times*, January 9, 1829.
122. *Journal of the Times*, December 26, 1828.
123. Richard S. Newman, *The Transformation of American Abolitionism: Fighting Slavery in the Early Republic* (Chapel Hill: University of North Carolina Press, 2002), 57-58.
124. Dillon, *Benjamin Lundy*, 137.
125. Garrison and Garrison, *Life*, I, 110.
126. *Journal of the Times*, October 10, 1828.
127. *Journal of the Times*, October 24, 1828.
128. *Journal of the Times*, November 14, 1828.
129. Garrison and Garrison, *Life*, I, 108-110. The "franking" privilege allowed postmasters to forward items through the mail postage-free. For much of the nineteenth century, it was a significant economic benefit to the postmaster as well as a source of political patronage and power. See Richard R. John, *Spreading the News: The American Postal System From Franklin to Morse* (Cambridge: Harvard University Press, 1995) and Richard B. Keilbowicz, *News in the Mail: The Press, Post Office, and Public Information, 1700-1860* (New York: Greenwood Press, 1989).
130. *Journal of the Times*, January 23, 1829.
131. *Journal of the Times*, January 30, 1829.
132. William Lee Miller, *Arguing About Slavery: The Great Battle in the United States Congress* (New York: Alfred A. Knopf, 1996), 105-7.
133. *Journal of the Times*, March 20, 1829.

134. Timothy J. Gilfoyle, *City of Eros: New York City, Prostitution, and the Commercialization of Sex, 1790-1920* (New York: W.W. Norton, 1992), 20.
135. *Journal of the Times,* March 27, 1829. Reference to the "triumph of the sword over the pen" was an oft used Garrisonian reference to Jackson's election in 1828.
136. Garrison and Garrison, *Life*, I, 120.
137. Dillon, *Benjamin Lundy*, 143-4. Dillon also confirms Lundy's visit with Garrison.
138. *The Liberator*, September 20, 1839.
139. Walter M. Merrill, ed., *The Letters of William Lloyd Garrison* (Cambridge: Belknap Press, 1971), I, 78-82, to Stephen Foster, March 30, 1829.
140. *Journal of the Times*, April 1, 1829.

Chapter Four

1. William Lloyd Garrison, Boston, to Mr. Marshall, April 27, 1877, Special Collections, Boston Public Library (Ms # A.1.1 v. 9, p. 27).
2. Erik H. Erikson, *Young Man Luther: A Study in Psychoanalysis and History* (New York: W.W. Norton, 1958), 229.
3. Most of the works published about the reform era argue that the majority of the participants had firm foundations in religion and the evangelical movements of the early nineteenth century. For example, see Ronald Walters, *American Reformers, 1815-1860*, rev. ed. (1978; reprint, New York: Hill & Wang, 1997,); Robert H. Abzug, *Cosmos Crumbling: American Reform and the Religious Imagination* (New York: Oxford University Press, 1989); James Stewart Brewer, *Holy Warriors: The Abolitionists and American Slavery*, rev. ed. (1976; New York: Hill & Wang, 1996); and Lawrence Friedman, *Gregarious Saints: Self and Community in American Abolitionism, 1830-1870* (Cambridge: Cambridge University Press, 1982).
4. Alexis de Tocqueville, *Democracy in America*, ed. J.P. Mayer, trans. George Lawrence (New York: HarperPerennial, 1988), 291.
5. Walter M. Merrill, ed., *The Letters of William Lloyd Garrison, Volume I* (Cambridge: Belknap Press, 1971), letter to Helen E. Benson, June 21, 1834, 368-9.
6. Stephen Thernstrom, *Poverty and*

Progress: Social Mobility in a Nineteenth Century City (Cambridge: Harvard University Press, 1964), 10. Samuel Eliot Morison, *The Maritime History of Massachusetts, 1783–1860* (London: William Heinemann, 1923), 191.

7. Francis Jackson Garrison and Wendell Phillips Garrison, *William Lloyd Garrison, 1805–1879: The Story of His Life Told by His Children* (Boston: Houghton, Mifflin, 1894), I, 14–20.

8. Garrison and Garrison, *Life*, IV, 305.

9. Walter Merrill, ed., *Behold Me Once More: The Confessions of James Holley Garrison, Brother of William Lloyd Garrison* (Boston: Houghton Mifflin, 1954), 7–31.

10. In late June 1823, and after a direct appeal from Fanny, Allen finally allowed Garrison to make the journey to Baltimore to see his dying mother. He returned to Newburyport at the end of July and Fanny died in Baltimore on September 3. Garrison and Garrison, *Life*, I, 53.

11. Garrison and Garrison, *Life*, I, 21–32.

12. August 29, 1817 letter, quoted in Garrison and Garrison, *Life*, I, 33

13. July 1, 1822 letter, quoted in Garrison and Garrison, *Life*, I, 44.

14. June 3, 1823 letter, quoted in Garrison and Garrison, *Life*, I, 51.

15. *The Salem Gazette*, June 11, 1824, Letter to the Editor signed "Aristedes." "The Crisis" series was primarily concerned with the upcoming presidential election and appeared on August 6, 10, 20; September 7; and October 22 and 29, 1824.

16. *Address Delivered Before the Members of the Franklin Debating Club on the Morning of the 5th of July, 1824, Being the Forty-Ninth Anniversary of American Independence* (Newburyport: Printed at the Herald Office, 1824), 6.

17. *Newburyport Herald*, October 14, 1825.

18. Merrill, *Letters*, I, 30–1, Garrison to Tobias H. Miller, October 14, 1825.

19. *The Free Press*, March 22, 1826.

20. *The Free Press*, June 29, 1826.

21. *The Free Press*, July 13, 1826.

22. William Lloyd Garrison, Boston, to Wendell Phillips Garrison, January 6, 1879, Special Collections, Boston Public Library (Ms # A.1.1 v. 9, p. 65).

23. Garrison and Garrison, *Life*, I, 71.

24. Garrison and Garrison, *Life*, I, 79.

25. Garrison and Garrison, *Life*, I, 220.

26. Garrison first shared a room with Nathaniel White who at the time was the printer for the *National Philanthropist* and who offered Garrison day work setting type. Garrison and Garrison, *Life*, I, 80.

27. "Biographical Sketch of the Late Rev. John Peak — Massachusetts," *The Baptist Memorial and Monthly Record* Vol. III, No. 11 (November 1844), 331-332; George Levesque, *Black Boston: African American Life and Culture in Urban America 1750–1860* (New York: Garland, 1994); and George A. Levesque, "Inherent Reformers-Inherited Orthodoxy: Black Baptists in Boston, 1800–1873," *The Journal of Negro History* 60, no. 4 (October 1975), 491–525.

28. "Biographical Sketch of the Late Rev. Wm. Collier, of Boston," *The Baptist Memorial and Monthly Record* Vol. III, no. 11 (November 1844), 327–328.

29. *National Philanthropist*, March 4, 1826. It is interesting to note that the Treasurer of the Massachusetts Society was Lewis Tappan. There is no indication that Tappan met or knew Garrison while he was in Boston or while he edited the *Philanthropist* in 1828 but, in few years, Lewis and his brother Arthur would come to know Garrison very well.

30. "Biographical Sketch of the Late Rev. Wm. Collier, of Boston," 327–328.

31. David Paul Nord, "The Evangelical Origins of Mass Media in America, 1814–1835" *Journalism Monographs* 84 (1984), 2, 7–10. See also Nord, "Religious Reading and Readers in Antebellum America" *Journal of the Early Republic* 15 (Summer 1995); and *Communities of Journalism: A History of American Newspapers and Their Readers* (Chicago: University of Illinois Press, 2001).

32. Garrison and Garrison, *Life*, I, 78.

33. *Boston Courier*, February 8, 1827.

34. Merrill, *Letters*, I, 37–8.

35. William Harlan Hale, *Horace Greeley; Voice of the People* (New York: Harper & Brothers, 1950), 65.

36. Andie Tucher, *Froth and Scum: Truth, Beauty, Goodness, and the Ax Murder in America's First Mass Medium* (Chapel Hill: University of North Carolina Press, 1994), 131.

37. *National Philanthropist*, January 18, 1828.

38. *National Philanthropist*, June 13, 1828.

39. *National Philanthropist*, March 14, 1828.
40. *National Philanthropist*, January 18, February 15, April 4 and 25, May 2 and May 23, 1828.
41. Merton L. Dillon, *Benjamin Lundy and the Struggle for Negro Freedom* (Urbana: University of Illinois Press, 1966), 127.
42. *Proceedings of the American Anti-Slavery Society at its Third Decade* (New York: American Anti-Slavery Society, 1864; reprint, New York: Arno Press, 1969), 120.
43. Dillon, *Benjamin Lundy*, 128–131.
44. Bertram Wyatt-Brown, *Lewis Tappan and the Evangelical War Against Slavery* (Cleveland: Press of Case Western Reserve University, 1969), 78–9.
45. Goodell became a very active abolitionist and close friend of Garrison's until they split in the 1840s over interpretation of the Constitution. Goodell also wrote the first history of the anti-slavery movement, *Slavery and Anti-Slavery: A History of the Great Struggle in Both Hemispheres with a View of the Slavery Question in the United States* (New York: William Goodell, 1853; reprint, New York: Augustus M. Kelley, 1970), and one of the first studies of slave law, *The American Slave Code In Theory and Practice* (London: Clarke, Beeton, and Co., 1853).
46. *Literary Cadet, and Saturday Evening Bulletin*, April 16, 1828.
47. Dillon, *Benjamin Lundy*, 131.
48. Garrison and Garrison, *Life*, I, 93–4 describes the meeting. The document signed by the ministers, which recommended the *Genius*, either was never issued or is not extant.
49. *National Philanthropist*, March 21, 1828.
50. Garrison and Garrison, *Life*, I, 94, states that the editorial "was clearly due to the inspiration of Lundy's visit."
51. Henry Mayer, *All on Fire* (New York: St. Martin's Press, 1998), 54.
52. Dillon, *Benjamin Lundy*, 133–9.
53. Garrison and Garrison, *Life*, I, 97.
54. Kenneth M. Stampp, *The Peculiar Institution: Slavery in the Ante-Bellum South* (New York: Vintage, 1956), 27–9; and John Hope Franklin and Alfred A. Moss, Jr., *From Slavery to Freedom: A History of African Americans*, 7th ed. (New York: Alfred A. Knopf, 1994), 188–92.
55. *Boston Courier* August 11, 1828, reprinted in the *National Philanthropist*, August 15, 1828.
56. *Boston Courier*, August 12, 1828.
57. *The Liberator*, August 22, 1835.
58. *The Liberator*, August 29, 1835.
59. *Boston Courier*, August 12, 1828.
60. Garrison and Garrison, *Life*, I, 98, also mentioned in the *Journal of the Times*, October 10, 1828, in which Garrison reported that the committee of "high-minded, spirited, and philanthropic men" were doing "bravely in Boston."
61. Charles M. Wiltse, ed., *The Papers of Daniel Webster Correspondence, Volume 2, 1825–1829* (Hanover, NH: University Press of New England, 1976), 347–8.
62. *The Liberator*, September 20, 1839.
63. *The Liberator*, September 20, 1839.
64. Dillon, *Benjamin Lundy*, 137.
65. *Journal of the Times*, October 10, 1828.
66. *Journal of the Times*, October 3, 1828.
67. *Journal of the Times*, October 10, see also October 24 and 31, 1828.
68. *Journal of the Times*, January 3, 1829.
69. Dillon, *Benjamin Lundy*, 143–4.
70. Mayer, *All on Fire*, 60–1.
71. Garrison and Garrison, *Life*, I, 118, and Dillon, *Benjamin Lundy*, 144.
72. *Genius of Universal Emancipation*, December 27, 1828.
73. *Journal of the Times*, January 16, 1829.
74. Dillon, *Benjamin Lundy*, 142–3.
75. *Journal of the Times*, October 10, 1828. Similar accusations were published October 31, 1828.
76. Dillon, *Benjamin Lundy*, 128–30.
77. *Journal of the Times*, February 13, 1829.
78. *Journal of the Times*, March 13, 1829.
79. *Journal of the Times*, February 6, 1829.
80. *Journal of the Times*, October 17, November 21, December 26, 1828, and January 23, 1829.
81. *Journal of the Times*, November 21, 1828.
82. *Journal of the Times*, March 27, 1829.
83. Garrison and Garrison, *Life*, I, 123.
84. Garrison and Garrison, *Life*, 123–4.
85. William Goodell, *Slavery and Anti-Slavery: A History of the Great Struggle in Both Hemispheres with a View of the Slavery Question in the United States* (New York: William Goodell, 1853; reprint, New York: Augustus M. Kelley, 1970), 400–1 (and footnotes).

Chapter Five

1. Henry Mayer, *All on Fire: William Lloyd Garrison and the Abolition of Slavery* (New York: St. Martin's Press, 1998), 61–2.
2. Walter M. Merrill, ed., *The Letters of William Lloyd Garrison* (Cambridge: Belknap Press, 1971), I, 82–84, to Jacob Horton, June 27, 1829.
3. *Address Delivered Before the Members of the Franklin Debating Club on the Morning of the 5th of July, 1824, Being the Forty-Ninth Anniversary of American Independence* (Newburyport: Printed at the Herald Office, 1824).
4. *Newburyport Herald*, July 5, 1825.
5. *The Free Press*, June 29, 1826.
6. *Newburyport Herald*, July 8, 1828.
7. The only complete printed record of Garrison's speech was published in two installments of the *National Philanthropist*, on July 22 and July 29, 1829, from which all of the following address quotes are taken.
8. *The Liberator*, September 16, 1842. Garrison completely abandoned his own participation in politics by early 1834, but became even more dismissive of politics later in the decade, especially as the movement to form an anti-slavery third party became more prominent.
9. *Boston Commercial Gazette*, July 6, 1829; *Boston Recorder*, July 9, 1829.
10. *American Traveller*, July 7, 1829.
11. Francis Jackson Garrison and Wendell Phillips Garrison, *William Lloyd Garrison, 1805–1879: The Story of His Life Told by His Children* (Boston: Houghton, Mifflin, 1894), I, 138.
12. *Boston Courier*, July 9, 1829.
13. *American Traveller*, July 14, 1829.
14. *Newburyport Herald*, July 21, 1829.
15. *Journal of the Times*, January 2, 1829.
16. *Journal of the Times*, January 23, 1829.
17. *Genius of Universal Emancipation*, September 25, 1829.
18. Peter Kolchin, *American Slavery, 1619–1877* (New York: Hill & Wang, 1993), 78–9.
19. *Genius of Universal Emancipation*, January 3, 1829 (erroneously printed "1828" on the paper itself).
20. Merton L. Dillon, *Benjamin Lundy and the Struggle for Negro Freedom* (Urbana: University of Illinois Press, 1966), 143.
21. *The Liberator*, February 13, 1852.
22. Garrison and Garrison, *Life*, I, 142.
23. Garrison and Garrison, *Life*, I, 140.
24. *National Philanthropist*, July 29, 1829.
25. Oliver Johnson, *William Lloyd Garrison and His Times; or Sketches of the Anti-Slavery Movement in America, and of the Man Who Was Its Founder and Moral Leader* (Boston: B.B. Russell & Co., 1880), 29.
26. *Genius of Universal Emancipation*, September 2, 1829.
27. A more complete discussion of the origins of immediate emancipation can be found in "The Emergence of Immediatism in British and American Antislavery Thought" in David Brion Davis, *From Homicide to Slavery: Studies in American Culture* (New York: Oxford University Press, 1986), 238–57.
28. George Bourne, *The Book and Slavery Irreconcilable* (Philadelphia: J.M. Sanderson & Co., 1816; reprint, New York: Arno Press, 1969), 3.
29. John W. Christie and Dwight L. Dumond, *George Bourne and The Book and Slavery Irreconcilable* (Wilmington: The Historical Society of Delaware and Philadelphia: The Presbyterian Historical Society, 1969), 1–82 gives a detailed biography of Bourne' life, work, and trials in America.
30. David Brion Davis, *The Problem of Slavery in the Age of Revolution, 1770–1823* (Ithaca: Cornell University Press, 1975), 33, 200.
31. Christie and Dumond, *George Bourne*, 83.
32. Dillon, *Benjamin Lundy and the Struggle for Negro Freedom*, 107–6. Serial publication of the pamphlet was in the *Genius of Universal Emancipation*, November 26, 1825; December 10, 17, 24, 31, 1825; AND January 7, 14, 21, 1826.
33. Ralph Korngold, *Two Friends of Mankind: The Story of William Lloyd Garrison and Wendell Phillips and Their Relationship with Abraham Lincoln* (Boston: Little, Brown, 1950), 33.
34. Christie and Dumond, *George Bourne*, 78–9.
35. Russel B. Nye, *William Lloyd Garrison and the Humanitarian Reformers* (Boston: Little, Brown, 1955), 24–26.
36. *Daily Evening Traveller* (Boston), October 15, 1878.
37. *The Liberator*, March 17, 1832.
38. *The Liberator*, August 25, 1832.
39. *The Independent*, January 30, 1868.

40. Johnson, *Garrison and His Times*, 45.
41. Norman Clark, *Deliver Us from Evil: An Interpretation of American Prohibition* (New York: W.W. Norton, 1976), 18.
42. Ronald G. Walters, *American Reformers, 1815–1860*, rev. ed. (New York: Hill & Wang, 1997), 126–7.
43. *Journal of the Times*, January 2, 1829.
44. George A. Levesque, *Black Boston: African American Life and Culture in Urban America, 1750–1860* (New York: Garland, 1994), 256.
45. George A. Levesque, "Inherent Reformers-Inherited Orthodoxy: Black Baptists in Boston, 1800–1873," *The Journal of Negro History* 60, no. 4 (October 1975), 496, 494.
46. James Oliver Horton and Lois E. Horton, *Black Bostonians: Family Life and Community Struggle in the Antebellum North* (New York: Holmes & Meier, 1979), 40–1.
47. Levesque, *Black Boston*, 266–272.
48. *The Liberator*, April 16, 1831.
49. Horton and Horton, *Black Bostonians*, 27–8.
50. James Oliver Horton, "Generations of Protest: Black Families and Social Reform in Ante-Bellum Boston," *The New England Quarterly* 49, no. 2 (June 1976), 248–9.
51. Henry Mayer, *All on Fire*, 68.
52. *Genius of Universal Emancipation*, September 2, 1829.
53. Merton L. Dillon, *The Abolitionists: The Growth of a Dissenting Minority* (DeKalb: Northern Illinois University Press, 1974), 150.
54. Leeds Anti-Slavery Series, No. 86, "Principles and Mode of Action of the American Anti-Slavery Society: A Speech by William Lloyd Garrison," *Anti-Slavery Convention Report* (London: William Tweedie, 1853), 5.
55. *Christian Register*, September 19, 1829.
56. *Genius of Universal Emancipation*, September 25, 1829.
57. *Genius of Universal Emancipation*, October 30, 1829.
58. Dillon, *The Abolitionists*, 38.
59. *Tributes to William Lloyd Garrison, at the Funeral Services, May 28, 1879* (Boston: Houghton, Osgood and Company, 1879), 39–40.
60. *National Philanthropist*, July 29, 1829.
61. Benjamin Quarles, *Black Abolitionists* (New York: Oxford University Press, 1969), 3–8.
62. Garrison and Garrison, *Life*, I, 148.
63. T. Stephen Whitman, *The Price of Freedom: Slavery and Manumission in Baltimore and Early National Maryland* (Lexington: University Press of Kentucky, 1997), 1–5.
64. Gary Lawson Browne, *Baltimore in the Nation, 1789–1861* (Chapel Hill: University of North Carolina Press, 1980), 99.
65. Christopher Phillips, *Freedom's Port: The African American Community of Baltimore, 1790–1860* (Chicago: University of Illinois Press, 1997), 2–3.
66. Browne, *Baltimore in the Nation*, 101.
67. Philips, *Freedom's Port*, 187.
68. *Genius of Universal Emancipation*, March 5, 1830.
69. Philips, *Freedom's Port*, 186.
70. Browne, *Baltimore in the Nation*, 100.
71. C. Peter Ripley, ed., *The Black Abolitionist Papers: Volume III, The United States, 1830–1846* (Chapel Hill: University of North Carolina Press, 1991), 96–7. See also Phillips, *Freedom's Port*, 220–1, and Leroy Graham, *Baltimore, The Nineteenth Century Black Capital* (Lantham, MD: University Press of America, 1982), 112.
72. Watkins biography has not received the attention it deserves; this brief summary is taken from two sources: Graham, *Baltimore, The Nineteenth Century Black Capital*, 93–141; and Bettye J. Gardner, "William Watkins: Antebellum Black Teacher and Anti-slavery Writer," *Negro History Bulletin* 39.6 (September-October 1976), 623–25.
73. Garrison and Garrison, *Life*, I, 145.
74. Graham, *Baltimore, The Nineteenth Century Black Capital*, 97–9.
75. "Memorial of Free People of Colour," *Baltimore Gazette and Daily Advertiser*, December 14, 1826.
76. "Original Communication for the Freedom's Journal," *Freedom's Journal*, July 6, 1827.
77. "Another Libel," *The Liberator*, January 8, 1831.
78. Garrison and Garrison, *Life*, I, 259.
79. Wm. Lloyd Garrison, *An Address Delivered Before the Free People of Color of Philadelphia, New-York and Other Cities During the Month of June, 1831* (Boston: Stephen Foster, 1831), 17–21.
80. Merrill, ed., *Letters*, I, 121–23, to Ebenezer Dole, July 11, 1831.

81. "Weymouth A.S. Fair," *The Liberator*, October 14, 1853.
82. "The Colored Citizens of Boston," *The Liberator*, December 10, 1852.

Chapter Six

1. *Genius of Universal Emancipation*, September 16, 1829.
2. *Genius of Universal Emancipation*, September 2, 1829. See also October 2; December 4, 11, 18, 25, 1829; January 15, 1830; and February 12, 1830.
3. Arthur M. Schlesinger, Jr., *The Age of Jackson* (Boston: Little, Brown, 1945), 80–1.
4. *Genius of Universal Emancipation*, December 18 and 25, 1829.
5. *Genius of Universal Emancipation*, December 4, 1829.
6. *Genius of Universal Emancipation*, October 16, November 6, and December 4, 1829.
7. Genius of Universal Emancipation, December 4, 1829.
8. Gary Lawson Browne, *Baltimore in the Nation, 1789–1861* (Chapel Hill: University of North Carolina Press, 1980), 100–1. Christopher Phillips, *Freedom's Port: The African American Community of Baltimore, 1790–1860* (Urbana: University of Illinois Press, 1997), 188–9.
9. *Genius of Universal Emancipation*, October 2, 1829.
10. *Genius of Universal Emancipation*, October 9, 1829.
11. William W. Freehling, *The Road to Disunion: Secessionist at Bay, 1776–1854* (New York: Oxford University Press, 1990), 162–177.
12. *Genius of Universal Emancipation*, October 9, 1829.
13. *Genius of Universal Emancipation*, October 16 and 23, November 6 and 20, 1829, and January 1 and 22, 1830.
14. *Genius of Universal Emancipation*, February 12, 1830.
15. *Journal of the Times*, March 27, 1829; Genius of Universal Emancipation, January 22, 1830.
16. *Genius of Universal Emancipation*, October 16, 1829.
17. Maurice G. Baxter, *Henry Clay and the American System* (Lexington: University Press of Kentucky, 1995), 199.

18. *Genius of Universal Emancipation*, October 16, 1829.
19. David S. Heidler and Jeanne T. Heidler, *Henry Clay: The Essential American* (New York: Random House, 2010), 19–22.
20. Heidler and Heidler, *Henry Clay*, 34–36, 131–32. See also Robert V. Remini, *Henry Clay: Statesman for the Union* (New York: W.W. Norton, 1991), 9–10, 179–80.
21. *Genius of Universal Emancipation*, January 15, 22, and 29, 1830.
22. *Genius of Universal Emancipation*, February 12 and 19, and March 5, 1830.
23. *Genius of Universal Emancipation*, September 25, December 11, 1829, and February 19, 1830.
24. *Genius of Universal Emancipation*, October 23, 1829.
25. *Genius of Universal Emancipation*, November 27, 1829.
26. *Genius of Universal Emancipation*, September 2, 1829.
27. *Genius of Universal Emancipation*, September 25, 1829. The publications recognized were *Mauch Chunck Courier, Record of the Times, Journal of Health, Le Papillon, Ladies Magazine, Providence Journal, Philadelphia Album*, and the *New England Weekly Review*.
28. *Genius of Universal Emancipation*, February 5, 1830.
29. Genius of Universal Emancipation, March 5, 1830.
30. Hazel Dicken-Garcia, *Journalistic Standards in Nineteenth-Century America* (Madison: University of Wisconsin Press, 1989), 97.
31. The history and effect of "newspaper exchange" has been addressed in Richard B. Keilbowicz, *News in the Mail: The Press, Post Office, and Public Information, 1700–1860s* (New York: Greenwood Press, 1989), and Richard D. John, *Spreading the News: The American Postal System from Franklin to Morse* (Cambridge: Harvard University Press, 1995).
32. *Genius of Universal Emancipation*, September 25, 1829.
33. *Genius of Universal Emancipation*, October 9, 1829. See *American Traveller*, July 14 and October 23, 1829.
34. *Genius of Universal Emancipation*, December 11, and 18, 1829.
35. *Genius of Universal Emancipation*, November 20, 1829.
36. Merton L. Dillon, *Benjamin Lundy*

and the Struggle for Negro Freedom (Urbana: University of Illinois Press, 1966), 119–20.

37. *Genius of Universal Emancipation*, October 23 and November 6, 1829.

38. Gerald J. Baldasty, "The Press and Politics in the Age of Jackson," *Journalism Monographs* 89 (1984), 8.

39. *Genius of Universal Emancipation*, November 20, 1829.

40. *Genius of Universal Emancipation*, January 1, 1830.

41. Dillon, *Benjamin Lundy*, 55–56.

42. G.J. Barker-Benfield, *The Culture of Sensibility: Sex and Society in Eighteenth-Century Britain* (Chicago: University of Chicago Press, 1992), 213.

43. *Genius of Universal Emancipation*, September 25, October 23 and 30, 1829.

44. *Genius of Universal Emancipation*, November 13, 1829.

45. *Genius of Universal Emancipation*, November 20, 1829.

46. *Newburyport Herald*, April 23, 1830.

47. *Newburyport Herald*, May 25, 1830.

48. *Genius of Universal Emancipation*, January 8, 1830.

49. Francis Jackson Garrison and Wendell Phillips Garrison, *William Lloyd Garrison, 1805–1879: The Story of His Life Told by His Children* (Boston: Houghton, Mifflin, 1894), I, 168.

50. Oliver Johnson, *William Lloyd Garrison and His Times; or Sketches of the Anti-Slavery Movement in America, and of the Man Who Was Its Founder and Moral Leader* (Boston: B.B. Russell & Co., 1880), 31.

51. Benjamin Quarles, *Black Abolitionists* (New York: Oxford University Press, 1969), 16–17.

52. Peter Hinks, *To Awaken My Afflicted Brethren: David Walker and the Problem of Antebellum Slave Resistance* (University Park: Pennsylvania State University Press, 1997), 118–9.

53. Marshall Rachleff, "David Walker's Southern Agent," *Journal of Negro History* 62, issue 1 (January 1977), 100.

54. *Boston Commercial Gazette*, June 30, 1830.

55. Peter Hinks, ed., *David Walker's Appeal to the Colored Citizens of the World* (University Park: Pennsylvania State University Press, 2000), xiv–xxv.

56. *The Liberator*, January 8, 1831.

57. In addition to the above, see *The Liberator*, January 1, 22 and 29, April 30, and May 14 and 28, 1831.

58. *Genius of Universal Emancipation*, January 15, February 26, and March 5, 1830.

59. Garrison and Garrison, *Life*, I, 168.

60. Henry Mayer, *All on Fire: William Lloyd Garrison and the Abolition of Slavery* (New York: St. Martin's Press, 1998), 85. Also, according to Norman Rosenberg, *Protecting the Best Men: An Interpretive History of the Law of Libel* (Chapel Hill: University of North Carolina Press, 1986), 120, between 1800 and 1830, civil suits had "replaced criminal prosecutions as the most common ... aspect of defamation law."

61. Dillon, *Benjamin Lundy*, 157.

62. *Genius of Universal Emancipation*, July 1830.

63. Phillips, *Freedom's Port*, 30–1.

64. William Lloyd Garrison, *Brief Sketch of the Trial of William Lloyd Garrison for an Alleged Libel on Francis Todd of Newburyport, Massachusetts* (Boston, Garrison and Knapp, 1834), 13.

65. Garrison and Garrison, *Life*, I, 168–71.

66. *Genius of Universal Emancipation*, March 5, 1830.

67. Johnson, *William Lloyd Garrison and His Times*, 33.

68. Garrison and Garrison, *Life*, I, 174.

69. *Genius of Universal Emancipation*, June 1830, 36.

70. Garrison and Garrison, *Life*, I, 174–7.

71. Walter M. Merrill, ed., *The Letters of William Lloyd Garrison, Volume I* (Cambridge: Belknap Press, 1971), letter to Harriet Farnham Horton, May 12, 1830, 91–93.

72. Garrison and Garrison, *Life*, I, 177.

73. Garrison, *Brief Sketch of the Trial of William Lloyd Garrison*, 15.

74. *Genius of Universal Emancipation*, May 1830, 18.

75. *Genius of Universal* Emancipation, June 1830, 33–4.

76. Genius of Universal Emancipation, June 1830, 35.

77. *Philadelphia Inquirer*, May 17, 1830.

78. *Nantucket Inquirer*, May 29, 1830.

79. *Mechanics Free Press* (Philadelphia), May 29, 1830.

80. *Commercial Advertiser* May 28, 1830; *Portsmouth Journal*, May 29, 1830; and *Schenectady Cabinet*, June 2, 1830.

81. Joseph Tinker Buckingham, *Personal Memoirs and Recollections of Editorial Life* (Boston: Ticknor, Reed, and Fields, 1852), II, 105-121.
82. *Boston Courier*, May 24, 1830.
83. Johnson, *Garrison and His Times*, 35-6.
84. *Newburyport Herald*, May 25, 1830.
85. Mrs. E. Vale Smith, *History of Newburyport: From the Earliest Settlement of the Country to the Present Time* (Newburyport, 1854), 260.
86. *Constitution of the Newburyport Debating Society Adopted January 24th 1823, with a List of Officers and Name of Members of the Society* (Newburyport: W & J Gilman, 1823), 8.
87. *Newburyport Herald*, June 11, 1830.

Chapter Seven

1. *Newburyport Herald*, June 11, 1830.
2. Lewis Bertram Wyatt-Brown, *Lewis Tappan and the Evangelical War Against Slavery* (Cleveland: Press of Case Western Reserve University, 1969, 78-9, and Francis Jackson Garrison and Wendell Phillips Garrison, *William Lloyd Garrison, 1805-1879: The Story of His Life Told by His Children* (Boston: Houghton, Mifflin, 1894), I, 190-1.
3. Oliver Johnson, *William Lloyd Garrison and His Times; or Sketches of the Anti-Slavery Movement in America, and of the Man Who Was Its Founder and Moral Leader* (Boston: B.B. Russell & Co., 1880), 38.
4. John B. Pickard, ed., *The Letters of John Greenleaf Whittier* (Cambridge: Belknap Press, 1975), "To the Editor of the Transcript," March 14, 1864, 62-4. See also *The Liberator*, January 15 and 22 and March 11 and 25, 1864.
5. Walter M. Merrill, ed., *The Letters of William Lloyd Garrison, Volume I* (Cambridge: Belknap Press, 1971), 106-7.
6. Merton Dillon, *Benjamin Lundy and the Struggle for Negro Freedom* (Urbana: University of Illinois Press, 1966), 160-1; and Garrison and Garrison, *Life*, I, 191-2.
7. Lewis Tappan, *The Life of Arthur Tappan* (New York: Hurd and Houghton, 1871; reprint, Westport: Negro University Press, 1970), 163.
8. Wyatt-Brown, *Lewis Tappan*, 79.
9. *Boston Courier*, June 11, 1830.
10. Merrill, ed., *Letters, Volume I*, to Ebenezer Dole, July 14, 1830, 104-7.
11. Walter M. Merrill, ed., *The Letters of William Lloyd Garrison*, vol. VI. Microform Supplement (Historical Society of Pennsylvania; Ann Arbor: University Microforms International, 1979), William Lloyd Garrison to Oliver Johnson, Roxbury, February 15, 1874.
12. *Genius of Universal Emancipation*, May 1830, 17.
13. *Newburyport Herald*, June 11, 1830.
14. Merrill, ed., *Letters, Volume I*, to Nicholas Brice, and to Richard W. Gill, May 13, 1830, 94-5.
15. Garrison and Garrison, *Life*, I, 195.
16. *The Liberator*, January 1, 1831.
17. *The Liberator*, January 15, 1831.
18. Garrison and Garrison, *Life*, I, 199; and William Lloyd Garrison, "Proposals for Publishing a Weekly Paper in Washington City, D.C. to be Entitled The Liberator, and the Journal of the Times" (Baltimore, 1830), Special Collections, American Antiquarian Society, Worcester, Massachusetts.
19. Merrill, ed., *Letters*, vol. VI. Microform Supplement, William Lloyd Garrison to Oliver Johnson, February 15, 1874.
20. *Essex Gazette*, September 11, 1830.
21. *Boston Recorder*, August 25, 1830; *New Hampshire Gazette*, August 17, 1830; *Portsmouth Journal*, August 21, 1830; and *American Traveller* (Boston), September 10, 1830.
22. *Augusta Chronicle*, September 22, 1830.
23. Algernon Sydney, *Discourses on Government*, vol. 1 (New York: Printed for Richard Lee by Deare and Andrews, 1805), 320-1.
24. Arthur Tappan, New York, to William Lloyd Garrison, Baltimore, August 9, 1830, quoted in Garrison and Garrison, *Life*, I, 202.
25. Wyatt-Brown, *Lewis Tappan*, 79.
26. Tappan, *The Life of Arthur Tappan*, 164.
27. Merrill, ed., *Letters, Volume VI*, to Oliver Johnson, February 5, 1874, 293-296.
28. Merrill, ed., *Letters, Volume I*, to George Shepard, September 13, 1830, 109-110.
29. Merrill, ed., *Letters, Volume V*, to Helen E. Garrison, June 8, 1864, 207-209.
30. *Philadelphia Inquirer*, August 31 and September 2, 1830.

31. Garrison and Garrison, *Life*, I, 203.
32. Elizabeth Cady Stanton, *Eighty Years & More: Reminiscences 1815–1897* (T. Fisher Unwin, 1898; reprint, New York: Schocken Books, 1971), 81–4.
33. *The Liberator*, November 10, 1849.
34. Gary B. Nash, *Forging Freedom: The Formation of Philadelphia's Black Community, 1720–1840* (Cambridge: Harvard University Press, 1988), 239–40.
35. Johnson, *Garrison and His Times*, 40.
36. Merrill, ed., *Letters, Volume VI*, to Oliver Johnson, February 5, 1874, 293, and Garrison and Garrison, *Life*, I, 204.
37. *Commercial Advertiser*, September 8, 1830; *Evening Post*, September 7 and 8, 1830.
38. Merrill, ed., *Letters, Volume I*, to George Shepard, September 13, 1830, 107–110.
39. Garrison and Garrison, *Life*, I, 207–9 and *Newburyport Herald*, September 28, 1830.
40. *Newburyport Herald*, September 28, 1830.
41. *Newburyport Herald*, October 1, 1830.
42. *Boston Evening Transcript*, October 2, 1830.
43. *Boston Evening Transcript*, September 28, 1830.
44. Garrison and Garrison, *Life*, I, 210.
45. *Boston Evening Transcript*, October 12, 1830.
46. *Boston Evening Transcript*, October 16, 1830.
47. Merrill, ed., *Letters, Volume I*, to Harriet Farnham, May 12, 1830, 91–93.
48. *Boston Courier*, October 11, 1830.
49. Garrison and Garrison, *Life*, I, 212.
50. Roderick French, "Liberation From Man and God in Boston: Abner Kneeland's Free Thought Campaign 1830–1839," *The American Quarterly* 32, no. 2 (Summer 1980), 202–4.
51. Merrill, ed., *Letters, Volume VI*, to Oliver Johnson, May 25, 1874, 323.
52. *Boston Evening Transcript*, October 15, 16, and 18, 1830.
53. Samuel J. May, *Some Recollections of Our Antislavery Conflict* (Boston: Fields, Osgood, & Co., 1869: reprint, New York: Arno Press, 1968), 17–19.
54. May, *Some Recollections of Our Antislavery Conflict*, 19–20.
55. Johnson, *Garrison and His Times*, 44. William Wilberforce (1759–1833) was a leading British abolitionist beginning in 1787; he was instrumental in passage of legislation to end Britain's participation in the slave trade and was leader in the 1833 passage of his nation's Slavery Abolition Act. Garrison met briefly with him during his first trip to England in 1833. See Merrill, ed., *Letters, Volume I*, footnote 136–7, 238–9.
56. May, *Some Recollections of Our Antislavery Conflict*, 331, 34.
57. Donald Yacovone, *Samuel Joseph May and the Dilemmas of the Liberal Persuasion* (Philadelphia: Temple University Press, 1991), 38–41.
58. *Genius of Universal Emancipation*, October 1830, 97.
59. Dillon, *Benjamin Lundy*, 162–3.
60. Letter from Elliot Cresson to R.R. Gurley, September 28, 1830, quoted in Henry Mayer, *All on Fire: William Lloyd Garrison and the Abolition of Slavery* (New York: St. Martin's Press, 1998), 101.
61. *London Times*, June 28, 1833.
62. Merrill, *The Letters of William Lloyd Garrison*, vol. VI. Microform, Garrison to Oliver Johnson, Roxbury, February 15, 1874.
63. *Genius of Universal Emancipation*, October 30, 1829 (italics are Garrison's).
64. William Lloyd Garrison, Roxbury, to Henry Wilson, May 2, 1872, Special Collections, Boston Public Library (Ms # A.1.1 v. 8, p. 14a).
65. Johnson, *Garrison and His Times*, 41.
66. *Newburyport Herald*, June 11, 1830.
67. Garrison and Garrison, *Life*, I, 217.
68. May, *Some Recollections of Our Antislavery Conflict*, 23–26.
69. *Boston Evening Transcript*, November 1, 1830.
70. *Boston Evening Transcript*, November 8, 1830.
71. *The Liberator*, January 1, 1831 (Garrison's italics).
72. Merrill ed., *Letters*, vol. VI, Garrison to Oliver Johnson, Roxbury, March 1, 1874.

Chapter Eight

1. *Newburyport Herald*, August 6, 1822.
2. *The Free Press*, September 21, 1826.
3. *National Philanthropist*, May 23, 1828.
4. *Journal of the Times*, February 13, 1829.
5. *Journal of the Times*, March 27, 1829.
6. *Newburyport Herald*, June 11, 1830.

7. *The Independent*, January 11, 1866.
8. *National Philanthropist*, July 22, 1829.
9. Walter M. Merrill, ed., *The Letters of William Lloyd Garrison*, vol. VI. Microform Supplement (Historical Society of Pennsylvania; Ann Arbor: University Microforms International, 1979), William Lloyd Garrison to Oliver Johnson, Roxbury, February 15, 1874.
10. Samuel J. May, *Some Recollections of Our Antislavery Conflict* (Boston: Fields, Osgood, & Co., 1869: reprint, New York: Arno Press, 1968), 20.
11. *Daily Evening Traveller* (Boston), October 15, 1878.
12. *Genius of Universal Emancipation*, February 12, 1830.
13. *The Liberator*, April 23, 1831.
14. *The Liberator*, April 30, 1831.
15. Walter M. Merrill, ed., *The Letters of William Lloyd Garrison, Volume III* (Cambridge: Belknap Press, 1973), to Henry Clay, March 16, 1849, 608–13.
16. "Prospectus of the Liberator," *The Liberator*, May 28, 1831.

Bibliography

Newspapers and Periodicals

American Traveller (Boston)
Augusta Chronicle (Georgia)
Baltimore Gazette and Daily Advertiser
Boston Commercial Gazette
Boston Courier
Boston Evening Transcript
Boston Recorder
Christian Register (Boston)
Columbian Centinel (Boston)
Commercial Advertiser (New York)
Daily Evening Traveller (Boston)
Eastport Sentinel (Maine)
Essex Gazette
Evening Post (New York)
The Free Press (Newburyport)
Freedom's Journal (New York)
Genius of Universal Emancipation (Baltimore)
The Independent (New York)
Journal of the Times (Bennington)
The Liberator (Boston)
Literary Cadet, and Saturday Evening Bulletin (Providence)
London Times
Mechanics Free Press (Philadelphia)
Nantucket Inquirer
National Intelligencer (Washington, D.C.)
National Philanthropist (Boston)
Niles' Register (Baltimore)
Newburyport Herald
New-Hampshire Gazette
North American Review
The Patriot (London)
Philadelphia Inquirer
Portsmouth Journal
The Salem Gazette
Schenectady Cabinet
The Yankee (Portland)

Books and Articles

Abzug, Robert H. *Cosmos Crumbling: American Reform and the Religious Imagination.* New York: Oxford University Press, 1989.

American Antiquarian Society. *Transactions and Collections of the American Antiquarian Society*, vol. VI. Albany: Joel Munsell, 1874; reprint, New York: Johnson Reprint, 1971.

Bailyn, Bernard. *Education in the Forming of American Society: Needs and Opportunities for Study.* Chapel Hill: University of North Carolina Press, 1960.

Bailyn, Bernard. *The Ideological Origins of the American Revolution.* Cambridge: Belknap Press, 1967.

Bailyn, Bernard, and John B. Hench, eds. *The Press and the American Revolution*. Boston: Northeastern University Press, 1981.
Baldasty, Gerald J. "The Press and Politics in the Age of Jackson." *Journalism Monographs* 89 (1984): 1–28.
Baldasty, Gerald J. *The Commercialization of News in the Nineteenth Century*. Madison: University of Wisconsin Press, 1992.
Barker-Benfield, G. J. *The Culture of Sensibility: Sex and Society in Eighteenth-Century Britain*. Chicago: University of Chicago Press, 1992.
Barnes, Gilbert Hobbs. *The Antislavery Impulse, 1830–1844*. New York: D. Appleton, 1933.
Bassett, T. D. Seymour, ed. "A Letter by William Lloyd Garrison, Written from Bennington, Vermont, on March 30, 1829." *Vermont History* XXXVIII, 4 (1969): 256–264.
Baxter, Maurice G. *Henry Clay and the American System*. Lexington: University Press of Kentucky, 1995.
Baym, Nina. *Novels, Readers, and Reviewers: Responses to Fiction in Antebellum America*. Ithaca: Cornell University Press, 1984.
"Biographical Sketch of the Late Rev. Wm. Collier, of Boston." *The Baptist Memorial and Monthly Record* III, no. 11 (November 1844): 327–328.
"Biographical Sketch of the Late Rev. John Peak — Massachusetts." *The Baptist Memorial and Monthly Record* III, no. 11 (November 1844): 331–332.
Blocker, Jack. *American Temperance Movements: Cycles of Reform*. Boston: Twayne, 1989.
Boorstin, Daniel J. *The Americans: The National Experience*. New York: Random House, 1965.
Botein, Stephen. "'Meer Mechanics' and an Open Press: The Business of Political Strategies of Colonial American Printers." *Perspectives in American History* 9 (1975): 130–211.
Bourne, George. *The Book and Slavery Irreconcilable*. Philadelphia: J. M. Sanderson & Co., 1816; reprint, New York: Arno Press, 1969.
Boyd, Julian, ed. *The Papers of Thomas Jefferson*, Volume II. Princeton: Princeton University Press, 1955.
Brewer, James Stewart. *Holy Warriors: The Abolitionists and American Slavery*, rev. ed. 1976. New York: Hill & Wang, 1996.
Brown, Herbert Ross. *The Sentimental Novel in America, 1789–1860*. Durham: Duke University Press, 1940.
Brown, Richard D. *Knowledge Is Power: The Diffusion of Information in Early America, 1700–1865*. New York: Oxford University Press, 1989.
Brown, Richard D. *The Strength of a People: The Idea of an Informed Citizenry in America, 1650–1870*. Chapel Hill: University of North Carolina Press, 1996.
Browne, Gary Lawson. *Baltimore in the Nation, 1789–1861*. Chapel Hill: University of North Carolina Press, 1980.
Browne, Patrick T. J. "'To Defend Mr. Garrison': William Cooper Nell and the Personal Politics of Antislavery." *New England Quarterly* 3 (1997): 415–442.
Buckingham, Joseph Tinker. *Personal Memoirs and Recollections of Editorial Life*. Boston: Ticknor, Reed, and Fields, 1852.
Cappon, Lester J, ed. *The Adams-Jefferson Letters*, vol. II. Chapel Hill: University of North Carolina Press, 1959.
Catalogue of the Merrimack Circulating Library Kept by W & J Gilman, Booksellers. Printed by W & J Gilman, State Street, circa 1821.
Chapman, John Jay. *William Lloyd Garrison*. Boston: Atlantic Monthly Press, 1921; reprint, New York: Beekman, 1974.
Chiasson, Lloyd, Jr. *The Press in Times of Crisis*. Westport: Greenwood Press, 1995.
Christie, John W., and Dwight L. Dumond. *George Bourne and The Book and Slavery Ir-*

reconcilable. Wilmington: The Historical Society of Delaware and Philadelphia: The Presbyterian Historical Society, 1969.

Clark, Charles E. *The Public Prints: The Newspaper in Anglo-American Culture, 1665–1740.* New York: Oxford University Press, 1994.

Clark, Norman. *Deliver Us From Evil: An Interpretation of American Prohibition.* New York: W. W. Norton, 1976.

Constitution of the Newburyport Debating Society Adopted January 24th 1823, with a List of Officers and Name of Members of the Society. Newburyport: W & J Gilman, 1823.

Cott, Nancy. *The Bonds of Womanhood: Woman's Sphere: in New England, 1780–1835.* New Haven: Yale University Press, 1977.

Craven, Avery. *The Coming of the Civil War.* Chicago: University of Chicago Press, 1950.

Crouthamel, James L. "The Newspaper Revolution in New York, 1830–1860." *New York History* 45 (April 1964): 91–113.

Crouthamel, James L. *Bennet's New York Herald and the Rise of the Popular Press.* Syracuse: Syracuse University Press, 1989.

Currier, John J. *History of Newburyport, Massachusetts, 1764–1909.* Newburyport: Printed for the author, 1909.

Cushing, Caleb. *The History and Present State of the Town of Newburyport.* Newburyport: Ephraim Allen, 1826.

Davidson, Cathy N. *Revolution and the Word: The Rise of the Novel in America.* New York: Oxford University Press, 1986.

Davis, David Brion. *The Problem of Slavery in the Age of Revolution, 1770–1823.* Ithaca: Cornell University Press, 1975.

Davis, David Brion. *From Homicide to Slavery: Studies in American Culture.* New York: Oxford University Press, 1986.

Dicken-Garcia, Hazel. *Journalistic Standards in Nineteenth-Century America.* Madison: University of Wisconsin Press, 1989.

Dillon, Merton L. *The Abolitionists: The Growth of a Dissenting Minority.* DeKalb: Northern Illinois University Press, 1974.

Dillon, Merton L. *Benjamin Lundy and the Struggle for Negro Freedom.* Urbana: University of Illinois Press, 1966.

Elkins, Stanley M. *Slavery: A Problem in American Institutional and Intellectual Life*, 3d ed. Chicago: University of Chicago Press, 1976.

Elkins, Stanley M., and Eric McKitrick. *The Age of Federalism.* New York: Oxford University Press, 1993.

Emery, Edwin, and Michael Emery. *The Press and America: An Interpretive History of the Mass Media*, 8th ed. Boston: Allyn and Bacon, 1996.

Erikson, Erik H. *Young Man Luther: A Study in Psychoanalysis and History.* New York: W. W. Norton, 1958.

Fanuzi, Robert A. "'The Organ of An Individual': William Lloyd Garrison and the *Liberator.*" *Prospects* 23 (1998): 107–127.

Ferling, John. *Adams vs. Jefferson: The Tumultuous Election of 1800.* New York: Oxford University Press, 2004.

Fischer, David Hackett. *The Revolution of American Conservatism: The Federalist Party in the Era of Jeffersonian Democracy.* New York: Harper & Row, 1965.

Foner, Philip S., ed. *The Life and Major Writings of Thomas Paine.* Secaucus: Citadel Press, 1974.

Franklin, John Hope, and Alfred A. Moss, Jr. *From Slavery to Freedom: A History of African Americans*, 7th Edition. New York: Alfred A. Knopf, 1994.

Freehling, William W. *The Road to Disunion: Secessionist at Bay, 1776–1854.* New York: Oxford University Press, 1990.

Freeman, Joanne B. *Affairs of Honor: National Politics in the New Republic.* New Haven: Yale University Press, 2001.
French, Roderick. "Liberation From Man and God in Boston: Abner Kneeland's Free Thought Campaign 1830–1839." *The American Quarterly* 32, no. 2 (Summer 1980): 202–221.
Friedman, Lawrence. *Gregarious Saints: Self and Community in American Abolitionism, 1830–1870.* Cambridge: Cambridge University Press, 1982.
Fuess, Claude M. *The Life of Caleb Cushing,* vols. I and II. New York: Harcourt, Brace & World, 1923; reprint, Hamden, CT: Archon Books, 1965.
Gardner, Bettye J. "William Watkins: Antebellum Black Teacher and Anti-slavery Writer." *Negro History Bulletin* 39.6 (September-October 1976), 623–625.
Garrison, Francis Jackson, and Wendell Phillips Garrison. *William Lloyd Garrison, 1805–1879: The Story of His Life Told by His Children,* 4 vols. Boston: Houghton, Mifflin, 1894.
Garrison, William Lloyd. *An Address Delivered Before The Free People of Color of Philadelphia, New York and Other Cities During the Month of June 1831.* Boston: Stephen Foster, 1831.
Garrison, William Lloyd. *Address Delivered Before the Members of the Franklin Debating Club on the Morning of the 5th of July, 1824, Being the Forty-Ninth Anniversary of American Independence.* Newburyport: Printed at the Herald Office, 1824.
Garrison, William Lloyd. *Brief Sketch of the Trial of William Lloyd Garrison For An Alleged Libel on Francis Todd of Newburyport, Mass.* Boston: Garrison and Knapp, 1834.
Garrison, William Lloyd. "Proposals for Publishing a Weekly Paper in Washington City, D. C. to be Entitled The Liberator, and the Journal of the Times." Baltimore, 1830. Special Collections, American Antiquarian Society, Worcester, Massachusetts.
Gilfoyle, Timothy J. *City of Eros: New York City, Prostitution, and the Commercialization of Sex, 1790–1920.* New York: W. W. Norton, 1992.
Gilmore, William J. *Reading Becomes a "Necessity of Life": Material and Cultural Life in Rural New England, 1780–1830.* Knoxville: University of Tennessee Press, 1989.
Goodell, William. *Slavery and Anti-Slavery: A History of the Great Struggle in Both Hemispheres with a View of the Slavery Question in the United States.* New York: William Goodell, 1853; reprint, New York: Augustus M. Kelley, 1970.
Graham, Leroy. *Baltimore, The Nineteenth Century Black Capital.* Lanham, MD: University Press of America, 1982.
Greeley, Horace. *Recollections of a Busy Life.* New York: J. B. Ford & Co., 1868.
Grimke, Archibald. *William Lloyd Garrison: The Abolitionist.* New York: Funk & Wagnalls, 1891; reprint, New York: Negro University Press, 1969.
Gross, Robert A. *The Minuteman and Their World.* New York: Hill & Wang, 1976.
Grossberg, Michael. *Governing the Hearth: Law and The Family in Nineteenth-Century America.* Chapel Hill: University of North Carolina Press, 1985.
Hale, William Harlan. *Horace Greeley; Voice of the People.* New York: Harper & Brothers, 1950.
Heidler, David S., and Jeanne T. Heidler. *Henry Clay: The Essential American.* New York: Random House, 2010.
Hemenway, Abby Maria, ed. *The Vermont Gazetteer: A History Embracing the History of Each Town,* vol. 3. Burlington, 1868.
Hinks, Peter. *To Awaken My Afflicted Brethren: David Walker and the Problem of Antebellum Slave Resistance.* University Park: Pennsylvania State University Press, 1997.
Hinks, Peter, ed. *David Walker's Appeal to the Colored Citizens of the World.* University Park: Pennsylvania State University Press, 2000.

Horton, James Oliver. "Generations of Protest: Black Families and Social Reform in Ante-Bellum Boston." *The New England Quarterly* 49, no. 2 (June 1976), 242–256.
Horton, James Oliver, and Lois E. Horton. *Black Bostonians: Family Life and Community Struggle in the Antebellum North.* New York: Holmes & Meier, 1979.
Howe, Daniel Walker. *What Hath God Wrought: The Transformation of America: 1815–1848.* New York: Oxford University Press, 2007.
Howells, William Dean. *Years of My Youth and Three Essays.* Bloomington: Indiana University Press, 1975.
Hudson, Frederic. *Journalism in the United States, from 1690 to 1872.* New York: Harper and Brothers, 1873.
Humphrey, Carol Sue. *The Press of the Young Republic, 1783–1833.* Westport: Greenwood Press, 1996.
Huntzicker, William E. *The Popular Press, 1833–1865,* Westport: Greenwood Press, 1999.
John, Richard R. *Spreading the News: The American Postal System from Franklin to Morse.* Cambridge: Harvard University Press, 1995.
Johnson, Oliver. *William Lloyd Garrison and His Times; or Sketches of the Anti-Slavery Movement in America, and of the Man Who Was Its Founder and Moral Leader.* Boston: B.B. Russell & Co.,1880.
Kerber, Linda K. *Women of the Republic: Intellect and Ideology in Revolutionary America.* New York: W. W. Norton, 1980.
Keilbowicz, Richard B. *News in the Mail: The Press, Post Office, and Public Information, 1700–1860.* New York: Greenwood Press, 1989.
Kett, Joseph F. *The Pursuit of Knowledge Under Difficulties: From Self-Improvement to Adult Education in America.* Stanford: Stanford University Press, 1994.
Kolchin, Peter. *American Slavery, 1619–1877.* New York: Hill & Wang, 1993.
Korngold, Ralph. *Two Friends of Mankind: The Story of William Lloyd Garrison and Wendell Phillips and Their Relationship with Abraham Lincoln.* Boston: Little, Brown, 1950.
Kraditor, Aileen S. *Means and Ends in American Abolitionism: Garrison and His Critics on Strategy and Tactics, 1834–1850.* New York: Vintage, 1967.
Leeds Anti-Slavery Series, No. 86. "Principles and Mode of Action of the American Anti-Slavery Society: A Speech by William Lloyd Garrison." *Anti-Slavery Convention Report.* London: William Tweedie, 1853.
Leonard, Thomas C. *News for All: America's Coming-of-Age with the Press.* New York: Oxford University Press, 1995.
Levesque, George. "Inherent Reformers-Inherited Orthodoxy: Black Baptists in Boston, 1800–1873." *The Journal of Negro History* 60, no. 4 (October 1975), 491–525.
Levesque, George. *Black Boston: African American Life and Culture in Urban America 1750–1860.* New York: Garland, 1994.
Levy, Leonard. *Emergence of a Free Press.* New York: Oxford University Press, 1985.
Lodge, Henry Cabot, ed. *The Works of Alexander Hamilton,* vol. X. New York: G.P. Putnam's Sons, 1904.
May, Samuel J. *Some Recollections of Our Antislavery Conflict.* Boston: Fields, Osgood, & Co., 1869: reprint, New York: Arno Press, 1968.
Mayer, Henry. *All on Fire: William Lloyd Garrison and the Abolition of Slavery.* New York: St. Martin's Press, 1998.
Merrill, Walter M. *Against Wind and Tide.* Cambridge: Harvard University Press, 1963.
Merrill, Walter M. "Prologue to Reform — Garrison's Early Career." *Essex Institute Historical Collection* XCII, no. 2 (1956): 153–170.
Merrill, Walter M., ed. *Behold Me Once More: The Confessions of James Holley Garrison, Brother of William Lloyd Garrison.* Boston: Houghton Mifflin, 1954.

Merrill, Walter M. and Louis Ruchames, eds. *The Letters of William Lloyd Garrison*, 6 vols. Cambridge: Belknap Press, 1971–1981.
Merrill, Walter M., ed. *The Letters of William Lloyd Garrison*, vol. VI. Microform Supplement. Historical Society of Pennsylvania; Ann Arbor: University Microforms International, 1979.
Meyers, John L., *Henry Wilson and the Era of Reconstruction*, Lanham, MD: University Press of America, 2009.
Miller, William Lee. *Arguing About Slavery: The Great Battle in the United States Congress.* New York: Alfred A. Knopf, 1996.
Mintz, Stephen. *Moralists and Modernizers: America's Pre-Civil War Reformers.* Baltimore: Johns Hopkins University Press, 1995.
Morison, Samuel Eliot. *The Maritime History of Massachusetts, 1783–1860.* London: William Heinemann, 1923.
Mott, Frank Luter. *American Journalism: A History of Newspapers in the United States, 1690–1960,* 3d ed. New York: Macmillan, 1962.
Nash, Gary B. *Forging Freedom: The Formation of Philadelphia's Black Community, 1720–1840.* Cambridge: Harvard University Press, 1988.
Newman, Richard S. *The Transformation of American Abolitionism: Fighting Slavery in the Early Republic.* Chapel Hill: University of North Carolina Press, 2002.
Nord, David Paul. *Communities of Journalism: A History of American Newspapers and Their Readers.* Chicago: University of Illinois Press, 2001.
Nord, David Paul. "The Evangelical Origins of Mass Media in America, 1814–1835." *Journalism Monographs* 84 (1984): 1–30.
Nord, David Paul. "Newspapers and American Nationhood, 1776–1826." *Proceedings of the American Antiquarian Society* 100, 2 (1990): 391–405.
Nord, David Paul. "Religious Reading and Readers in Antebellum America." *Journal of the Early Republic* 15 (Summer 1995): 241–272.
Nord, David Paul. "Tocqueville, Garrison and the Perfection of Journalism." *Journalism History* 13.2 (Summer 1986): 56–63.
Norton, Mary Beth. *Liberty's Daughters: The Revolutionary Experience of American Women, 1750–1800.* Boston: Little, Brown, 1980.
Nye, Russel B. *William Lloyd Garrison and the Humanitarian Reformers.* Boston: Little, Brown, 1955.
Nye, Russel B., ed. *Autobiography and Other Writings by Benjamin Franklin.* Boston: Houghton Mifflin, 1958.
O'Brien, Frank M. *The Story of the Sun.* New York: George H. Doran, 1918.
Parsons, Lynn Hudson. *The Birth of Modern Politics: Andrew Jackson, John Quincy Adams, and the Election of 1828.* New York: Oxford University Press, 2009.
Pasley, Jeffery. *"The Tyranny of Printers": Newspaper Politics in the Early American Republic.* Charlottesville: University of Virginia Press, 2001.
Phillips, Christopher. *Freedom's Port: The African American Community of Baltimore, 1790–1860.* Chicago: University of Illinois Press, 1997.
Phillips, Ulrich Bonnell. *American Negro Slavery: A Survey of the Supply, Employment and Control of Negro Labor As Determined By Plantation Regime.* New York: D. Appleton, 1918; reprint, Baton Rouge: Louisiana State University, 1966.
Pickard, John B., ed. *The Letters of John Greenleaf Whittier.* Cambridge: Belknap Press, 1975.
Potts, Louis W. "The Franklin Debate Society: Culture in the Missouri Frontier." *Missouri Historical Review* 86.1 (1991): 1–21.
Proceedings of the American Anti-Slavery Society at Its Third Decade. New York: American Anti-Slavery Society, 1864; reprint, New York: Arno Press, 1969.
Quarles, Benjamin. *Black Abolitionists.* New York: Oxford University Press, 1969.

Rachleff, Marshall. "David Walker's Southern Agent." *Journal of Negro History*, 62, issue 1 (January 1977): 100–103.
Reilly, Timothy F. "Le Liberateur: New Orleans' Free Negro Newspaper." *Gulf Coast Historical Review* 2.1 (1986): 5–24.
Remini, Robert V. *Henry Clay: Statesman for the Union*. New York: W. W. Norton, 1991.
Rhodes, James Ford. *History of the United States from the Compromise of 1850*. New York: Harper & Brothers, 1893.
Ripley, C. Peter, ed. *The Black Abolitionist Papers: Volume III, The United States, 1830–1846*. Chapel Hill: University of North Carolina Press, 1991.
Rock, Howard B., Paul A. Gilje, and Robert Asher, eds. *American Artisans: Crafting Social Identity, 1750–1850*. Baltimore: Johns Hopkins University Press, 1995.
Rohrbach, Augusta. "'Truth Stronger and Stranger Than Fiction': Reexamining William Lloyd Garrison's *Liberator*." *American Literature* 74 (2001): 727–755.
Rorabaugh, W. J. *The Craft Apprentice: From Franklin to the Machine Age in America*. New York: Oxford University Press, 1986.
Rosenberg, Norman. *Protecting the Best Men: An Interpretive History of the Law of Libel*. Chapel Hill: University of North Carolina Press, 1986.
Schlesinger, Arthur M. *Prelude to Independence: The Newspaper War on Great Britain*. 1957. Boston: Northeastern University Press, 1980.
Schlesinger, Arthur M. Jr. *The Age of Jackson*. Boston: Little, Brown, 1945.
Schouler, James. *History of the United States of America Under the Constitution*, Volume IV. New York: Dodd, Mead, 1892.
Schudson, Michael. *Discovering the News: A Social History of American Newspapers*. New York: BasicBooks, 1978.
Schudson, Michael. *The Good Citizen: A History of American Civic Life*. Cambridge: Harvard University Press, 1999.
Scudder, Horace E., ed. *The Complete Poetical Works of James Russell Lowell*. Boston: Houghton Mifflin, 1917.
Sears, Donald A. *John Neal*. Boston: Twayne, 1978.
Silver, Rollo. *The American Printer, 1787–1825*. Charlottesville: University Press of Virginia, 1967.
Smith, Mrs. E. Vale. *History of Newburyport: From the Earliest Settlement of the Country to the Present Time*. Newburyport, 1854.
Stampp, Kenneth M. *The Peculiar Institution: Slavery in the Ante-Bellum South*. New York: Vintage, 1956.
Stanton, Elizabeth Cady. *Eighty Years & More: Reminiscences 1815–1897*. T. Fisher Unwin, 1898; reprint, New York: Schocken Books, 1971.
Steward, Donald H. *The Opposition Press in the Federalist Period*. Albany: State University of New York Press, 1969.
Sydney, Algernon. *Discourses on Government*, vol. 1. New York: Printed for Richard Lee by Deare and Andrews, 1805.
Tappan, Lewis. *The Life of Arthur Tappan*. New York: Hurd and Houghton, 1871; reprint, Westport: Negro University Press, 1970.
Taylor, Alan. *William Cooper's Town: Power and Persuasion on the Frontier of the Early American Republic*. New York: Vintage, 1996.
Thernstrom, Stephan. *Poverty and Progress: Social Mobility in a Nineteenth Century City*. Cambridge: Harvard University Press, 1964.
Thomas, John L. *The Liberator, William Lloyd Garrison: A Biography*. Boston: Little, Brown, 1963.
Thomas, John L. "Romantic Reform in America, 1815–1860." *American Quarterly* (Winter 1965): 656–681.

Tocqueville, Alexis de. *Democracy in America*. J.P. Mayer, ed., George Lawrence, trans. New York: HarperPerennial, 1992.
Tonsing, Paul Martin. *The Power of the Press: History and Development of Printing Presses From the Fifteenth to the Twenty-First Century*. Fort Worth: P & T, 1998.
Tributes to William Lloyd Garrison, at the Funeral Services, May 28, 1879. Boston: Houghton, Osgood and Company, 1879.
Tucher, Andie. *Froth and Scum: Truth, Beauty, Goodness, and the Ax Murder in America's First Mass Medium*. Chapel Hill: University of North Carolina Press, 1994.
Unger, Harlow Giles. *Noah Webster: The Life and Times of an American Patriot*. New York: John Wiley & Sons, 1998.
Villard, Fanny Garrison. *William Lloyd Garrison on Non-Resistance, Together with a Personal Sketch by His Daughter, Fanny Garrison Villard and a Tribute by Leo Tolstoi*. New York: The National Press Printing Co., 1924; reprint, New York: Haskell House, 1973.
Walters, Ronald G. *The Antislavery Appeal: American Abolitionism after 1830*. Baltimore: Johns Hopkins University Press, 1976.
Walters, Ronald. *American Reformers 1815–1860*, rev. ed. New York: Hill & Wang, 1997.
Warfel, Harry R., ed. *Letters of Noah Webster*. New York: Library Publishers, 1953.
Whitman, T. Stephen. *The Price of Freedom: Slavery and Manumission in Baltimore and Early National Maryland*. Lexington: University Press of Kentucky, 1997.
Wilentz, Sean. *Chants Democratic: New York City and the Rise of the American Working Class, 1788–1850*. New York: Oxford University Press, 1984.
Wilentz, Sean. *The Rise of American Democracy: Jefferson to Lincoln*. New York: W.W. Norton, 2005.
Wilson, Henry. *The History of the Rise and Fall of the Slave Power in America*. Boston: James R. Osgood and Company, 1872.
Wiltse, Charles M. ed. *The Papers of Daniel Webster Correspondence, Volume 2, 1825–1829*. Hanover, NH: University Press of New England, 1976.
Wolf, Hazel Catherine. *On Freedom's Alter: The Martyr Complex in the Abolition Movement*. Madison: University of Wisconsin Press, 1952.
Wyatt-Brown, Bertram. *Lewis Tappan and the Evangelical War Against Slavery*. Cleveland: Press of Case Western Reserve University, 1969.
Yacovone, Donald. *Samuel Joseph May and the Dilemmas of the Liberal Persuasion*. Philadelphia: Temple University Press, 1991.

Index

abolition 1–2, 8–14, 16, 18, 25–27, 42, 71–72, 95, 98, 100, 116, 119, 121, 126, 129, 139, 156, 158–161, 163, 165–170, 172, 179
Adams, Henry 11
Adams, John 4, 20–21, 46–47, 49, 60–61, 87
Adams, John Quincy 4, 46, 48–50, 66–67, 75–77, 79, 81, 138, 174
Adams, Samuel 19
Africa 105–106, 113, 121, 124–125, 127, 140
African Abolition Society (Boston) 118
African Methodist Episcopal (AME) Church 123, 142
The African Society (Boston, 1796) 117
Albany, NY 100
Alcott, Bronson 166
Allen, Ephraim W. 2–3, 31, 54–57, 63, 65, 88, 104, 110; and Caleb Cushing 37, 42, 56; dispute with Garrison on Jefferson's death 60–63, 87, 174; Garrison's apprenticeship 31, 35–37, 41, 45–46, 54, 85; on Garrison's 1830 tour 163–164; on Garrison's trial in Baltimore 140–141, 151–153, 156, 170, 176; *see also Newburyport Herald*
American Anti-Slavery Society (AASS) 58, 65, 119
American Colonization Society 51, 92–93, 95, 100, 104–105, 118, 121, 125–126, 132–133, 138, 155, 161, 163, 168
American Manufacturer 89, 101, 135
American Revolution 10, 14, 19–21, 32–33, 38, 40, 42, 45, 48–50, 66, 72, 104, 117, 170
American Society for the Promotion of Temperance 116
"The American System" 68, 75, 105, 129–130, 132, 135, 158, 178
American Tract Society 26

American Traveller (Boston) 110, 137
Ames, Fisher 35, 48, 72
Amesbury, Massachusetts 162–163
Andover Seminary, 35
Andrews, Ferdinand, 41
The Anti-Masonic Tract 89
anti-slavery 3–4, 9, 11–17, 19, 27, 37, 52, 73–74, 76, 79–81, 91–100, 102, 109, 111–117, 120–121, 124–127, 130, 134, 139, 141, 151, 154–155, 158, 163, 167, 169–172, 174, 177–178
Anti-Slavery Convention (London, 1840) 161
An Appeal to the Colored Citizens of the World 142; *see also* Walker, David
apprenticeship system, early 19th century 32–34; *see also* Garrison, William Lloyd
"Aristides" 46–47
Augusta Chronicle (Georgia) 137, 159

Baldasty, Gerald 19, 23
Baldwin, Reverend Dr. 88
Baltimore 3, 34, 50, 74, 95, 98; Black community's influence in 122–126, 128, 141, 144, 179; Garrison in 5, 8, 30, 45–46, 81, 85, 88, 102–104, 110–115, 121–122, 124, 126, 128, 130–131, 137–138, 140–142, 144–149, 152–158, 160, 163–165, 171, 175–176, 179
Baltimore American 137
Baltimore City Jail 145–146
Baptist Preacher 89
Barlow, Joel 50
Barnes, Gilbert 13–15
Bartlett, Deacon Ezekiel 30–31, 85
Beecher, Reverend Lyman 90, 115–116, 151, 166–167, 178
Belknap Street Church 65, 88, 116–118

207

Bennett, Thomas 35, 65, 88
Bennington, Vermont 4, 8, 26, 75–77, 79, 81–82, 88, 98–101, 107, 129, 174
Bennington Academy 79
Bethel Church (Baltimore) 124
Black Literary Society (Baltimore) 124
"BLACK LIST" 139–141, 143, 145, 157
Blackwood's Magazine 50
The Book and Slavery Irreconcilable 113–114
Boston 2–6, 17, 27, 31, 33, 35, 38, 44, 50, 57, 64–69, 73–75, 79, 87–89, 91–98, 100, 102, 104–105, 107, 109–111, 113–119, 121–122, 126–128, 137, 142–143, 150–151, 154–155, 160–162, 164–174, 178–179; Black Community's influence in 5, 116–119, 121–122, 126–128, 143, 164; Garrison in 2–3, 5–6, 17, 27, 35, 65–69, 73–75, 79, 88–89, 91–98, 102, 104–105, 107–111, 116–118, 143, 154–156, 160, 162, 164–174, 178–179; Lundy in 3–4, 73–75, 79, 91–100, 107, 109
The Boston Chronicle 19
Boston Clique 17
Boston Commercial Gazette 109, 142
Boston Courier 65–68, 94, 96–97, 110, 150–151, 156, 165
Boston Evening Transcript 164–166, 171–173
Boston Recorder 109, 158
The Boston Statesman 40
Bourne, George 113–115, 119
Breckinridge, John C. 36
Brewer, James Stewart 17
Brice, Judge Nicholas 137, 145, 147–148, 156
"Brief Sketch of the Trial of William Lloyd Garrison" 148, 153, 160
Broadway Hall (New York) 161
Brooklyn, Connecticut 94, 166, 168
Brown, Nicholas 140, 157
Brown University 88
Buckingham, Joseph 65, 67–68, 150, 155, 165
Bunker Hill 6, 173
Burr, Aaron 23
Butler, Eliza 143

Calhoun, John C. 178
Catskill Recorder 137
Chandler, Elizabeth Margaret 112
Channing, William Ellery 90, 97–98, 102, 167–168
Chapman, John Jay 13
Chapman, Maria Weston 11
Charleston, South Carolina 34, 59, 142, 170–172
Charlestown, Massachusetts 88–89
Child, David Lee 65
Christian Constitutional Society 22
Christian Register 119–120, 134

Christianity 7, 9, 22, 61, 89, 109, 126, 161, 165, 178
Cicero 35, 42
City Gazette (Charleston) 171
Civil War (U.S.) 10, 13–17, 19, 24, 26, 32, 51, 97, 111, 169
Clay, Henry 48, 72, 81, 132–135, 153–154, 158, 178; on colonization 132–134; effort to release Garrison from Baltimore jail 153–154; 1824 Election 48, 81; Garrison's support for 72, 81, 132–135, 158, 178; and Thomas Jefferson 132–133
Coffin, Robert Stevenson 50
Collier, Rev. William 65, 69, 73, 88–89, 92, 97, 101–102, 117, 135, 166; Baptist ministry 88–89, 117; Boston boarding house for printers 65, 73, 88–89, 92, 97, 102, 166; publisher of reform newspapers 65, 69, 89, 101, 135
The Colored American (Baltimore) 126
"A COLOURED BALTIMOREAN" 125–127; *see also* Watkins, William
"A COLOURED CANADIAN" 126; *see also* Watkins, William
Colton, Walter 168
Commercial Advertiser 150, 161
Concord Library Society 33
Congress (U.S.) 4, 52, 56–57, 63–64, 73, 79–81, 87, 95, 97, 107–108, 111, 129–130, 158
Connecticut 94, 166
Constitution (U.S.) 1, 12, 21–22, 44, 48, 53–54, 59, 78–79, 105–107, 129, 148, 152, 160
Convention of the Free People of Color 127
Cooper, James Fenimore 51
Cooper, Judge William 33
Cornish, William 124
Cowley, Robert 124
Craven, Avery 14
Crawford, William 48–49, 66
Cresson, Elliot 168–169
"The Crisis" (in *Salem Gazette*) 47–50, 86
Crocker, Daniel 123
Crocker, William Goss 35–36, 39–40
Cuffee, Paul 161
Cunningham, William 46
Currier, John J. 39
Cushing, Caleb 41, 60–61, 105; assistance for Garrison 36–38, 42; conflict with Garrison 52, 56, 63–64, 68, 87, 91, 107, 151; editorship at *Newburyport Herald* 37, 42, 44, 59; and Newburyport Debating Society 38–39, 52

Dana, Daniel 162
Dana, Richard Henry 50
Davis, David Brion 114

Day, Benjamin 18
Deaver, James 124
Declaration of Independence 7, 40, 75, 86, 105, 137
Democratic Party 36, 45, 131
Democratic-Republicans (Jacksonian) 56
democratization (Jacksonian) 23–24, 32–33
Dicken-Garcia, Hazel 24
Dillon, Merton 16, 94, 121, 139
Dimmick, Luther 162
District of Columbia 79–80, 91, 95, 100, 111, 158
Dole, Ebenezer 127, 154–155
Douglass, Frederick 127; *see also* *Frederick Douglass' Paper*

Edgeworth, Maria 51
Elections 4, 11, 13, 21–23, 44–48, 52, 58, 62–68, 75–79, 81–82, 85, 87, 91, 99–100, 107, 129–131, 175; 1823 Massachusetts Governor 44–45, 67, 85; 1824 Presidential 46–48, 66–67; 1826 Newburyport Congressional 52, 62–64, 87; 1827 Boston Mayor 65; 1828 Presidential 4, 23, 66, 68, 75–79, 82, 99–100, 107, 129, 175; 1829 Maryland House of Delegates 130–131; 1832 Presidential 81; 1860 Presidential 11, 13
Electoral College 77
Elkins, Stanley 14–15, 44
emancipation 6–7, 9, 11, 13, 15–18, 25–27, 37, 72, 74, 76, 80, 83, 93, 95, 104, 106, 111–115, 119–121, 128, 132–133, 145–146, 151, 156, 162, 166, 169, 171, 173, 178–180
Embargo Act (1807) 23, 29, 32, 44, 48, 84
Emerson, Ralph Waldo 168
England 30, 42, 50, 54, 114, 139–140, 168–169
Episcopal Church 29, 84
Essex Courant 55
The Essex Gazette 158
Eustis, William 45, 49
evangelization 17, 26, 32, 91, 109
Evans, Estwick 51, 62
Evans, Sarah Ann 51
Evening Post (New York) 22, 161
Everett, Edward 37

Faneuil Hall 66, 96
Fanuzi, Robert A. 25
Farnham, Frances 30
Farnham, Martha 85, 147
Federal Street Baptist Church (Boston) 90, 94
Federalism 3, 8, 35, 44
Federalist Party 8, 21–22, 34–35, 44–48, 52, 54, 56–57, 61, 63, 65–67, 72, 87
Fessenden, Thomas 50
Finney, Charles 13

First Amendment to the U.S. Constitution 79; *see also* freedom of the press
First Society of the Free Thinkers 165, 169, 178
Fischer, David 56
Fleeming, Thomas 19
Forten, James 161
Foster, Stephen 82
Franklin, Benjamin 20, 40–41
Franklin Debating Society 39–40, 52, 59, 86, 104
Franklin Typographical Club 27
Frederick Douglass' Paper 126–127
The Free Press (Newburyport) 3, 8, 25, 31, 55–65, 82, 86–88, 105, 107, 115, 120, 136, 138, 148, 151, 158, 174–175
Free Thinkers 165, 169, 178
freedom of the press 19–20, 55, 140, 148–150, 152, 156–157, 174
Freedom's Journal (New York) 126, 143
French Revolution 48, 108
Friedman, Lawrence 17

"Gag Rule" 80
Gales, Joseph 138, 158
Gannett, Ezra 166
Garrison, Abijah 29, 84–85
Garrison, Caroline Eliza 29
Garrison, Frances Maria Lloyd (Fanny) 8, 29–30, 37, 45–46, 70, 84–86, 147
Garrison, Francis Jackson 11
Garrison, Helen Benson 12, 84
Garrison, James Holley 29–30, 85
Garrison, Maria Elizabeth 29–30
Garrison, Wendell Phillips 11
Garrison, William Lloyd 1, 7, 10–15, 18, 25, 53, 110, 114, 128, 146, 148; anti-slavery ideology 112, 124, 133, 159; apprenticeship 2, 6, 8, 18–19, 24, 26–27, 30–42, 44–46, 49, 51–56, 63, 65, 74–75, 85–86, 104, 115, 140, 151, 174–175, 177; "Aristides" 46–47; and Clay, Henry 72, 81, 132–135, 158, 178; and colonization 5, 93, 106, 110, 113–114, 119, 121–123, 126, 128, 132, 141, 160–161, 168–169, 175, 179; and Cushing, Caleb 36–38, 42, 52, 56, 63–64, 68, 87, 91, 107, 151; and deaths of John Adams and Thomas Jefferson 60–62, 87; on democratic politics and ideology 3–4, 24–25, 35, 40, 42, 47, 49, 65, 75, 107–109, 152, 159, 175, 177–178, 180; on editorial freedom, 4, 57; on editorial integrity and responsibility 26, 47, 53, 55, 57–58, 62–63, 71, 86, 99, 121, 136, 138–139, 173–175; England tour (1833) 54, 168–169; on freedom 2, 40, 43, 49, 105–107, 118, 157, 169–171; funeral eulogy by Wendell Phillips 28–29, 40; Garrisonian abolition 10–11, 14, 16–17, 25, 42, 111, 117, 119, 170;

education 2, 8, 30–33, 35–36, 41–42; and Immediate Emancipation 5–7, 11, 112–121, 129, 134, 141, 160, 163, 168–169, 172, 175; and Jackson, Andrew 4, 47–49, 61, 66, 68–69, 76–79, 81–82, 99–100, 107–108, 129–131, 133–134; jailed in Baltimore 146–154; Jefferson, Thomas 46, 48, 50, 60–61, 65–66, 72, 78, 87, 90, 104, 174; journalism 7–8, 18, 24–25, 35, 44, 57, 61, 78, 86, 91, 134, 156; journeyman printer experience 3, 6, 36–37, 40, 46, 54, 65, 102, 104; libel trial in Baltimore 140–141, 144–146; mottoes for his newspapers 45, 55, 69, 76, 112, 116, 159; on newspapers and reform 7–10, 25–27, 32, 41, 54, 70–71, 76, 79, 88, 90–91, 93, 99, 101, 135–136, 174–176, 179–180; on novels and novel reading 26, 36, 51, 61, 69–70, 86; Park Street Address 53–54, 111–112, 118, 128, 137, 177, 179; on political elections, 4, 21–24, 44, 46, 56, 58, 68, 81, 91 (*see also* elections); political ideology 3, 9, 35, 40, 42, 75, 108–109, 159, 178, 180; on the printer's craft 8, 26–27, 44, 54–55, 59, 62, 101, 111–112, 152, 171–172, 180 (*see also* printers and printing); on republicanism 54, 61, 106, 124, 128, 132, 138, 165, 178; on the value of education 4, 25, 59, 69–71, 76, 90, 99, 105–106, 117, 120, 127, 137, 175; *see also* Baltimore; Bennington, Vermont; Boston; *The Liberator*; Lundy, Benjamin

Genius of Universal Emancipation 5, 8, 74, 81, 88, 91, 110–111, 126, 129, 134, 140, 146, 152, 175–176
Georgia 49, 129, 142, 145, 159
Gill, Richard 156
Gilman Bookstore 36
Glorious Revolution 42
Goodell, William 92, 102, 109, 115, 135
Gorham, Benjamin 67–69
Grant, Pres. Ulysses 10, 36
The Great Awakening 17
Great Britain 113, 118, 124
Greece 62, 70, 104
Greeley, Horace 24, 35, 91
Grimké, Archibald 12
Gross, Robert 33

Haiti 81, 93, 101–102, 106, 112–113, 117, 121
Hamilton, Alexander 21–23, 46, 48
Hanover Street Church (Boston) 90
Harper, Charles 124
Harris, John 61, 63–64
Hartford, Connecticut 160, 162
Hartford Convention (1814) 34, 44, 47–48, 66
Harvey, Remus 124
Haverhill, Massachusetts 30, 64, 158
Hawthorne, Nathaniel 51

Henshaw, David 69
Heyrick, Elizabeth Coltman 114–115, 119
Hill, Isaac 101
Hinks, Peter P. 142
Hollis Street Church (Boston) 90
Holy Alliance 45, 49
"Honestus" 110
Horton, Harriet Farnham 147, 156
Horton, Jacob 104, 109
Howells, William Dean 35
Hudson, Warden David W. 146
Hull, Henry 82

Immediate Emancipation 113–115; *see also* Garrison, William Lloyd
Immediate, Not Gradual Abolition 114
Independence Day 4, 38–39, 41, 52, 59–60, 62, 75, 87, 104, 108–109
The Independent (New York) 9, 115
Investigator and General Intelligencer (Providence, RI) 92

Jackson, Andrew 4, 23–24, 44, 47–49, 61, 66, 68–69, 73, 76–79, 81–82, 99–100, 107, 129–131, 133–134
Jefferson, Thomas 50, 72, 78, 90, 104, 174; Garrison on his death 60–62, 87; on newspapers and the press 2, 20–22; and politics 29, 34, 44, 46, 48, 65–66
Jeffersonian-Republican Party 21–23
Johnson, Pres. Andrew 9
Johnson, Oliver 10, 13, 18, 115–116, 141, 150–151, 153, 158, 170, 177
The Journal of the Times (Bennington) 4, 8, 76–77, 79, 81–82, 88, 98–101, 107, 111, 116, 132, 158, 174–177
journalism 8, 18–19, 24–25, 35, 61, 156; *see also* Garrison, William Lloyd
Julien Hall 165–166

Kentucky 81, 96, 132–133, 144
Kentucky Colonization Society 133
Kett, Joseph 33
King, Martin Luther 18
Knapp, Isaac 35–36, 39–40, 55, 88, 173
Kneeland, Abner 165, 178
Korngold, Ralph 14–15, 114
Kraditor, Aileen 15–16

Ladd, William 91, 101, 135
Lafayette, Marquis de 38
Lane Seminary 13
Latrobe, John H.B. 124
The Liberator 18, 36, 51–52, 54, 58, 74, 88, 96, 115, 117, 143, 154–155, 157, 160; decision to end publication 1–2; decision to publish in Boston 168–170, 172–179; final editorial

INDEX

7; inaugural editorial 28–29; as instrument of reform 6–11, 24–27, 43, 72; motto 45, 159; proposal for Washington, D.C. paper 158–159, 168, 177; William Watkins in 124, 126–127
The Liberator and the Journal of the Times 158
Liberia 36, 93, 106, 121, 123
library associations 33–34, 36–38, 41
Lincoln, Abraham 10–11, 13–14, 160
Literary Subaltern (Providence) 101
Lundy, Benjamin 3–5, 73–75, 79, 81, 88, 91–102, 104, 107, 109–115, 121, 124, 130, 137–139, 141–142, 144–149, 153–154, 156, 161, 168, 170, 174–175; and Bennington, Vermont 81, 91, 100; and Boston 3–4, 73–75, 79, 91–100, 107, 109; on colonization 74, 95, 141, 168; Garrison's obituary of 74, 91; *Genius* in Washington, D.C., 154, 156, 168, 170; Haiti 81, 101–102, 112, 121; libel trial in Baltimore 138, 141, 144–145, 148; partnership with Garrison 5, 88, 110–115, 124, 130, 139, 141–142, 145–146, 148–149, 153–154, 156, 174–175; and Tappan, Arthur 153; and Woolfolk, Austin 137, 147
Luther, Martin 83
Lynn, Massachusetts 30, 136
Lynn Record 136

Malcom, Rev. Howard 94–96
Maryland Abolition Society 130
Massachusetts General Colored Association 143
Massachusetts Society for the Suppression of Intemperance 69, 89
May, Samuel J. 10, 168, 170, 177
Mayer, Henry 18, 94, 144
McKitrick, Eric 44
Mechanics Free Press (Philadelphia) 150
Medical Advertiser (Boston) 89
Mein, John 19–20
Merrill, Walter 15, 42
Merrimack Library 36, 40
Merrimack River 162
Miller, Tobias H. 35, 86
Mitchell, Charles 145
Monroe Doctrine 45
More, Hannah 51
Mott, James 161
Mott, Lucretia 161

Nantucket Inquirer 149
National Bank (U.S.) 21, 129
National Gazette 46, 49
National Intelligencer (Washington) 138, 158
National Philanthropist 3, 8, 65, 69–75, 82, 89–94, 102, 105, 116, 130, 135, 149, 174–175, 177

National-Republican Party 45, 55–57, 64
Native Americans, rights and treatment 4, 76, 90, 126, 129, 134, 174
Neal, John 50–51, 72, 74–75, 99, 175
New England 2–5, 13–14, 29, 35–36, 44, 48, 52, 56, 59, 62–63, 65, 71, 73–74, 77, 79, 87, 92, 94–95, 98–99, 101–102, 106, 109, 136, 147, 154–155, 159, 165, 167, 169–172
New England Anti-Slavery Society 65
New England Inquirer 101
New Hampshire 62, 75, 86, 158
New Hampshire Patriot 101
New Haven, Connecticut 160, 162
New Jersey 73, 111
New Orleans 44, 78, 139–140, 165, 170
New York City 17–19, 22, 24, 33–34, 88, 91–92, 98, 100, 115, 117, 126, 136, 150, 153–154, 160–162, 169–170
New York Tribune 24, 91
Newburyport 8, 27, 29, 31, 34, 36, 38–39, 44, 52, 55–56, 59–60, 84, 105, 107, 151, 164
Newburyport Athenaeum 36
Newburyport Debating Society 38–39, 52, 151
Newburyport Female Asylum 39
Newburyport First Baptist Church 36, 85, 88
Newburyport Herald 19, 27, 31, 35, 37–44, 46, 49–51, 54–62, 64, 66, 68, 75, 85–86, 110, 140, 151, 163, 174
Newburyport Library 36
Niles, Hezekiah 154
Nord, David Paul 25–26, 89
North American Review 37
North Carolina 96, 142
Northern Chronicler (Newburyport) 55
Nova Scotia 29, 84
novels and novel reading 26, 34, 36, 50–51, 61, 70, 86
Nye, Russell 14–15, 115

"An Old Bachelor" (A.O.B.) 41–43, 45, 50, 85, 94
Oliver, Gamaliel 30
Otis, Harrison Gray 35, 44–45, 49, 66–68, 85, 91, 10

Paine, Thomas 47–48
Park Street Address 53–54, 111–112, 118, 128, 137, 177, 179
Park Street Church (Boston) 4, 104, 121, 126
Parsons, Theophilus 50
Pasley, Jeffery 21–22
The Patriot (London) 169
Paul, Rev. Thomas 88, 116–117
Peak, Rev. John 88, 117
penny press 18–19, 24, 31, 71

Philadelphia Inquirer 149
Philanthropist see *National Philanthropist*
Phillips, Christopher 122
Phillips, Wendell 13–14, 28–29, 40
Pickering, Timothy 35, 46–47, 49
Pierpont, John 90
Poe, Edgar Allan 51
Pope, Alexander 42
Portland, New Hampshire 34, 51, 75, 94
Portsmouth, New Hampshire 62, 86, 94
Portsmouth Journal 150
printers and printing 19–20, 22, 24, 31, 34, 65, 88–89; *see also* Garrison, William Lloyd
The Protestant (New York) 115
Providence, Rhode Island 92
Public Advertiser (London) 42

Quakers (The Society of Friends) 3, 5, 30, 73–74, 91, 94, 97, 112, 114, 124, 138–139, 146, 149, 161, 169, 178
Quarles, Benjamin 121
Quincy, Edmund 11, 176
Quincy, Josiah 65–66

Raymond, Daniel 130–131
Reed, David 119
Republican Party 13, 160
Republican Party Convention (1864) 160
Resignation: An American Novel 51, 86
Rhode Island College 88
Rhodes, James Ford 12–13
Richmond, Virginia 6, 170
Rochester, New York 126–127
Rochester Observer 138
Ruchames, Louis 15
Rush, Benjamin 89

sabbatarianism 70, 76, 174
Salem, Massachusetts 34, 50, 64
Salem Courier 99, 101
The Salem Gazette 41, 46–50, 86
Savannah, Georgia 142
Schenectady Cabinet 150
Schlesinger, Arthur 19
Schouler, James 12–14
Schudson, Michael 24–25
Scott, Sir Walter 36, 43, 51
Seaton, William 158
Second Congregationalist Church (Newburyport) 162
Second Presbyterian Church (Newburyport) 105, 162
Sedition Act (1798) 20–21
Senate (U.S.) 10, 36, 66, 73, 79
Seward, William 1
Sewell, Samuel E. 11, 166
Shakespeare, William 36, 42

Sharp Street Church (Baltimore) 123–124
Shepard, George 162
slaveholder/slaveholding 5, 7, 73–74, 78, 94, 96, 101, 107–108, 114, 125, 127, 131–134, 137, 139–140, 142, 149, 155, 157, 163, 165, 167, 169, 171, 178
South America 43, 49, 104
southern anti-slavery 94–95
Southwick, Sylvester 92
Southworth, Sylvester 101
Stacy, George W. 8
Stamp Act (1765) 19–20
Stanton, Henry 10, 58
Swain, William 54
Sydney, Algernon 159

Tappan, Arthur 92, 153–154, 160–161, 166
Tappan, John 166
Tappan, Lewis 153–154, 161, 166
tariff 67–68, 72–73, 130, 134
"Tariff of Abominations" 73
Taylor, Alan 33
temperance 3–4, 8, 33, 65, 69–73, 75–76, 85, 89–90, 93, 99–100, 116–117, 129, 134, 152, 158, 174, 179
Thayer, Abijah W. 158
Thirteenth Amendment to the U.S. Constitution 1, 115, 119
Thomas, Isaiah 22, 31
Thomas, John L. 15
Tilton, Theodore 9, 115
Times (London) 169
Tocqueville, Alexis de 25–26, 38, 83
Todd, Francis 5, 140–141, 144–145, 148–151, 154–157, 168–170, 176
Toronto, Canada 123, 126
Tract Societies 26, 89, 99, 170
Treaty of Ghent (1814) 34, 44
Turner's Revolt (1831) 94

Unitarian Church 97, 119, 134, 166, 168, 170
United States Gazette 140

Varnum, John 56, 63–64, 87
Vermont 4, 26, 75, 77, 79–82, 99, 107, 111, 174
Vermont Chronicle 101
Vesey, Denmark 37, 59, 142
Village Record 138
Virginia 6, 49, 74, 95–96, 113, 131–132, 139, 144
Virginia Constitutional Convention (1829) 131–132, 134
Virginia House of Delegates 143

Walker, David 142–144, 168; *see also An Appeal to the Colored Citizens of the World*

INDEX

Walsh, Robert 46–47
Walter, Lynde 164–165, 171–172
Walters, Ronald 16, 33
Ware, Rev. Henry, Jr. 170
Washington, George 40, 44, 48, 104
Washington, D.C. 5–6, 44, 74, 79, 81, 95, 138, 158–160, 164, 168–170, 177
Washington Spectator 168
Watkins Academy 123
Watkins, William 123–127; *see also* "A COLOURED BALTIMOREAN"; "A COLOURED CANADIAN"
Webster, Daniel 57, 61, 66, 68, 73, 97, 107, 167
Webster, Noah 46
Wedgewood, Joseph 139

Weld, Theodore 13, 15
Whig Party 138, 158
White, Nathanial H. 69, 74
Whittier, John Greenleaf 11, 135, 153–154
Wilberforce, William 167
Wilentz, Sean 23, 54
Williamstown Advocate 101
Wilmington, North Carolina 142
Wilson, Henry 10–11
Wolf, Hazel Catherine 14
Woolfolk, Austin 137–138, 147, 151
Wyatt-Brown, Bertram 92
Wythe, George 132

The Yankee (Portland) 51, 72, 75, 99
Young, Alexander 167

www.ingramcontent.com/pod-product-compliance
Ingram Content Group UK Ltd.
Pitfield, Milton Keynes, MK11 3LW, UK
UKHW041957140426
5217IPUK00015B/849

9 780786 474257